THREE VERSE PLAYS

JEHANNE D'ARQUE

THE COURTSHIP OF SOREN KIERKEGAARD

BESS AND BOB

by

JOHN GURNEY

Illustrated by Paul Peter Piech

UNIVERSITY OF SALZBURG

SALZBURG - OXFORD - PORTLAND

First published in 1997 by **Salzburg University** in its series:

**SALZBURG STUDIES IN ENGLISH LITERATURE
POETIC DRAMA & POETIC THEORY**
186

EDITORS: WOLFGANG GÖRTSCHACHER & JAMES HOGG

ISBN 3-7052-0064-X

INSTITUT FÜR ANGLISTIK UND AMERIKANISTIK
UNIVERSITÄT SALZBURG
A-5020 SALZBURG
AUSTRIA

Front Cover: Reputed portrait of Jeanne d'Arc, originally in the church of St. Maurice, Orleans, now in the Musée du Trocadéro, Paris.

Woodcuts: Paul Peter Piech († 1996) ©

© John Gurney

Distributed by
    Drake International Services
    Market House, Market Place,
    Deddington OXFORD OX15 0SF
    England
    Phone 01869 338240
    Fax N°: 01869 338310

Distributed in the U.S.A. by
    International Specialised Book Services Inc.
    5804 NE Hassalo Street
    Portland
    Oregon 97213-3644
    Phone 503.287.3093
    Fax: 503.280.8832

Introduction

Verse drama is an exacting art form. The demands it makes on the playwright are considerable - Simone Weil was of the opinion that Shakespeare only wrote one first-rate play - *King Lear*. Certainly the history of the genre is littered with failures. The problem lies in the power, concentration, range of insight and quality of aesthetic sensibility needed by the synthesising, organic imagination of the writer and in the depth and complexity of lived experience required to develop the experiences he portrays. The verse dramatist is well served by a long and difficult apprenticeship in life. He offers his opus in fear and trembling. The critics lie in wait.

He also faces ethical problems. These are common, of course, to all literature, but especially so to the tragic mode. As the dramatist invents and is invented by his characters and actions and invests them with all the glamour of his Creative Idea, as he fills his text with decisive emotion, intelligence, will and intuition and transcends selfhood in the act of constructing new forms for old harmonies and disharmonies, deep within him there stirs a profound Manichean fear, especially in the making of tragedy, that his broad "passive capacity" may make him an open road for the demonic. Plato's anxiety about the transgression of archetypes is often near. The dramatist, attempting his spiritual catharis, may, when submitted to the operation of opposites, end not by producing a vision of beatitude, but a despairing revelation of decadence, a subtle corruption.

But the attempt to create has to be made. For better or worse the dramatist, driven by the mystery of poetry on the one hand, and by the fear that he may become no more than a mere asterisk and footnote in the divine "futuribilia" on the other, creates his angels and his devils, trusting that his identity as a maker emanates from the light-ground of his soul, and is not just one among the many masks and vizards of the Trickster within him; that his art derives from the very centre of his creatureship, its core of creative love-wisdom, the Benign Unknown.

The three plays in the present volume come from a time when I was questioning the concept of redemption through pain, of there being a special grace in suffering, and elaborating the idea that affliction is intrinsically evil. The play on Soren Kierkegaard helped articulate some of this malaise. I came to think that his form of existentialism involved a corruption both of conscience and consciousness. The seminal idea for the play came from psychology. Kierkegaard, I felt, seemed an example of the inverted Oedipus complex, and I experienced an urge to explore the cyclothymic and schizoid dynamics of his personality. Identified and identifying with his father, he, like Hamlet before him, seemed commanded by him to do the very thing most calculated to destroy himself, in Kierkegaard's case, to marry. The bungling attempt to construct a simplistic ethical salvation half-maddened him with the threat of annihilation. What could have been a celebration of faith in life became a dance of spiritual death.

Jehanne d'Arque also originated as a possible case-study - of paranoid schizophrenia. But I was only a few sheets into the text when I realised that I was engaging with the personality of a saint in the making. Like Kierkegaard, she appeared driven by a Hegelian "supra-morality" deriving from a different level of consciousness. Under the onslaught of evil, she became a holy, he an unholy satirist.

Bob, Robert Devereux, second Earl of Essex, would have loved to have fitted such a Hegelian scenario. Lacking depth of self-knowledge, he quickly steps upon the webs of *Bess*, Elizabeth Ist. Drawn into the role of a rebellious son, both by his own nature and by that of the Queen, he becomes her sacrifice to fate, an oblation to win her eternal youth from the gods. *Bess*, cultivating inertia as an antidote to mutability, having passed a proclamation stopping her age at thirty-five, and washing her hands of all complicity in those very events that her own unconscious has brought about, drifts towards death, her frustrated passion gaining regular displaced relief only through a ritualised sequence of orgiastic angers, in which, following the classical Freudian passion of hysteria, she finds only a transient satisfaction. It is the ending of an era.

Bexhill, October 1996

Table of Contents

JEHANNE D'ARQUE

A VERSE PLAY IN ELEVEN SCENES

DRAMATIS PERSONAE

JEHANNE D'ARQUE
ROBERT DE BAUDRICOURT, Commander of Vaucouleurs
PIERRE FOURNIER, a priest

CHARLES, The Dauphin
GEORGES DE LA TREMOUILLE, Commander of the French Army
YOLANDE OF ARAGON, Queen of Sicily
DUC D'ALENCON
REGNAULT, Archbishop of Rheims
FOOL

DUNOIS, the Bastard of Orléans
JEAN PASQUEREL, a confessor
A PRIEST, AN OFFICER

THE DUKE AND DUCHESS OF BEDFORD
THE EARL OF WARWICK
PIERRE CAUCHON, Bishop of Beauvais
JEAN D'ESTIVET, the promoter of the trial
JEAN BEAUPERE, a clerk
MAUGIER LEPARMENTIER, a torturer

GRAY, MOUTON, guards
SOLDIERS 1, 2, 3

SCENE I

Vaucouleurs. ROBERT DE BAUDRICOURT *is looking through an embrasure in his tower towards the square. He watches* JEHANNE D'ARQUE, *who kneels below with over a hundred citizens, praying for France, and awaiting his predestined third summons.* PIERRE FOURNIER, *a priest, hovers behind him, anxiously folding and unfolding a stole, possibly for use in a trial of spirits. His left eyelid twitches intimately.*

DE BAUDRICOURT
Fournier.

FOURNIER
      Monsieur de Baudricourt?

DE BAUDRICOURT
How do your books define a sorceress?

FOURNIER
A sorceress is a woman who attains
her ends by commerce with the Devil.

DE BAUDRICOURT
Look down there. What do you see?
Would you say she was a sorceress?

FOURNIER (*looking down*)
Ah! The girl from Domremy. The one they call
La Pucelle.

DE BAUDRICOURT
      Exactly. Well, is she a witch?

FOURNIER
She does not look like one. Not many
sorceresses will pray upon their knees for
weeks on end.

DE BAUDRICOURT
        The Devil can appear
in many forms.

FOURNIER
        Of course. Even as a
woman wearing trousers, now and then.

DE BAUDRICOURT
You confessed her yesterday.

FOURNIER
        I did. Yes.
And the day before that. And the day
before that. For the whole week she's been pouring
out her heart. It's cleaner than the river.

DE BAUDRICOURT
Well?

FOURNIER (*perceiving his meaning*)
        I know I am an incompetent priest,
a very dirty servant of the Lord,
but even I... The seal of the confessional
cannot be broken.

DE BAUDRICOURT
        Of course. But you could
quietly drop a hint. Stand on your left
leg, for example. Or the right.

FOURNIER
        I cannot
break the seal. Not even for the devil
himself.

DE BAUDRICOURT
        A most ambiguous answer.
A week ago she prophesied a
serious defeat. Today this letter
came. A battle at Rouvray. Another

disaster for the Dauphin. It appears
Orléans is almost done for. When it falls,
then we can bury France. That woman is
clairvoyant. And clairaudient. I should have
had her horse-whipped through the streets, ravished by
the garrison, then thrown into the river
in a sack. What's this augury that keeps
on blowing round the town?

FOURNIER
                    There are two of them.
One is very old. That France will be lost
by a woman, but saved by a maid. The second's
this. Merlin also made a prophecy.
It foretold the coming of a virgin
from on oakwood in Lorraine. An oakwood
covers the hills about her village.
It can be seen from her father's doorway.
I myself have spoken with a man
who knows the place. He says the wood is half
a league away.

DE BAUDRICOURT
                    All France is overgrown with
oakwoods. These voices that she hears. That tell
her she must cut her hair, wear male clothing,
raise the siege of Orléans, then have the
Dauphin crowned as King of France, what do we
make of that, then? Is she mad? Simple? Is she
an exhibitionist? A visionary? A
mystic? Or is she just a witch? If so,
what is the colour of her craft? If it's
black, then we all know how to deal with her. If
white, then she is harmless. But if she's grey -
the grey ones are the trouble. With a grey
witch, you don't know where you are. One day she
cures, the next day she will kill. Your grey witch
is most dangerous. Which is why I've called
you here, master priest. To earn a little
of your stipend. To try the spirits. Find out
whence her power comes. From heaven, or from hell.

Or somewhere else that's hidden in-between.
(*He gestures to a* MAN-AT-ARMS *who leaves the room.*)
This whole affair must finish here and now.
She makes us look incompetent, two fools.
(The MAN-AT-ARMS *returns with* JEHANNE, *prodding her forwards with the point of his sword. She is dressed in a male tunic, male hose and male leggings.*)

JEHANNE (*to the* MAN-AT-ARMS)
Sheathe your sword. I bring no harm to you.
(DE BAUDRICOURT *signals to the* MAN-AT-ARMS *who returns his sword to its scabbard, then guards the door.*)

DE BAUDRICOURT
So. For the third time. The girl from Domremy.
What do you bring us now, girl from Domremy?

JEHANNE
Nothing.

DE BAUDRICOURT
         Nothing? Then we shall soon dispose
of nothing.

JEHANNE
         I was nothing before I
was born. I am nothing now. And very soon
I shall be nothing once again.

DE BAUDRICOURT
                         Then you will
not fear annihilation.

JEHANNE
                  I was
annihilated many years ago.
May God allow that to continue.

DE BAUDRICOURT
You make a great deal of noise for such a
piece of nothing. A nothing wearing hair
cropped like a man's. A nothing wearing
masculine leggings. Surely all this
nothingness adds up to something?

JEHANNE
                              Of course it does.
(*quietly*) To Everything.

DE BAUDRICOURT
                    Ah! I wondered when we
should get to that. By being nothing you
are everything. Is that what you would say?

JEHANNE
Despite yourself, you are a man of insight.
You glimmer with the Spirit.

DE BAUDRICOURT
                         Well, since you
are now everything, let me put you
to the test. I'll try out your omniscience.

JEHANNE
That would be very foolish. Quite unworthy
of you. It would not please God.

DE BAUDRICOURT
                         Just a simple
test, that's all I ask. Tell me what I'm thinking.

JEHANNE
That the evil spirits have penetrated
my body. That I must be bled. Smoked.
Beaten. Shrieked at. (*Pulling at* FOURNIER'*s stole*)
                    Even exorcised.

DE BAUDRICOURT
                         Go on.

JEHANNE
You wonder whether I am a lunatic.
A simpleton. An exhibitionist.
A visionary. Or a witch pretending
she's possessed by an insane St. Catherine
and by a mad St. Margaret.

DE BAUDRICOURT
Continue.

JEHANNE
If I am a witch, what colour am I? Black?
Or grey? Or white? If white, do I fly through
the air like St. Michael does, on four wide
wings? If black, will you have to burn me?
If grey, well that could be most difficult.
That is what you're thinking about me.
That is how you react. What's the matter, then?
Don't you like being spoken to like this
by a mere woman? Do I make you afraid
of losing all your male authority?
Do you fear your spirit's mixing with
my spirit? That you are struggling hard
against me? Choking back strange words? Subduing
unusual impulses? Don't be afraid
De Baudricourt. I am not a witch. I
am not possessed. You have no need of
exorcism here. Poor priest. You look so
scared. You are right to be afraid. You have
so little faith. How can you have access to
the spiritual power? Poor man. He would be
obliterated, finished in a flash.

DE BAUDRICOURT
Try her spirits, Fournier. Test them. Now!

(FOURNIER *produces a quivering crucifix which he holds before him.*)

FOURNIER (*stuttering, hesitating*)
I conjure you, in the name of Almighty God, that if there be
any bad thing in you, that you depart from this place
immediately. If there be any good thing, then let you approach
us, and fall down to your knees. (JEHANNE *approaches him
very slowly, until her eyelids are almost touching his, then she
steps back rapidly and slowly kneels.*)

JEHANNE
See what a very good girl I am. There,
priest, I kneel before your office, not your soul.
Just as I knelt before you yesterday
when making my confession. That should have been
enough.

DE BAUDRICOURT
          By whose authority do you come
disturbing us like this?

JEHANNE
                    You waste my time.
Almighty God's.

DE BAUDRICOURT
               And he instructed you
to wear this clothing?

JEHANNE
                    My dress is nothing.
Less than nothing.

FOURNIER
               You think it is a good
thing, to appear like this?

JEHANNE
                    Ask God. He
ordered it.

FOURNIER
How does God communicate
with you?

JEHANNE
I have told you that before.
Through voices.

DE BAUDRICOURT
But what kind of voices?
Angels' voices? Saints' voices? Or do they
come straight from God Himself, from the Holy
Spirit?

JEHANNE
Mainly I hear the voices of Saint
Catherine and St. Margaret.

FOURNIER
How do you know
that they are saints?

JEHANNE
Because they smell
quite differently from you. Their heads wear
glorious crowns.

DE BAUDRICOURT
How do you distinguish one
from the other?

JEHANNE
By the way they speak to me.
They are quite the opposite to you. I
also get great help from Michael, from Saint
Michael. His was the first voice I received.
He was surrounded by all the angels of heaven.

FOURNIER
St. Michael and all the angels, you saw
them bodily, in full reality?

JEHANNE
As I now see you there before me. When
St Michael first went away I wept. I
would greatly then have liked to leave with him.

DE BAUDRICOURT
How old were you when this occurred?

JEHANNE
                              Thirteen.

DE BAUDRICOURT
And where did it happen?

JEHANNE
                    I was racing
in the meadow with my friends.

DE BAUDRICOURT
                              Continue.

JEHANNE
I was lying in the grass to get my breath.
Then suddenly a person came to me.
A boy up from the village, as I thought.
He said my mother wanted me back home.
I went, but when my mother saw me come
she called out in a loud and angry voice
demanding why I'd left the flock of sheep
untended in the meadow. Then I turned.
The sun was hot, my shadow underfoot.
It was in my father's garden. Suddenly
my right side was a brilliant blaze of flame -
quite different from the sunlight in the fields.
I stood there, dumb with wonder, terrified.
A voice came from the brightness. It was kind.
It told me that I had no need to fear.
That I was good, that I should stay devout,
continue in obedience. Then it left.
I stood there in the orchard, dark at noon.

DE BAUDRICOURT
And the vision, did it keep returning?

JEHANNE
Gradually I came to lose my fear.
Sometimes it would come to me at night,
at others in the evening, when the bells
were chiming down the valley, through the farms.
Most often, though, at noontime, in the woods,
so softly, from a luminous white cloud
that gradually assumed a human form,
St Michael's, the archangel.

DE BAUDRICOURT

                              Continue.

JEHANNE
At first I was afraid it was some trick,
some glamour of the Devil, of some witch
that hid inside the hollows of a tree
and wished to practise evil. Nonetheless
he always spoke so gently to my face.
He told me of the sufferings of France,
informed me of my God, of his command
that I should carry arms and serve the king,
that all things would be ordered through my arm.
I often wept. To me it seemed a dream.
But then my other saints came to my aid.
Always they encouraged and assured
that God would hold me up and strengthen me
because I was his daughter. When they went
I'd sigh, and weep the night away for France,
my heart a fire of pity for the world.

FOURNIER
And did you tell your father what they said?

JEHANNE
They told me to be silent, and I was.

DE BAUDRICOURT (*sitting on the edge of his table*)
And now you're here, to bear arms for the king?

JEHANNE
The voices are quite clear upon that point.
Three times I must approach you. At the third
you'll give me what I want. Armour. Horses.
Men to ride with me. An introductory
letter to the Dauphin, at Chinon. You
have already written to him. And
yesterday, he replied. News has reached you
of his latest serious defeat. My
voices give me information. It is
of the greatest importance. Prophecies
to calm his troubled soul and bring him peace.

DE BAUDRICOURT
But why male clothes?

JEHANNE
               It's right for me to wear them.
They hide the contours of my body as I ride.
They protect my limbs from rape.
Before this Lent is more than half-way through
I must be on my way to see the Prince,
yes, even if I walk there on my own,
arrive there with my legs worn to the knees.
He must be crowned the King of France at Rheims.
I must lead his armies, no one else.
The English will be driven in the sea. (*Approaching*)
I look into your eyes, De Baudricourt.
I see what time has fixed into your brain.
The boredom and frustration of your life.
All day you sit and listen to complaints,
to farmers, with their whining grievances,
to peasants, filing in with crafty eyes,
demanding compensation for the war,
pretending that their buildings have been fired,
their cattle carried off, their crops forced down.
All grumble at the taxes you collect.
The place, of course, is very dangerous,

a frontier town, right next to Burgundy,
its people weakened, terrified by war.
All feel the world is coming to an end.
Changes in the currency each month.
Taxes from the Prince increase each year.
The trade routes close, all commerce is destroyed.
Rumours, endless rumours everywhere,
with constant threats of famine. Look at us.
Back home at Domremy our barns are burned,
our winter fodder pillaged, carried off.
Our sheep scarce have the strength to wade the mud.
They trample down the last grey blades of grass
that struggle through the pastures. Look around!
Your town is in disorder, falls apart!
It's flooded with the ordure of the world,
deserters from the army, mountebanks,
students, ruined tradesmen, artisans,
adventurers and beggars, routiers,
a thousand types of criminal and rogue.
All France will soon be living like the beasts,
existing, like its ancestors, in caves,
in forests, quarries, marches, rivers, isles,
in swamps of desolation, anywhere.
The English range from Calais to Cadiz.
France is at the brink, is all but gone.
Salisbury's laying siege to Orléans.
If that should fall, the Dauphin's cause is lost.
And that will not be good for Baudricourt.
You know, of course, what Burgundy will do.
That head of yours will leave its resting-place
and roll down to the river for the fish.
Consider well these sentences I say.
Your people know my mission is from God.
Their only chance of safety lies with me.
You're caught up in a pattern of events
you cannot understand. It does your soul
no good at all to stand against your God.

DE BAUDRICOURT (*succumbing, worn down by her rhetoric*)
All right then. Tell me what you require.

JEHANNE
The journey will be very difficult.
We have to pass Burgundian territory.
It's better that we travel through the night.
By day we'll use the cover of the woods.
I shall disguise myself. Change into a
page. Here. Write this down. I shall need a
woollen tunic, dyed in grey. With a high
neck, hooked up to the chin, and belted in
with leather round the waist.

DE BAUDRICOURT
                        Got it. What else?

JEHANNE
A sleeveless leather jerkin, dyed in black
and laced up at the front with leather thongs.
Woollen stockings. A knitted cap, that winds
around the head. And some money, of course.
I have none of my own. Also I shall
need another horse. And I should also
like to have a sword. I shall not need to
use it.

DE BAUDRICOURT
            How long will you take?

JEHANNE
                        Eleven
days. I shall arrive on the twenty-third
of February.

DE BAUDRICOURT
            Very well. It will be done.

FOURNIER
You understand the dangers that you run?
The écorcheurs strip everyone they meet.
Throw the peasants into bins. Rape their wives
above them on the lids, then leave them there
to suffocate in flour. They rip

out infants from the womb, grope in women's
bellies for their jewels, for hidden plunder.
They roam the land like maddened animals.

JEHANNE
I have good news for my king.

DE BAUDRICOURT (*throwing down his pen*)
                              Your confidence
destroys me. Well, perhaps you are from God.
Sleep between the furrows if you must.
I'll see you get the uniform you need.
I fear you'll sink your outline in the turf
before you sniff a battle. Our country
needs a miracle. Charles has never been
so weak. You also seem to understand
Orléans is the key to central France.
If Orléans falls, so too, does all the rest.
Bedford now is massed for an attack.
Such an act's without a precedent
and ruptures all the rules of chivalry.
Dunois now has charge of the defence.
The town is well-provisioned, nonetheless
our feckless Prince is planning his retreat -
to run for Spanish sun or Scottish rain.
God knows how you'll cope with things at court.
Make towards the Queen of Sicily.
Yolande is the one who rules his mind.
Get her on your side and you will find
her lapdog is your weapon. Watch Tremouille.
Friend Georges will be your natural enemy.
He controls the Army, understand?
Once he followed Burgundy, but when
he lost that King's protection, rapidly
he turned his coat and galloped south to Bourges.
A great inflated bladder of a man
who now is made Grand Chamberlain, no less.
He fixes all his rivals through intrigue
and blatant acts of murder. Watch for him!
Burgundy leans this way, and then that.
Plays one against the other, comes and goes.

Yesterday the English, now the French,
conceding nothing definite to each
but holding close his hand till such a time
that he can be the master of all France.
Such are the delights of politics!
Fear success. Remember, when the wheel
has fully risen, it's about to fall.
Go, and save our France, if go you must.
But write this on your mind, ingrain it there.
At court men find all opposites are bad.

[CURTAIN]

SCENE II

Chinon. CHARLES', *the Dauphin's, decrepit Court of Love.*
TREMOUILLE, *Commander of the Army,* YOLANDE OF
SICILY, ALENCON, REGNAULT THE ARCHBISHOP OF
RHEIMS *and others are dressed fantastically, not unlike
circus characters.* CHARLES *is stamping round the chamber,
tearing his hair in anguish, largely ignored by the others.*

CHARLES
This is most unnerving! Most unnerving! Here am I, just about
to abscond from my disasters, to build myself a private
metaphysical world in the highlands of Scotland or the deserts
of Castile, when along comes this teenage cowgirl from the
borderlands of Lorraine bellowing to the world that she is the
voice-box of the Absolute, insisting that I modify my being and
my life to suit the needs of the community, that I exemplify
within myself the unity of man with the cosmos, that I realise
the wisdom of conforming my actions to the divine universal
laws and practise the virtue of incessantly striving to achieve
such an end by labouring to advance from a lower to a higher
state of perfection. It is all too much! This peasant-girl is the
last straw! Bullying me with the orders of Almighty God!
Dragging me back to reality with some horrible feminine

protest, just when I am about to establish a uniquely individual structure of reasoning to isolate me from the external terrors of existence and the internal horrors of the wrath of God.

YOLANDE
When you are already half-mad.

CHARLES
Exactly. When I am already half-mad. Who wouldn't be at least three-parts crazy in a place like this? It's the only way to stay sane! I mean, just look at you all! Look at the court! What a festival of dreams! What a circus you all are! The brutality of it all! Man fights with man. Woman with woman. Hermaphrodite with hermaphrodite. What a terrible struggle for existence! What an elimination of the unfit! What a ruthless annihilation of the inferior! (*Stiff with rage*) Oh why can't she just leave me alone! Let me live inside the existence of my fictions, my luminous delusions? Oh, if only I could be an unconscious rock, a thoughtless tree! Or simply drop off into death!

ARCHBISHOP
Pull yourself together, Charles. As you requested, we have been considering the question of this so-called Maid.

CHARLES (*dully*)
Yes. Go on.

ARCHBISHOP
We have looked into all the available aspects of the case.

CHARLES
So?

ARCHBISHOP
And our opinions are divided.

CHARLES
Fancy that!

ARCHBISHOP
Equally divided. The problem is her source of inspiration.

CHARLES
I could have told you that.

ARCHBISHOP
God, it appears, if not in her plackets, is most certainly in her pockets. You have not met her yet, but she claims He speaks to her both mediately, through saints and angels, and immediately, through the noise of his own voice. (*Sighing deeply*) Poor Pope John must now be turning in his grave to hear such things! These days not even the blessed in heaven have the sight of God before the final judgement. Not one quick leper's squint. So much for Pope John! Yet there she rides, ranges through the black flints of the fields, confounding modern doctrine with her howls of beatific inspiration. Not every grunt from a peasant's snout has a divine origin, you know. God is far more distant nowadays. Those in heaven itself can scarcely see His light.

CHARLES
Pope John was dead and buried long ago.

ARCHBISHOP
She has absolutely no respect for authority. Everything she does is arrogant! In Paris, at the University, the centre of our intellectual world - their patron saint is Catherine by the way, the saint that she keeps on seeing in the trees - our foremost theologians argue year by year upon the doctrine of Christ's mother, about her immaculate conception. A *furor theologicus* no less. All our leading theologians! And has Catherine herself appeared for one brief instant to arbitrate their quarrels, or pour her wisdom on their thoughts? Of course not! She has been far too busy out in cold Champagne appearing to a mere slip of a girl, an illiterate, unlettered and untaught farm-hand, filling her childish mind with fantasies and foolish dreams of saving the civilised world! Great men now spend their whole life-times, break their brains upon one single point of thought that she herself settles with a wink, a quiver of an eyelid! It's absurd! She makes the Church superfluous, God himself a heretic, no less. A fine thing it will be for all of us when every jumped-up seer, each idiot visionary instructs us on the ordering of the world, usurping all the work of Providence, of Holy Church,

the company of saints and all the hosts of heaven! There's a thought! Each man his own godhead! His own Lord! What an absurd nightmare, when there is no truth, only an opinion. Then we are only one step from the position that there is no justice! Worse yet - that justice is only the advantage of the strong! The woman must have water on the brain! Take my word for it. She's too devout a girl. Too keen on her devotions and her prayers. I see it all too often. And it always leads to arrogant presumption, cruel inhuman pride.

CHARLES (*clapping his hands derisively*)
A long speech, Archbishop. Well-turned. One to grace the mouth of the most accomplished sophist. Oh dear! I see there's more to come.

ARCHBISHOP
The child is a fanatic! Cast her out! Consider how she works! She uses woman's weapons. She titillates your interests, stokes your fears. Plays on your credulity. Look at her letters. *"God predestines many joys for you. I myself know much for your own good. Have messages to comfort you from God. I will even pick you out among a crowd."* Fortune tellers', necromancers' tricks. We meet them in the palace every day. She treats you like a mistress, like a whore. Then, if all else fails, she summons up her infantry of tears.

CHARLES
Alencon. You have met the girl. You're an expert in the ways of women. Is she, as she claims, diaphanous and chaste?

ALENCON
As straight as light. As clear as noon. When she
prays the jewelled windows melt across her head
and colour her with heaven.

CHARLES
You sound quite smitten. Still, there's nothing unusual in that! (*Digging him in the ribs with his elbow*) What is she then, a blonde or a brunette? She's always got a helmet jammed on her head when I catch sight of her, thundering up and down the field with that lance of hers, for all the world looking as though

she were riding some sort of overweight unicorn.

ALENCON
Her hair is black. She cropped it thick and short.

CHARLES
How does the girl speak? Tell me truthfully.

ALENCON
A strong deep voice, that comes from underground.
A sound that you could hear a mile away.
That's good for rallying defences.
But musical, so musical it is!
Her build is like a peasant's, tall and wide.
The sort of frame that rides a horse all day.
At home she spins and weaves and cleans the house.
She cannot read or write or sign her name.
Her age is sixteen years. She's fully grown.
Her tunic and her boots are as a man's.
Behind her strong right ear a bright red scar
is blazing like the outline of a flame.

ARCHBISHOP
Obviously a witch-mark! What surer sign
of heresy?
The girl is a demoniac, possessed.
Of course she has a burning certainty.
These people always do. I've met them all.
They drag you to disaster. Keep her out.
Woman is redemption's enemy.
Her navel is the black hub of the world.
All Nature groans in suffering through her flesh.
Her soul is like a cauldron, full of spells.
It boils with all the passions of the earth.
She chains men to their senses, to their sins,
and smells of a cloaca, death and hell.

YOLANDE
Yet Baudricourt speaks highly of the girl.
He says she is consistent. That her
testimony never alters. That he

could find no fault in her, however hard he tried -
and Baudricourt is shrewd to a degree.

CHARLES
Tremouille, what have you got to say?
Do you need this virgin, this Penthesilea
from Lorraine to help you run the army?
Shall I obey God and demote you now?
Make her my Chef de Guerre? How would you like
the voice of God behind you on the field,
jabbing at your arsehole with her sword?

TREMOUILLE
I shall continue to do the best I
can with the resources available.
Wars are won by politics. By treaties.
By discussion, and by compromise.
The battlefield is just the smallest part
of the overall picture.

CHARLES
                              I see.
So you would argue that you do not need
an illiterate peasant to show you
the way to victory? No new virgin
Amazon?

TREMOUILLE
            That would be my position.

CHARLES
Never mind, Tremouille. You're still my favourite.
Defeatist through and through, aren't you, little
piggy-eyes? Risk nothing, egh? Risk nothing.
I owe you money, don't I? Far too much.

YOLANDE
And what has he achieved? What's left for you
to lose now? Just look around you, Charles.
All your former glory is quite gone.
We live in fear, our ears turned to the door,

our eyes on the horizon. Everywhere
each citizen is listening for the bell,
the trumpet from the tower telling him
the brigands have returned. Just look at France.
He's turned her to a land of animals,
all her peasants killed and put to flight,
from here, down by the Loire, up to the Seine,
from Champagne down the Meuse, right on to Chartres,
all pastures overgrown and choked with weeds,
one endless desolation. Think of France!
The wolves and bears advance right to the towns.
The marshes are recaptured by the sea.
Floods rush across the landscape, swamp the fields.
The churchyards fill with brambles, ferns and trees.
The monks have been reduced to eating grass.
They champ the leaves like cattle. Think of France!
Perhaps this child is really sent from God.
If so it is a sin to turn her out,
another curse to add to your account.

CHARLES
My sins! My sins! Oh, very well, then. We'll
see this deviation from her sex,
this intermediate being. Her letters say
she'll quickly pick me out. Apparently
I have a certain light above my head,
a sort of mystical illumination,
so she says. We'll see if she can spot it.
Call in the Fool. [*Enter* FOOL] Come here, dear boy.
I see you're ready, dressed up just like me
in common melancholia, bent and boned.
Now, I shall wear this cloak of Alencon's
and you, you are the Dauphin, France's Prince.
Enjoy your new authority my friend.
For all I care it's yours perpetually.
I know you would not want it, would you boy?

FOOL
I'd be a fool to do so.

CHARLES
                    That's my boy.
I've told you what to do. So make us laugh.
A wager, then Tremouille. A thousand livres
she picks me out immediately? Agreed?

TREMOUILLE
One thousand livres. Provided that
you hide behind that screen.

CHARLES (*smacking his palm*)
                          Done, then. Done!
Bring in the Voice of God. It's time we had
a different entertainment. Well, summon her.
(*to* FOOL)You, sit on my throne, and make us grin.
(CHARLES *withdraws behind a screen.*)

FOOL
Bring in the maid called *La Pucelle*.
(PAGE *stamps the floor with a stick. Enter* JEHANNE. *There
is an intake of breath at her male dress. The* FOOL *parodies
the accent of the Dauphin.*)
                                Ah, my dear!
I'm glad to see you here. Right glad you've come.
Allow me first to introduce myself.
I am the echo of my noble ancestors.
First, of Charles the Bold, then Charles the Fat.
Then Charles the Simple. Then of Charles the Fair.
Then Charles the Wise, my grandfather.
And then my idiot father, Charles the Mad.
Some call me Charles the Dauphin, by the way.
But most, just Charles the Bastard. Kiss my shoe!
(*He extends and wiggles its fantastic tip.*)

JEHANNE
You mock me, Fool. I come see my king.

FOOL
Close that door. The draught is terrible!
Come girl, approach! Don't be overawed.
I always dress in velvet, as you know.

I like to wear this fragrant pod of cloth.
We living ghosts, we tend to feel the cold.
Yes, even in the summer. Touch those pads.
Furred right to the knuckles, like a mole.
Well, what sort of figure do I cut?
Knock-kneed, with bony wrists. This bulbous nose.
The sort of face you find at Mardi Gras.
A sulking melancholic's.
(*Approaching her, placing an arm round her shoulders*)
You like our carious court? Egh? Answer me!
(*Tilting her head*)
These women dressed with horns. Their odious sleeves?
Their yard-long shoes? Their monstrous shaven heads?
You must meet our most important fiends.
Here's a devil. One you'll often meet.
The Duke de la Tremouille, no less.
The Army Chief. You'll quickly pick him out.
Secreting like a pig, a pregnant sow.
And next to him, a most religious man.
All gas and admonition. The Primate
of all France. His see is Rheims.
But that's a place he'll never see again.
He even went there once, long years ago.
Some twenty at the least. This man's my page.
The one that banged the floor when you came in.
You like my court, this comic carnival?
You see the way God punishes poor France?

JEHANNE
You ape the Prince. You will not be the King.
He's in the room. You've hidden him from me.

FOOL
It's beautiful to have you in the court.
Still smelling of dry daggings and the piss.
A sour stench of old milk upon your hands. (*Sniffing them*)
A shepherdess, true representative
of what the people stand for. The real source
of French culture. The creators of our
language. Art. Epic. Lyric poetry.
Ah my dear! We of the upper classes,

we have risen above the masses, but
have impoverished ourselves. Our one resort's
to come to you in full humility,
but not to teach, to learn. (*General laughter*) Or, rather,
to unlearn our civilised lies, to scrap
the fictions and illusions of our goals.
When were you born, my simple little child?
The Feast of the Epiphany, they say.
When you descended, joined this vale of tears,
did cockerels really crow from dusk to dawn
and beat their golden bodies with their wings?

JEHANNE (*walking round the chamber, searching*)
I met a man. He stood upon a bridge.
He cried, *"If I can have you for a night*
you will not be a virgin very long!"
I turned towards him, looked into his eyes.
"Would you deny Him, you so close to death!"
I murmured as I passed. His face turned white.
Already he has drowned. Has ceased to be.
Death strikes us like an arrow in the eye
so swiftly, none can see its fatal flight.
(*She stands before a curtain. She draws it aside then falls*
upon her knees before the Dauphin.)
Noble prince, they call me *La Pucelle*.
The King of Heaven sent me here to you
and ordered me to give to you a sign.
(*A general gasp of amazement*)

CHARLES (*trembling, terrified of witchcraft*)
Keep your distance, witch! Look towards the wall!
Those eyes, those eyes, those overlooking eyes!
They're bulging like a hare's in middle March!
I am the Dauphin. Do as I command!

JEHANNE (*fixing him with her eyes, and advancing towards him*)
You order me to disobey your God?

CHARLES
Kiss my heel, then.

JEHANNE (*fervently*)
>With all my heart.

CHARLES
>That's nice.

All right, then. Kiss the other. Oo! You're warm!
Just you stay there for a while. Keep looking
at the floor. Prostrate yourself. That's better.
My head feels weak. It's spinning like a top.
You, you others, go away. Clear off!
Back now. Back. We need to speak alone.
She has messages from God. (*They withdraw a little.*)
>Up now, girl!

My God, how big you are! That great stout neck!
You're far too large for me to haul about.
Up now, on your feet. You're six foot tall!
Now come with me, and step behind this screen.
That's better. See? The air smells sweeter here.
My asthma! Now at last I start to breathe.
Forgive that entertainment I devised.
A test, you know, of your integrity.
But one that's won at least a thousand livres.
Inherently I'm flippant, through and through.
It made a laugh, though - well, it did for me!
It seemed a clever way to find you out. (*Nudging her*)
I like your hairstyle. Really dangerous.
These clothes as well. You'll start a fashion off.
All our women will be wearing hose.
And leggings too. (*Sniffing her*) They still smell of a horse.
Well, let's get straight to the point. No pleasantries.
You said that God has sent you with a sign.
What sort of sign?

JEHANNE
>It is near you now.

CHARLES
I can't see anything. (*Spinning round*) Which direction?

JEHANNE
It is above your head.

CHARLES
Above my head?

JEHANNE
It is carried by an angel.

CHARLES
An
angel? I can see no angel.

JEHANNE
Then I
shall have to spit upon your eyes. (*She spits.*)

CHARLES
Good Lord!

JEHANNE
I spit upon your eyes. Now they can see.

CHARLES (*rubbing his eyes in wonderment*)
Well I never! There is a light up there.
A small round light. It's like a circle.
It is shining like a crown. (*He cries with amazement as the crown begins to descend towards him. He jumps up to clutch it, but it remains just out of his range.*)
I need a stick.
A bishop's crozier! That will do the trick!
A floating crown of gold, with inlaid jewels!

JEHANNE
An angel stands a lance-length from your side.
He holds it there above you. You'll be crowned
the King of France. Yes. You can touch the crown.

(CHARLES *seizes it avidly. He taps it suspiciously, then bites it with his teeth.*)

CHARLES
Good Lord! It's solid! Solid gold! Out of
thin air! Gold, out of thin air! What are you, then?
Some sort of magician? A female alchemist?
I've heard that they exist. You hold the *lapis*?
I'll make you my official treasurer.
I'll be the richest king in all the world.
You don't mind if I try it on for size?

JEHANNE (*taking it and placing it on him*)
There now. How does that feel? It fits you
perfectly. Exactly right. Now you can
set it in your treasury. Keep it with
your other precious metals till you're crowned.

CHARLES (*unhappily*)
Crowned?

JEHANNE
            It must be so. At Rheims. God has
foreordained it.

CHARLES
            But Rheims is full of Englishmen.

JEHANNE
Then we must drive them out. God has sent me
to take charge of your army.

CHARLES
            My army?
That's a joke! Just take one look at it!
The army is a shambles. It's no use,
you know. (*Removing the crown sadly*)
            Crown or no metaphysical
crown, I'll never make a warrior king for you.
I'm not a man of action. I am more
a man of contemplation. I might just
poke my head outside the surface of the
heavens for an hour or so to watch the
formless forms, whatever they might be, but

I would soon get bored with that. I'm hopeless
at all forms of consistent action. I
am inconstant. Erratic. Sad. Lazy.
And nothing can be done about it.

JEHANNE
But I have come to change all that, my lord.
These are merely the effects of guilt.
The punishments of a stricken conscience.
Come closer in. I have more signs for you.
I'll now reveal your secret words to God.
Things that you have wept to Him alone,
confided to none other. God Himself
has shown these things to me, to cure you of
your sickness. If I should tell you them,
will you believe that I've been sent by Him?

CHARLES
You're sure you're not a witch? You promise?

JEHANNE
Last November, the first day of the month -
All Saints' Day. Do you remember? At Loches.

CHARLES
Ah!

JEHANNE
    You went into the oratory to pray.

CHARLES
Go on.

JEHANNE
    You asked three things of God.

CHARLES (*clapping his hands*)
                                        I did.
I did.

JEHANNE
  You spoke of those three things to no one.
No friend at court. No minister. No priest.

CHARLES
Not one word.

JEHANNE
      Your first request was this.
You prayed to God that if you weren't the true
heir to the throne, legitimate in blood,
that God Himself should take away your will
from any thought of gaining back the crown
because of all the suffering it would cause.

CHARLES
Correct! Amazing! What about the second?

JEHANNE
That if the French were suffering for your sins
that you alone should take the punishment.
You'd suffer any penance, even death.

CHARLES
That death should wrap me up in darkness. And
the third?

JEHANNE
      That God should turn away His wrath,
forgive the people, if it was their sins
that caused this tribulation.

CHARLES
          True! All true!
Will you take my pain away?

JEHANNE
          Evil must
be purified, or life is just not
possible. But God alone does that.

CHARLES
But you, what do you know of suffering,
who overflow with energy and joy?

JEHANNE
Time bears us all towards the thought we cannot
bear, but which must come to us in time.
Each second brings some being in the world
much closer to the thing that he or she
will find intolerable. I, too, must be
unfaithful to myself, will mock my God.

CHARLES
The centre of the eye is always black,
a window to the darkness of the brain.
My mother is the lawful Queen of France.
Before my birth my father had been mad
a dozen years. I was conceived upon
Whit-Sunday. Such a comic Pentecost!
Imagine it, the King my father
strapped down to a bed, his head boxed up
in blackness, a red gag soaked in bloodstains
in his lips. A most submissive lover!
My mother's tastes were always odd, you know.

JEHANNE
Poor, poor prince.

CHARLES
                    My mother once was beautiful.
Poets worked her body into verse.
Singers sang her lyrics, throbbing songs.
But she was married to a madman. What a life!
Always filled with children. Twelve of us.
Someone born or dying all the time.
Have you watched your siblings carried off?
Stamped down in a casket underground?
Heard the dead soil drumming on their heads?
Probably they're happier where they are.
And where's her beauty now? Yes, where indeed?
Chained up to that lecher Burgundy,

her body like a common lavatory,
a closet where he drops his excrements.
Still, such is life. She drinks too much, you know.
She suffers from the gout. Can scarcely walk.
A sensuous beast who's wheeled round in a chair
and claims that I'm a bastard. She should know.
At night she often lies across my dreams.
I feel the monstrous burden of her thighs
and think about my father.

JEHANNE

                    Dream no more.
The true blood of the Valois runs through you.
God Himself assures me of the fact.

CHARLES (*laughing*)
The true blood of the Valois! What is that?
You see the sort of man you'd make a king?
Suppose I was anointed, oil and all?
What happens if a madness strikes me down,
my father's sins are visited on me?
If I should kill my children! Mutilate!
I hate all kinds of violence. Can't stand blood.
It makes me faint. I have quite frequent blackouts.
My legs give way. Just suddenly collapse.
I feel I'm full of sexual disease.

JEHANNE
I shall give you courage. I, and God.
We two shall cleanse this century of its sins.
We'll drive the English out of Orléans,
from Paris and the coast of Normandy
and sweep them in the Channel. You will see!
I'll lead you in procession up to Rheims,
will see you in full glory, crowned with shouts
that lift away the vaulting of the roof
and echo right to England. All will yield.
The French will rise again like wheat in Spring.
The English drop like dung upon our fields.

CHARLES
Well, you certainly have a way with words.
If rhetoric can win a war I'll soon
be king of China. But we shall see.
On this we must speak further. You're looking
rather pale, girl. White as milk. This business
of being a medium. It must be
rather tiring. Yes. Quite exhausting.
They say you keep your fast up, right through Lent.
Is that correct? You eat one meal a day?
We're going to find you something rich to eat.
Wars aren't fought on fish, but meat, you know!
Meat! Some good red meat, that's what you need.
I'll take you in to meet my kitchen staff.
We get on well. Especially the cook.
He lends me money. I need lots of it.
The sleeve's torn on my tunic - look at me!
The only thing for me's a cardboard crown.
So watch me dear, I'm not worth much you know.
At best I am an aimless fainéant.
A nothing clad in language. Or, at worst,
a clandestine betrayer. Trust me not!
My favourite there, the Duke de la Tremouille
is watching you. He's green with envy. See?
He's pushed his face half-way into the screen!
Like pastry through a mould. A clever man.
I think he's trying to lip-read what we say. (*Waving*)
Defeatist through and through. There's murder on
his conscience. Watch his eyes. As tiny as
a hog's. But very shrewd. They won't give much
away. He bullies me. I owe him money, too.
Risk nothing! That's his motto, always was.
A policy quite different from yours.
Your presence here has put me in a spin.
My mind is always changing, blowing round.
It alters like the weather.

JEHANNE
                    Change no more.
God Himself has entered in your life.
Now all must fall before you.

CHARLES
                    We shall see.
I think that I shall keep you in the tower.
A view in all directions. Lots of sun.
My servants will be there to wait on you -
my page, my major-domo, and his wife.
A chapel is attached where you can pray.
I hear you're keen on that. So, pray away!
The people have such filthy habits here.
All sorts of poisons creep into the skin,
from France, from Spain, from Northern Germany.
You must look out. Be holy, good and true.

JEHANNE
It sounds more like a prison than a home.

CHARLES
You'll have free right of access to myself.
Come and go exactly as you please.
Within the limits of decorum, obviously.
Yolande there, that woman sporting horns,
she'll be coming up to see you very soon.
A quick examination, that is all.
A check on your virginity. A quick
up-skirt inspection. Or, in your case,
a rapid trousers down. You understand?
Nothing that's unpleasant, rough or crude.
I do not disbelieve you in the least.
The bishops, though, insist. It's all this
witchcraft business. You will understand.
They don't like women, at the best of times.
Nothing personal. I'm quite sure you are
as chaste as Christ's own mother. Certainly
your voices are impressive. I myself
believe them absolutely, but you see,
they have to be juridically approved
before you lead my army. We have to
try the spirits, as it were. The Friars
Minor will inquire into your general
stability and credibility.
Then you will go to Poitiers, where

doctors of theology and law
will study you. When they at last decide
you're not a witch or heretic, are full
of voices, and not vices, well, who knows?
Perhaps you'll drive the English clear of France!
Well, anyway, that's quite enough of that.
It's time for lunch. Now you'll sit next to me.
I want to know the story of your life.
Your friends, your parents, special interests.
Every pet and rabbit on your farm.
You're going to be my six-foot favourite!
My strapping girl, my saviour and my queen!
Come follow me, my dear. I lead the way.
Accompany my nose towards the food!
I have a fine confessor you must meet.
All piety and white intelligence.
You'll love the way he shines into your soul!

[CURTAIN]

SCENE III

By the Coudray Tower, Chinon. YOLANDE *and* ALENCON
are watching JEHANNE *tilting with a lance, and organising
various military manoeuvres.*

YOLANDE
You men. You can't take your eyes off her, can you? She's got
you in a proper body-lock. Are you in love with her?

ALENCON
We are the greatest of friends.

YOLANDE
Friends? What is friendship?

ALENCON
Equality made of harmony.

YOLANDE
You speak of friendship, but you deceive yourself. Love is a great daimon.

ALENCON
One looks on her and starts to understand. There's nothing in the field she cannot do. Leading the cavalry. Organising the line of battle, the pikemen, the archers. Placing the cannon. The way she scales a ladder! It's all quite remarkable, you know. It all comes to her quite naturally. The men love her.

YOLANDE
Of course they do. I see now why she wears male clothing. Climbing walls and suchlike. Leading from in front with the next man's helmet thudding up her buttocks. It all looks most uncomfortable.

ALENCON
You see the way she manages a lance?

YOLANDE
She was born half-horse. She charges like a centaur.

ALENCON
The men adore her. They're flocking in from all over France to join the army. Volunteers, the lot of them. All their services for free. She shames their manhood.

YOLANDE
I'm sure she does. The Dauphin will like that. Not having to pay the army, I mean. He's all for sacrifice, provided he doesn't have to make it himself. But what about the theologians? How are things at Poitiers? You're supposed to be the Dauphin's official observer. Or is all that too confidential to disclose?

ALENCON
Everyone is talking about her. Your testimony on her virginity
was taken very seriously. It was considered of the greatest
importance. She was believed far more readily once they knew
she was uncorrupted. Witches, it appears, are never virgins. It's
against the devil's rules.

YOLANDE
What did they discuss, then?

ALENCON
Oh, all sorts of nonsense. Occult phenomena. Devils. Spirits.
Perispirits. Reincarnations. Astral bodies. Leaders. Spirit
controls. Materialisations and the rest. What is understood by
the word *natural*, and what is designated by the term
supernatural. Esoteric and exoteric denominations. They
talked a great deal about Adam and Eve. The sanctifying grace
by which they received the infused virtues - so that they should
act in a way to merit heaven. What else did they say? How in
paradise, God was known by virtue of a spiritual light which he
imparted to the human spirit, an expressed resemblance of the
uncreated light. They discussed whether Jehanne had herself
experienced this light, whether someone purely human such as
she could receive a small participation in the kind of
knowledge possessed by the angels in their pure spirituality.

YOLANDE
And what did they decide?

ALENCON
That her voices were quite genuine. That she was a type of
lucid medium. That she could have ecstatic intercourse with
God, since she was largely free from the obstacles caused by
carnal passion, unaffected by a disorderly imagination or an
evil disposition, or by the frailty of forgetfulness.

YOLANDE
Those Armagnacs can soon smell out success, especially when
it rebounds to them. She'll triple their prosperity and power.
Just imagine it. Charles the Seventh. The new Melchisedech.
The powers of a thaumaturge, no less. Miracles are happening

everywhere. As common as the sunrise nowadays. And yet
there is a sort of logic in it all. The doubt about the monarchy
will go. The faithful will have to rally to our side for fear of
being traitors, as well as through their terror of damnation. A
king that one can sniff and hear and touch, whose rival's just a
seven-year English boy that nobody in France has ever seen -
that could be quite a useful thing to have. And Burgundy, well,
he'll be on the spot. He too would seem a traitor. She's coming
back toward you once again. Our Lady of the gisarme and the
lance, the cannon and the culverin, the sword. She carries all
before her. Everyone is pushing to enlist. Our knights all paint
her face inside their shields. And all for nothing. No one asks
for pay. The Dauphin is delighted. A fiery army, only needing
food! What more could he demand?

[*Enter* JEHANNE, *hot and flushed from scaling ladders,
brandishing a hand-axe.*]

JEHANNE
Mon tres beau Duc. You bring me bright good news?

ALENCON
What do your voices tell you, my dear saint?

JEHANNE
Ah! I see you come to disappoint me.
My voices tell me to be patient, not to fret,
that all things will be ordered in due time
provided I obey them. Am I right?

ALENCON
The theologians incline towards you.
So does the Dauphin.

JEHANNE
                    I understand.
The Dauphin must be driven like a mule.
Once the whip is dropped he stops to graze
then wanders through the pastures... Ah, these men!
My time is short, yet always they delay!
The way their minds go round and round and round,

as twisted as a staircase! And so I wait
in golden sloth, in beautiful decay.
They store me in this tower, this great stone jar
and bury me in honey. Talk and talk.
They say that women gossip. Men are worse.

ALENCON
Armies can't be furbished overnight.
Things are on the move now, down at Tours.
Consider the equipment and the men,
the horses and the cattle and the sheep!
A quartermaster's nightmare! Dear Jehanne,
you understand so little of these things,
the details of the planning, the expense.
Agere sequitur esse, but in you
the action must be instant as the thought!
How can men fire crossbows without bolts?
A horse attack unless its feet are shod?
Who checks the shields, the cannon and the shot?
Such things can't come by magic, can they dear?
What really matters now is our morale -
the way you've changed us since the day you came.
You alter us by being what you are.
You save us, give direction to our lives,
new vision, greater order, deeper love.

YOLANDE
Six months the English now have laid their siege.
Consider all the trouble that they face.
Ten thousand men to furnish and to feed.
Each day grows more expensive, the delay
more serious for the English self-esteem.
The money starts to fail, the troops desert.
The mercenaries ride off to other wars.
Disaffection spreads. The Dauphin says
we merely have to wait till finally
the English pack, and simply slouch away.

JEHANNE
The Duke of Bedford does not work like that.
Such reasons must persuade him to attack.
The English still maintain the upper hand.
Still have the stronger purpose, greater will.
France cowers like a rabbit at a stoat.
Don't you see? Our course is obvious.
We have to show we're not afraid to die.
Must pour ourselves in thousands at their forts
and bleed for our beliefs, our liberties!
The war has reached its crisis, yet we wait,
and I, whom God has sent to lead you all,
to clean out France, and then the Holy Land,
to liberate Jerusalem at last,
am made to sit on benches, answer men
who pry into the clothes my angels wear,
the accents of their voices, whether they
are tainted by some rustic dialect
or use the proper grammar! Oh what fools!
Next they'll ask the colour of God's hair
and if He changes clothing every day
or sleeps upon a silken bed at night.
If only they could see! We must attack!
Attack, and then the whole world will be ours!
Yet all they do is plot and counterplot
and speak of secret treaties, and delay. (*Pause*)
What is that?

ALENCON (*offering her a packet he has taken from his pocket*)
                    It's for you.

JEHANNE
                    For me? A
present? You have brought me a present?

ALENCON
From my wife.

JEHANNE
          What is it? Does it open?

ALENCON
There. See. Like that. Just so. What is it then?

JEHANNE
Une vierge ouvrante. How beautiful she is!
And such a kind expression on her child.
Jesus Maria! Oh, Our Blessed Lord!

ALENCON
My wife did not expect to make you weep.
You see the way the sculpture is designed?
The Father is revealed inside the Maid.

JEHANNE
It's beautiful! You'll thank her, soon, from me?
You know I cannot write.

ALENCON
                              You must not cry.
You weep like Rachel for her children.
France will soon be altered, that I know.
And here is something else.

JEHANNE
                              Something else? What
is it?

ALENCON
        A poem.

JEHANNE
            A poem?

ALENCON
                    From the
Duke of Orleans. From England. It's for you.
I'll read it to you later, if you wish.
A perfect evocation of the Spring.

JEHANNE
You are my perfect friend.

ALENCON
                        Your servant and
your slave. Yes, Paris will be saved. And all
of France. We'll even cross the Channel. Free
the Duke. The court is all so different now
you're here. And everybody feels it.
Everything's electric, edged with light.
We glitter with the supernatural will!

[CURTAIN]

SCENE IV

Chinon. CHARLES. ARCHBISHOP OF RHEIMS.

CHARLES
You're taking too long. I feel restless. In need of a good battle.

ARCHBISHOP
It's not like you to be impatient. Or so warlike.

CHARLES
This girl turns everything upside down. What was her effect on you?

ARCHBISHOP
Oh, she bewildered us. We felt polytheistic. Part of a new order. Of a many-souled world. There she stood, a huge transvestite, proud and tall as Artemis, keeping herself at a distance, holding everyone at bay, a virgin soul among her brothers and her sisters. And there sat the rest of us, old, decrepit, yet young again at heart, like most ill-made knights. We all had a most peculiar double-feeling. You could say our sense of soul returned. We felt a stronger, new identity, much more personally important, yet at the same time aware of our subjectivity as being made of many components, shifting, elusive, now wise and informative as Athene, now wily as

Persephone, as she seduced us through the earth down deep dark holes. Then she would whisper like Aphrodite, lifting us from her pink sea. Then stride into an Artemis again. It was disconcerting - so much unity, so much multiplicity. How have you reacted towards her?

CHARLES

Rather childishly, I'm afraid. I have been re-reading Gottfried von Strassburg. Strassburg! Ah! Not far away from where she was born. I fear I am in love with her. I fantasise continually that together we have escaped from the world. Found refuge in the forest at Morrois. There we live in that fantastic cave. The grotto is high. It is round and perpendicular. Its whole circumference is as white as snow and smoothly even. On the keystone of the vault is set a crown elaborately fashioned with goldsmiths' work and encrusted with precious stones. Below us there stretches a pavement of beautifully shining marble, as green as grass. At the centre is a bed most perfectly carved from a slab of crystal. It has been dedicated to the Goddess of Love. Small windows have been cut in the upper part of the grotto to let in light. Through these the sun shines in full apotheosis. Such simplicity, such power, such aspiration! The transparency, the translucency of my desire! Every window pictures kindness, rich humility. True breeding. On every figure I project her name and face. In that place, love is still honour, though the world would see it otherwise. I hold her as a sister. I feel no carnal motions. None at all. The sweetness of virginity, Archbishop! The purity, the power! As you must doubtless know. There human passion is turned to inspiration. From us flows all the good in the world. No one can take leave of her disheartened. She knows what each person needs, and the way to please him according to his truest desires.

ARCHBISHOP

A form of inborn suffering turns your brain. Do not meditate upon her excessively. That woman embraces nobody but Christ.

CHARLES
Pathetic, isn't it? I'm like an adolescent boy! But then, all my acts are ridiculous.

ARCHBISHOP
Not necessarily. It was a shrewd manoeuvre on your part to make us responsible for checking the girl. Now you can blame us if anything goes seriously wrong. The emotions aroused by chivalry are still very strong, even in this day and age. Honour can still appear in an heroic light, armed with lance or sword. Jehanne is already served and venerated like a queen. Already they have lifted her to an unreal level of perfection. Defend her inaccessible virginity. Desire to hack to bits as many Englishmen as their axes can reach.

CHARLES
How did she manage your examination?

ARCHBISHOP
Oh, *she* examined *us*.

CHARLES
And what was her verdict?

ARCHBISHOP
She was not at all impressed with us. She sat upon a bench-end, crossed her legs, and looked us up and down. Her clothes caused consternation. Quite a stir. I think they smelt of stables. Anyway, she told us all to start, get on with it. A Carmelite professor, Frère Séguin - a thin streak of a man, a Limousin - he speaks a sort of patois - he began. He asked about her voices, the style of language that they used. *"A better one than yours!"* was her reply. *"Do you believe in God?"* - I hear his voice. *"A better one than yours!"* she answered back. Then he said it could not be God's will for them to take her up on trust alone. They could not give the Dauphin their advice to give her the requested men-at-arms without some proof deserving of their trust. At this she lost her temper, shouting out, *"I have not come to conjure up mere miracles! Lead me to Orléans,"* she bellowed out, *"and I shall show the sign for which I'm sent!"*

CHARLES
Which silenced Frère Séguin.

ARCHBISHOP
It took him back. She outlined then the plans of Providence.
Orléans would be liberated. The Dauphin crowned at Rheims -
by me, of course - Paris would be taken once again. And last of
all, the Duke would then be freed.

CHARLES
No doubt that staggered them.

ARCHBISHOP
Of course. Another man, one Guillaume Aymerie, returned
then to her voices. He said if God desired to free the French
from all their wars then she did not need an army.

CHARLES
And what did she say to that?

ARCHBISHOP
She swore at him. She said the men must fight, then God
would give them victory. Then there was the affair of the letter.

CHARLES
The letter?

ARCHBISHOP
To the Duke of Bedford. Instructing him to leave. To surrender
the keys of all the towns he had captured. Otherwise a terrible
fate would fall on all the English.

CHARLES
Arrogant!

ARCHBISHOP
It took our breath away.

CHARLES
But you did it. You wrote the letter, then sent it for her.

ARCHBISHOP
Yes.

CHARLES
You see. She always gets what she wants. I can imagine what it
was like for you. Day after day. But you reached your decision.

ARCHBISHOP
Yes.

CHARLES
To trust her. To let her act.

ARCHBISHOP
Blood and prayers and tears and endless hymns. That's what
the girl has got in store for you. She'll turn her troops to monks.
Already they're confessing all their sins and attending mass.
The best of soldiers must be the best of men, she says. She
drives away all prostitutes and whores. Beats them with the flat
blade of her sword until they bleed.

CHARLES
So we shall raise the siege?

ARCHBISHOP
Things have now reached such a state it would be too
dangerous for you not at least to attempt to.

CHARLES
So. Officially you pronounce her orthodox?

ARCHBISHOP
Yes. Eccentric, yes, but orthodox. Miraculous. Puzzling.
Unusual. Very strange. But orthodox. For the time being.
There's little left of France. Give her her flag, her armour and
her lance. Use the girl. Make her feel she's free. Lead her up
and down before the men. Let her flash her standard at the sky
and wave her little hand-axe now and then but keep her out of
battle. Let the soldiers treat her as a saint. A saint that leads
them on their holy war. Already they're enlisting in their
droves. They want to fight for nothing. Just for her.

CHARLES
I can't afford to equip them, let alone pay them.

ARCHBISHOP
You will not have to. A victory or two would serve us well.
Give more strength for a treaty. The Church, you know, must
disapprove of war. By treaties - that's how modern war
proceeds. So. Let war return. We place our trust in God!

[CURTAIN]

SCENE V

JEHANNE, *in full armour, her helmet in her hand, meets*
DUNOIS, *the Bastard of Orléans, on the banks of the Loire to
the south of the city. She bellows through the wind.*

JEHANNE
This wind! This driving wind! You there!
Are you the Bastard of Orléans? Answer me!

DUNOIS
I am. And I rejoice at your arrival.

JEHANNE
Who advised these men to bring me here, to
the south side of the river, not the north?

DUNOIS
I, and others wiser than myself.

JEHANNE
Those wiser than yourself. Who are these men that
you call wiser than yourself? Point them out to me.

DUNOIS
The men stood over there. The Maréchal de Rais.
Saint Sévère. Louis de Culen, Admiral
of France. De Vignolles. Those who have you in
their charge.

JEHANNE
     Who have me in their charge? Their charge?
You set those men above the word of God?
You think those men superior to him,
that they can contradict my voices, turn them round
to do as they command? Answer me!
You know what God has ordered me to do?

DUNOIS
To free Orléans. To crown the king. To
enter Paris, liberate our Duke,
then unify the country in a great
crusade to loose Jerusalem.

JEHANNE
     Quite so.
What am I then? A talisman? A charm?
A flag of propaganda you can wave,
parade along the ramparts from a wall?
A toy girl on an ornamental horse?
A mascot, egh? Some simple animal
to wash and comb and manicure, a beast
with quaintly painted hoofs and gilded horns
to tether to a stake behind the tents
as soon as battle's started? Answer me!
You Dunois, you! The Bastard of Orléans!
You think I've come from Chinon for a game?
Have travelled from Lorraine, through Burgundy,
have slept and prayed and fasted, ridden, marched,
have bruised my aching body night on night
by sleeping in my armour till the blood
has seeped out through the hinges just for this?
My army is confessed, prepared to die.
It prosecutes a glorious, holy war.
Their souls fly straight to heaven when they fall

as white doves rise in April to the clouds.
Their spirits are all poised for an attack.
They wait to make their northerly approach,
yet where have you now brought us? To the south!
How then will you get us all across?
What do you propose that we should do?
Float there in full armour? Swim in mail?
Walk upon the bottom, file by file?
What are we then? Mere ornaments of war?
Mere drovers for your cattle, your supplies?
I come to make those forts an abattoir,
to drive the English northwards from the land
and you do this, you play these tricks on me!
Why aren't I consulted by your men?
You think that God's unworthy of your plans?
His wisdom insufficient for your needs?
Am I the one in charge of all these troops,
the envoy of the Dauphin, and the Lord?

DUNOIS
All Orléans awaits you. Come. Look there.
See the way the English lay their siege.
A ring of forts:- to north, to west, to south.
Only by the east can we move through,
but even in the east we're vulnerable.
I have this large flotilla of small boats.
You see them? In the middle of the stream,
between that pair of islands. Already
they are being loaded up with fresh supplies.
They'll land you after nightfall. I've arranged
a feint attack upon St. Loup bastille,
you see? The north side of the river. There!
With luck we'll steal unnoticed in the town.

JEHANNE (*contemptuously*)
Unnoticed! Yes. And what about the wind?
It blows from the north-east. It's far too strong
to move against. It pins you to the south.

DUNOIS
Exactly. The wind is now a problem.

JEHANNE
Have you prayed to God to cut its strength
or alter its direction? Answer me!

DUNOIS
Of course we have. Our prayers aren't strong enough
to influence the meteorology.

JEHANNE
But what if I should pray and make it change?
Spin it on its axis half-way round?

DUNOIS
That indeed would be a miracle.

JEHANNE
My saints have told me this. The wind will change.

DUNOIS
Of course it will. The problem, though, is when. (*Laughter*)

JEHANNE (*trancing*)
Watch the tents!

DUNOIS
            Good Lord! They've stopped swaying.

JEHANNE
And what is happening to the river?

DUNOIS
The waves! They're falling!

JEHANNE
                And what of the
direction of the wind?

DUNOIS
          It's backing.
Even as I speak. Towards the south!

JEHANNE
A good obedient wind. He's finished now.
Now all your boats can start to sail across.

DUNOIS
Come down to the boats.

JEHANNE
I take no orders.
Only those from God. You go over with
the rest. I shall ride along to Reuilly
and spend the night with my confessor.
Make sure the town is told that I am here.
Tomorrow I shall pass in through the gates.
No one will attempt to stop my path.
Already I can see the English fall.
Their forts are all on fire. I hear their screams.
They pitch into the river - God be praised!
They lie, a bridge of faggots for our feet.
Now you are invincible, my men!
Arrowheads will shatter on your skin.
Cannonballs can't harm you. You are all
invulnerable as metal! All will drop.
Talbot, Glasdale, many will lie dead.
The end is now beginning for them all.

[CURTAIN]

SCENE VI

PASQUEREL, PRIEST, OFFICER. *Sounds of battle.*

PASQUEREL
How's the Maid?

PRIEST

Her body's drenched with blood.
A six-inch wound is pouring from her breast.
Its runs with oil and honey. She won't stop!
Everywhere she's foremost in attack.
Men charge the walls like beasts, like maddened bulls.
The Lord of Heaven have mercy on their souls.
Battle is a dreadful way to die!

OFFICER
The English are in panic. Look at them!
Their bodies burn like torches, balls of fire.
The drawbridge is collapsing. See! They drown
beneath their heavy armour. Hear the bells?
The bells, the bells are ringing! And the crowds!
They jeer down at the English as they sink!
That culverin has shot down twenty men.
It took them out like pigeons, one by one.
Glasdale is already hoisted up.
They've carved him into pieces, boiled his flesh,
and set about embalming his remains
to sell back to the English! Ah, the Maid!
The Maid now comes towards us, stiff with gore.

[*Enter* JEHANNE]

JEHANNE
He called me a cowgirl. A witch and a whore!
That Glasdale was no English gentleman,
although he was their leader. How they burn!
To save themselves they jump into the stream.
There's nothing we can do to stop them drown.
I watched them cut away a soldier's leg.
A quick slash with the knife, and then the saw.
It scarcely took a second. Then the smoke.
The cauterizing torment of the torch!
However will that suffering soldier live?
By begging for his living on the streets?

OFFICER
He'll speak with pride of how he fought for you.
His wounds will gain him charity for life.

JEHANNE
The women we have widowed here today!
The children lying fatherless and cold.
I held a dying soldier with these hands.
He made his last confession in my arms.
I had to pull the arrow from my wound.
My breasts are badly bruised, and red with blood.
They dressed the cuts with lard and olive oil
then rubbed the pain with honey. I grow weak.

[*Enter* DUNOIS]

DUNOIS
It is a great victory. All Orléans
rejoices. You are our miracle!
Our miracle sent down to us from God!

JEHANNE
The fools begin to treat me like a saint.

DUNOIS
They use you as an oracle. Your words
are treasured and interpreted by seers!
The women name their children after you.
They touch your cloak as if it cured all ills.
One glance from you will raise the three-day dead.

JEHANNE
I fear they rob the godhead of its power
and venerate its shadow. More fools they.
There's little I can do to alter that.
The labour is my soldiers', theirs alone.
To them belongs the glory, not to me.
The sun glints like the moon behind the flames.
I wish it were a white hole in the sky
where I could rise to heaven. Why this pain?
Whyfore all this suffering, all this blood?

PASQUEREL
The heart of man is evil and corrupt.
It feeds upon illusion.

JEHANNE
                    That is true.
If only they had listened to the truth.
I told the English what my God would do
but always they deceived, were double-tongued.

PASQUEREL
Your soldiers, though, were different.

DUNOIS
It's good to see them in this state of grace.
She's sentenced them to heaven, one and all.
How ill they wear their new-found purity.
Deprived of their diseases and their whores
they scarcely dare to catch each other's eye.
You're looking tired. What have you eaten today?

JEHANNE
Some bread dipped into water, that is all.
I am not hungry.

DUNOIS
                    The siege is raised.
Talbot sends a message.

JEHANNE
                    So?

DUNOIS
                              He offers
us a battle.

JEHANNE
        When?

DUNOIS
                Tomorrow.

JEHANNE

Tomorrow

is the Sabbath.

DUNOIS

We must attack him.
Finish him off.

JEHANNE

No. We don't fight on the
Sabbath. Not unless our enemy
attacks us. If he does, well then, we shall
have to defend ourselves.

DUNOIS (*angrily*)

So. You have fallen
for his trick? When they're drawn up in battle-line
you'll simply stand and watch them, is that so?

JEHANNE
A priest will take an altar to the field.
A table and a marble block will do.
Two masses will be said.

DUNOIS

And after that?

JEHANNE
They'll go away.

DUNOIS

Withdraw to Meung?

JEHANNE

Oh you

will kill them all, don't worry. But on
some other day.

DUNOIS
You'll let them get away?
Regain their nerve? More French will have to die
later.

JEHANNE
If you do not obey me I
shall ride away and leave you to your
usual defeats and to the mercy
of the English. My work is over here.
My voices tell me I must go
to Loches. My time is short. The Dauphin must
be crowned. There is no other way. No
other way at all.

[CURTAIN]

SCENE VII

Rheims. JEHANNE, PASQUEREL, TREMOUILLE,
CHARLES, ALENCON *and the* ARCHBISHOP *move into a
rest-room after the consecration of the new king. There is an
air of tension, rather than celebration.*

CHARLES
Well Jehanne, I did it. I kept my word for once. I am crowned
true king of France. (*to* ARCHBISHOP) Can you smell
anything strange?

ARCHBISHOP
Smell something, Your Majesty?

CHARLES (*nervously walking around, stretching his limbs
and dabbing his forehead*) Yes. Something rather peculiar. It's
all right. (*He sniffs his hands.*) It's only me. That stuff you
smeared on my forehead. That shrivelled oil you pricked out of
that filthy old ampulla. Like a lump of ear-wax. Only black and

red. That consecrating stench! But then the whole place stank, didn't it? And every seat taken. I told you we should have charged an entrance fee. How much for a ducal seat, egh, Alencon? A hundred crowns? Two hundred for a bishop's? All of that, at least. A pity more of *them* weren't there. I hope you made a list, Archbishop! Just think of all the trade you've missed. The sale of your indulgences. The offices we could have put on hire! Still praying, Jehanne? (*to* ARCHBISHOP) I hope you marked exactly where she stood? Be sure to set a shrine there when she dies. A useful source of income that will be. Odd feeling, you know, being the centre of it all, yet knowing that no one's all that interested in you. (*He slumps into a chair.*) All eyes were on you, Jehanne. You quite upstaged the lot of us. Your opera of pomp, your great display! Four hours I sat there in the summer heat. My bladder in an agony of pain. I can't control my water like a woman, you know! I thought she might have fainted in the heat. Pretty though, wasn't she? Stood there in the window-light. Coloured by evangelists and kings. But not without her touch of drama, egh? Flinging herself to her knees like that with a great crash of armour when everyone started bellowing *"Noel! Noel!"* What a noise! I thought a chandelier had fallen from the ceiling. The height of exultation, my dear child! The height of exultation! Our Regnault did quite well, didn't he? All that macaronic Latin. Do you think that anybody really understood it? Still, who worries about all that? I thought that he was going to drop the crown. What a size it was! You didn't feel the weight. The Chapter lent it me. The real one's with the English. (*the* ARCHBISHOP *begins to pace around.*) Can't say, though, that it feels all that much different to be a king, apart from the smell of that filthy oil. People will blame me more when things go wrong, I suppose. Oh do sit down Archbishop, pacing round like that! You're not going to give me another of your sermons! I can see it in your eyes.

ARCHBISHOP (*annoyed*)
I do wish, Charles, that you would start to act more like a king. Society, in order to survive, must shape its individuals in such a way that they wish to do the things they have to do. Their outer function must be made an inward urge, so that they feel compelled to do their tasks from deep within - driven on by

dark unchallenged absolute values that brook no contradiction. Therefore you must activate their instincts in such ways that force them down their predetermined paths. Now you are our consecrated king. The foremost of the princes, with the power of working holy miracles. You understand? Now you are the autograph of God. You must embody that dark numen in yourself. Impel men to venerate your glory, your wonder and your power. Now you're ceremonials, shows of strength - gorgeous trains, festivities at court - a style of life that puts you in your setting, hard at work, deserving all the endless prophecies, the epics and the legends of the kings, the sermons and the noble eulogies, both rational and philosophical, that prove your human will is most divine. Think now of the myths that aid your rule. The golden age. The tale of the crusade. The new idea of Empire with its tree that roots you in a Trojan origin. The catalogue is endless. Now you rule. The emperor in his kingdom. You alone. You hold it by your God and by your sword. By your authority of goodness. Your wish is now the law.

CHARLES
Indeed it is. Now I shall show my power!
The first thing I shall do is shut your jaw.
I, the Infinite, the Universal Truth
now order you to silence. Go away
you boring fool. Clear off and wash your body.
And clean yourself. Wipe of that muck and sweat!
Your breath is foul. It's stinking like a jakes!
Thank God we don't have crownings every day.
The things these idiots claim that I can do!
Can I command the moonlight, make it shine?
And if I wink, does blackest night descend?
Can I piss out the oceans, spit out lakes?
Fart and carve a valley through the hills?
The idea is ridiculous. Absurd!
Thank God the air is cooler in this room.
The vaults feel like an ice-well underfoot.
As cold as winter. Chill as coming death.
                                        [*Exit* ARCHBISHOP]
Still silent, Jehanne? Still Praying? Come to me.
Now, sit you down beside me. Aren't you pleased?

My strapping Saint, my virgin medium,
you got what you desired.

JEHANNE

Not half of it.

CHARLES
Today's events displeased you?

JEHANNE

Tomorrow
we must march. Before us Paris waits.
We lose good time if we do not attack.

CHARLES
Paris will be bought. No shedding blood.
I totally forbid it, utterly!
I swore I'd never see that place again.
My father, mad, sat gibbering in his room.
The German whore, my mother, at his side,
her belly crammed with bastards! And the town!
Those narrow stinking alleys, thick with filth,
disgusting as the people that they hide.
All seething with intrigue and discontent.
Twelve years ago my leaders were in jail.
The mob attacked the prison, tore it down,
then ripped my men to pieces, just like beasts!
Heads, legs and all. They threw them in the Seine.
I know full well they'd do the same to me.
No. Paris will be bought. No drop of blood.
I will sign a treaty, make a truce,
a time of rest to ease you from your toil.

JEHANNE
Those men of Burgundy that come to make
this truce. You've seen them smile and turn aside?
The way they hide the purpose of their eyes?
They stay here for a week to scent the air,
promise that all France will come to you,
but what are they all up to while you wait?
They're reinforcing Paris. With the best

from Normandy and England. Can't you see
their truces are a mockery, a farce!
We must attack tomorrow! Straight away!

(JEHANNE *stamps over to a window and glares towards the
sky.* TREMOUILLE *takes his opportunity and approaches the
new king.*)

TREMOUILLE
Our Artemis! Still standing head and shoulders above the rest
of her brigade! *Potneia theron.* Our Lady of the Beasts! One
nod from her, the dogs devour their former master.

CHARLES
Come closer, Tremouille. (TREMOUILLE *recoils from the
smell*) I know. I smell like stinkweed. Swinecress. Hemlock.
It's that oil. These dog-days boil us all.

TREMOUILLE
Plato acknowledged two gifts granted by this particular season.
Fruit, and Dionysian joy.

CHARLES
Dionysian joy?

TREMOUILLE
Do not gaze on naked Artemis. There is a dark side to
innocence. Do not be too innocent my king. Think of her
woman's instincts. Think of her female impulses. They will tear
you apart like raw meat. Look at her. See? Waiting for her
voices. For her silver intuitions to flitter in. Imperious as Eve.
Primitive with longing. She will sever you. She will dismember
you, just as she has castrated the English. She makes your life
too deep. Avoid her joy. Do not step into terror and pity. Be the
hunter, cultured and educated, dally at the edge of the
woodland, but do not become the hunted one, red, dark-
forested and horned. Already you have one foot in her
unknown. Set both feet there and all will be reversed. You will
be utterly altered. Completely broken up. Remember your
father. She came from the shadows of the oakwoods, gleaming
with the prophecies of Merlin. Let her return to them. Already

she starts to fill all space with yearning. Her female smell is everywhere. Subjugate her. Subjugate her, now.

CHARLES
Her posture is upwards. She takes attention to the heavens.

TREMOUILLE
Artemis Orthia! The upright goddess! Remember how they worshipped her in Sparta. But man's natural look is downwards, into the street dirt. Into the gutters and their shadows.

CHARLES
She could weigh me down with horns. Set upon my head her immense hubris. Her terrible spiritual aspiration.

TREMOUILLE
You are already distressed by her gross excess of spirit.

CHARLES
Her gross excess of spirit. Yes. I like that phrase immensely. *Her gross excess of spirit.* Yes. That's good.

TREMOUILLE
Nailed up to a tree.

CHARLES
Lifted on a cross.

TREMOUILLE
Crucified by her vision of the Trinity.

CHARLES
Afflicted by perfectionism.

TREMOUILLE
Her neurotic punctiliousness.

CHARLES
Her impossible purity.

TREMOUILLE
You'll have her on your back for the rest of your life.

CHARLES
Must I betray her innocence?

TREMOUILLE
Protect yourself. Have no thought of betrayal.

JEHANNE (*approaching*)
You have much to talk of, my good lord.

CHARLES
I too must listen to my voices. Your
voices told me I'd be king, and king I am.

JEHANNE
It was your destiny, my lord.

CHARLES
I have one great regret. That I did not
see more of you upon the battlefield.
Ordering the ranks. And laying guns.
You have it all by nature, people say.
The new du Guesclin, fearless in the fight.
Never any hint of a defeat.
You push your pennants up into the sun
and terror strikes the English. They're a rout!
They think you're Hecate's daughter. Quite a witch.
Wild and dangerous, unpredictable.
Such is the omnipotence of thought!
First you pluck a crown from empty air.
Then you pluck a kingdom, by sheer will.
No wonder that the English are afraid.

JEHANNE
Do I look as though I ate children? Suckled
adders? What's the matter, sir? Am I a
problem?

CHARLES
      Leave us, Tremouille. No, Pasquerel,
you stay.

TREMOUILLE
      As the king wishes.   [*Exit* TREMOUILLE]

CHARLES
      Jehanne.

JEHANNE
Yes, my lord.

CHARLES
      We must have a little chat.
Come close to me. Does my smell worry you?

JEHANNE
No, my lord. It is a holy smell.

CHARLES (*confidentially*)
I'm very glad. It's not going to work, you know. This trick of
yours. This anointing. I am no David. I refuse to be infused by
the Holy Ghost. I firmly intend to remain who I am. We are
opposites, you know, you and I. Real opposites.
Philosophically I lean towards pessimism. Like a half-uprooted
tree. My will - well you know all about my lack of will-power.
The wish is there, but that's as far as it goes. I'm constantly
deflected, being bent. Whereas you, you are indivisible. As
straight as that crusader's sword of yours you had dug up
behind the altar at... where was it?

JEHANNE
At the church of St. Catherine de Fierbois.
My voices led me there.

CHARLES
Exactly. Your voices. Now as you know I like to reflect on
causes, whereas your orientation is teleological. Your vision is
pure and idealistic, whereas I, I defend myself by macabre
fantasies. I am oppressed by guilt, by the neuroticism of

conscience. You are glorified by it. The world outside these walls depresses me. But you, you impose upon it your magnificent will. I adore sexual surrender. You think it's not worth the bother. It never enters your brain. I brood upon the horror of my parents. You monopolise your siblings. I suffer hell at the mere thought of death. You abandon all self-interest in your vision of the ideal society and your responsibilities to the community. As I have said before, you proclaim the oneness of the universe, the unity of mankind, the wisdom of conforming to universal laws. Life for you means a constant effort, the struggle to renew virtue, to strive, as has been said before, continuously from a lesser towards a greater perfection. Whereas I prefer to build a private metaphysical world quite different from the one that others inhabit. My court is just such an area. Already I am half-way to developing my own personal and unique style of reasoning. I am, as you would say in your blunt and country fashion, half-mad, whereas you, dear visionary, you are super-sane.

JEHANNE
What are you trying to tell me? That I have become a nuisance to you? That you will no longer support me against the English?

CHARLES
I admire you, Jehanne. I admire you intensely, with an admiration bred from the deepest inferiority. But I must forbid the shedding of any more French or English blood. I must tell you this. I have signed a secret treaty with Burgundy and the English. I shall disband the army forthwith. It can't do much in winter anyway, and that's just round the corner. Diplomacy will now achieve the rest. Our strength now lies in words, since you have given substance to our nouns.

JEHANNE
I see.

CHARLES
You feel betrayed?

JEHANNE
Yes.

CHARLES
I thought you would.

JEHANNE
Treaties with the English are useless.

CHARLES
You doubt my judgement?

JEHANNE
Always.

CHARLES
Well doubt it, then. But I am tired of war. We need a time of
peace, of clearing up. The Church advises it. Your efforts won't
be needed any more. I'm hungry now. I need to have a wash.
But no more battles. No attacks on Paris. Enough has already
been achieved. We'll talk of all this later. Yes, later. There is
too much eating and drinking to be done. You have given me
too much responsibility. I will see you at the banquet.
Somewhere around the place. Till then, farewell!

[*Exit* CHARLES]

PASQUEREL
You have been betrayed.

JEHANNE
                         Yes.

PASQUEREL
                                   You expected it.

JEHANNE
Yes.

PASQUEREL
    The king must be obeyed.

JEHANNE

What if he is bad?

PASQUEREL
Well, then he is a punishment from God.

JEHANNE (*angrily*)
I thought that France had suffered quite enough.

PASQUEREL
Who are we to read the mind of God?

JEHANNE
We ought to sweep the English in the sea.
That fainéant Tremouille. I know he's bribed.
He plays upon the terrors of the king.

PASQUEREL
What do your voices say?

JEHANNE

Nothing. They have left.
They offer me their silence. Nothing more.
How quickly one's meridian is passed.
Suddenly the sun feels less intense.
One knows that one has ceased to ride the light,
dismounts into a shadow. I saw my
father in the crowd. He spoke to me.
He did not like my gold and crimson robe.
He thought it far too gorgeous, too ornate.
When I asked him then to choose a gift
he asked for tax remissions back at home,
so he should not collect them any more
and so avoid the peasants' curses.
I said I would request it from the King.
I gave him sixty livres. The Dauphin gave
me them. He said that they would help him patch the barn.
One's origins grow distant, too apart.
It seemed we came from very different worlds.
I still prefer the cowshed to the court.
What is happening to the present?

PASQUEREL
                              You find
it disappoints you?

JEHANNE
                    I feel that I could
fall straight through it, into nothingness.

PASQUEREL
Nothing could be better than that, my child.
To surrender the past, but also to
surrender the future. For the future
pollutes the nothingness of the present.
For what we all call the present is not
really the present. It is a veil,
a cloud. And it shifts. There is nothing
eternal about it. No finality.
Just as there is no real finality
in the future. The future is a word,
a hope. An expectation, and an
illusion. It is the ideal present
we have projected onto what is to come
and which will eventually become the present.
Do you understand? One must penetrate
the here and now. Pierce straight through into
its nothingness. And there, within that
nothingness is the end that you seek.
You have encountered the eternal.
It is good to be frustrated by events.
You are frustrated because you have expected
an illusion. Something that came, but was
not. It is absurd to desire the
future to be here and now without
ceasing to be the state it is. An idea.
A concept. A feeling. You know the cure.

JEHANNE
Eternity.

PASQUEREL
It is painful, entering the present.
Only when suffering seems everlasting,
only when we can gaze upon awful
affliction with complete acceptance
and the beatitude of agape
can we be separated, and enter
the everlastingness. There is still
much pain for you to undergo, my child,
much pain.

JEHANNE
              What shall I do?

PASQUEREL
                        You must pray to God
as nothingness. As non-existence. As
non-entity. Pray to Him as the
absolute Other. Then you will comprehend
His will. No longer dwell upon the future,
but listen for your voices. They will sing.
The same corruption follows from the sword,
whether one holds the grip or feels the blade.
But in the supernatural there is no
coercion, no compulsion, and no force.
Nor will that love protect your soul against
the coldness of that force, the sickness of
its metal. Killing chills the soul, whether
as agent or receiver. As does all
whose essence is mere violence. If you wish
to make your soul invulnerable to wounds
then you must find some other god than ours.

JEHANNE
I understand your words. And yet I know
I must follow my own reason. Others still
insist that we attack, and I agree.

PASQUEREL
You place yourself in danger if you
disobey your king.

JEHANNE
My king lacks will,
and I shall give it him. I grow of age.
My voices do not speak. It's time that I
now took my own decisions. We shall fight.
First Paris, then the cities of the north!
The Western world, then dear Jerusalem!
I know it, for I feel it in my heart!

[*Exit* JEHANNE, *clanking her armour.* PASQUEREL *shakes his head and sighs.* CURTAIN]

SCENE VIII

Paris. THE DUKE AND DUCHESS OF BEDFORD *admire a painting which* THE DUKE *is uncovering.*

DUCHESS
Ah! The wedding present for the Duke of
Burgundy.

DUKE
How do you feel about it?

DUCHESS
It's very different. Very human.
Almost too much so. Who painted it?

DUKE
An
Italian called Masaccio. He died
quite recently, aged twenty-eight. The same
age as Praxiteles.

DUCHESS
How sad!

DUKE
                         Yes. Those
whom the gods love, die young. It is an
interesting portrait. Three dimensional.
Man is changing, my dear. Soon he'll have no
need of kings, nor even churches. He is
starting to become himself, God help us!
But at the present we must still destroy
our most gifted individuals, our
future evolution. It is all too
difficult for little folk like us,
the Duke and the Duchess of Bedford,
to deal with.

DUCHESS
                    How is the trial going?

DUKE
Slowly. The Church never hastens over her
murders. She does not like to have a
dirty conscience. She has to make sure she
has shifted the guilt, or at least shared
it out correctly.

DUCHESS
                    Do you feel guilty?

DUKE
Of course I do, my dear. In a world like
ours, guilt is the price of authority.
No. The trial is proceeding in its own
laborious manner. But we are having
to suspend the public hearings.

DUCHESS
                         Oh? Why?

DUKE
The girl's enjoying the notoriety.
She makes the prosecutors seem too
foolish. Too much like what they are.

That's always the problem with real virtue.
It dirties the others, like you and me.
They are having to proceed with the
examination within the shadows
of her cell.

DUCHESS
        She knows what she is talking
about.

DUKE
        That's right, my dear. And they do not.
She knows exactly what to do in
order to frustrate them. She refuses
to answer any questions on the
orders from her voices. She refuses
woman's clothes, insists upon her right
to run away, and insults the lot of them.
Not that I rebuke her for such things.
They're an unpleasant nest of traitors, all
of them.

DUCHESS
        But is she really a French witch?

DUKE
Good Lord no! But our soldiers think she is.
She terrifies them, even in her irons.

DUCHESS
Then why don't you have done with her? Do what
you have to do, and let her rest in peace.

DUKE
Politics is not a simple craft.
To kill her now would be too dangerous.
The girl is still a legend and a myth.
She'd soon become a martyr and inspire
ten times as much devotion than she's done
already. The dead sustain their myths.
While they're alive, there's still sufficient room

to slander them, degrade and vilify.
We must destroy her claim that all she's done
has been the work of heaven, God-inspired.
That must be done by her own countrymen,
and not by us. You understand the plan?
Once she's been proved a dark limb of the Fiend,
King Charles's crown will soon appear as black
as all the tangled alleys of his brains.
His tenure then will seem as feeble as
his constancy and reason.

DUCHESS

>That is cruel.

DUKE
No crueller than the things she does to France.
We bring them law and order, stop their brawls
and offer them a double monarchy
and how does she respond? By setting a
degenerate on the throne. Just look at him!
A beast who has no morals and no will.
A cheat, a thief, a common murderer.
A man who keeps a mistress, changes faith
more often than the wind along the shore.
And all done in the name of Holy God!
How does he thank her, once his crown's achieved?
He betrays her to her enemies. Like that!
Does he once attempt a rescue? Not at all.
Offer a ransom? No sign of such a thing.
The man's a coward, reeking parasite.
He gives away the land she wins for him
and peasants die so he can rot at ease.

DUCHESS
Why do you bring this charge of heresy?

DUKE
The easiest accusation one can make.
And the hardest to disprove.

DUCHESS

                            You trust your
hirelings? This man you've put in charge, this
Bishop Cauchon?

DUKE

                   A most ambitious man.
He's changed his side to make a new career.
The Maid's invasion robbed him of Beauvais.
She tore the see of Rouen from his grasp.
Now he has a chance to get it back
and make himself immortal.

DUCHESS

                         By the fire.
By burning her.

DUKE

                   Our motives aren't the best.
But justice will be done. She has to die.
That moment she was dragged down from her horse,
that moment that the drawbridge lifted up
her fate was sealed. She was as good as dead.
But still she is a force to reckon with.
No one can predict what she will do.
She still could make a fool of all of them -
the Church, the University, the Court
of Holy Inquisition. Yes, the lot!
The cardinals and bishops, all those priests
and countless theologians. They all know
too much, of course, lack holy ignorance.
Time will show us when her fate will come.
Fortune governs all. On runs the sun!

                    [CURTAIN]

SCENE IX

Rouen. JEHANNE's *prison cell.* GRAY *and* MOUTON, *guards.* JEHANNE *is at prayer, kneeling, despite a sound of hammering.*

MOUTON
Hear that sound, Master Gray?

GRAY
What sound is that, Master Mouton?

MOUTON
That sound in the yard, Master Gray.

GRAY
Sounds like a 'ammering, Master Mouton.

MOUTON
Quite right, Master Gray. A right royal 'ammering. That sound is the 'ammer of the locksmith.

GRAY
And what's the locksmith 'ammering, Master Mouton?

MOUTON
'e's fitting up a cage. A cage with thick iron bars.

GRAY
What are they going to do with the cage, Master Mouton?

MOUTON
Fill it with a witch. Chain her by the hands, the feet, the throat. Then hang her in the square. That locksmith is a devil. A very devil.

JEHANNE
You do wrong to interrupt my prayers.

MOUTON
Remember when they burnt that Paris witch? How she shat across the faggots? What a stench! Fair gassed the whole bloody garrison, that one did. I can see her now. The roasting flesh all sliding from the bones. The arms both dropping off. The left leg, then the right, till all was left was her naked torso, all black and charred, in flames.

JEHANNE
You do wrong to interrupt my prayers.

MOUTON
Hear that, Gray? The witch rebukes us. A French witch rebukes a good honest English soldier. What do you think of that, Master Gray?

GRAY
I think the witch deserves to be taught a lesson. A girl of her age shouldn't be interested in prayers. It's unnatural.

MOUTON
Then what should she be interested in, Master Gray?

GRAY
You know as well as I do, Master Mouton. A good strong piece of English meat!

JEHANNE
You dare to interrupt me at my prayers, and you so close to death?

GRAY
She threatened you, Mouton. Did you hear that? She threatened to kill you. Nasty!

MOUTON
Evil little bitch.

GRAY
Filthy witch.

MOUTON
We'll have to put her in her place won't we, Master Gray? And
what is the proper place for a woman, Master Gray?

GRAY
Flat on her back, Master Mouton.

MOUTON
Exactly. Flat on her back, Master Gray. Nothing too unnatural,
egh, Master Gray? Even if she does dress like a man. You have
her first. You open her up. I'll shut her mouth for her. (*Striking
her*). Go on then. (*Struggling with* JEHANNE) Tear it away.
Quickly. Get your knees between her legs, my fine old warrior!
Open her up!

GRAY
They say the virgin pisses ice.

MOUTON
Then we shall have to melt her, won't we? Come here you
bitch. You've had this coming to you for a long, long time.
(JEHANNE *bites his hand through to the bone.* MOUTON
*screams in an agony of rage and springs to his feet seizing his
sword.*) I'll cut her fuckin' 'ead off, I will. She's bit me to the
bone.

JEHANNE
Rape! Rape! Rape! Houcepailliers! Houcepailliers! Rape!
Rape! Rape!

MOUTON
The blood! The blood! She's cut me to the bone!

JEHANNE
Rape! Rape! Rape! Houcepailliers! Houcepailliers!
Houcepailliers!

[*Enter* THE EARL OF WARWICK, SOLDIERS]

WARWICK (*to* MOUTON)
You! Drop your sword! Get back to the wall! Move!
(*to* GRAY) You too. Or I'll take your head off! Now!
Take them to the dungeon. Get them out of here,
before I slit their stomachs with my sword!

[*Exit* GRAY, MOUTON, *guarded*]

JEHANNE
Your soldiers tried to rape me at my prayers.

WARWICK
They broke their orders. I'll hang the pair of them.

JEHANNE
You break the law to keep me locked in here,
in irons and in a common prison cell.

WARWICK
You're lucky that it's not a dungeon.

JEHANNE
Despite my pleas you offer me no bed,
put chains around my body every night.
All Rouen interrupts me at my prayers.
And now you plan to hang me in the square
as if I were some common lunatic.
This is bad. You do your soul no good to keep me here.
A dog within its kennel gets more rest.

WARWICK
The cure is in your hands. Give your oath
you won't escape, then you can have a room
and women too. Your chains are self-inflicted.
You bring these daily sufferings on yourself.

JEHANNE
You yourself would act no differently.

WARWICK
Did they harm you?

JEHANNE

My lips feel bruised. My gums
are rather sore. I broke the soldier's finger.
Will you really hang him?

WARWICK

He will hang. Slowly.

JEHANNE
I think a simpler punishment's enough.

WARWICK
That is my decision. Alter your mind.
Swear an oath. Change your clothes. Then you can live
quite differently. You'll find we're not barbarians.

JEHANNE
Never.

WARWICK

I know. You're far too much the soldier.

JEHANNE
Am I to be suspended in the square?

WARWICK
There are many ways of destroying a witch.
All painful.

JEHANNE

You will not frighten me.

WARWICK
Wait till you see the flames. One can stand
the *idea* of burning. A real fire's different.

JEHANNE
How much longer will I be in here on trial?

WARWICK
Ask your assessors. Only they will know.
Do you feel fit to see them?

JEHANNE
                    Lead them in.
It makes no difference, does it? Let them come.
The sooner this is over, we can rest.
[*Exit* WARWICK. *Enter* BISHOP CAUCHON, D'ESTIVET,
the promoter, BEAUPERE, *a clerk and* LEPARMENTIER, *a*
torturer.]
Bishop Cauchon. You're in charge of this.
Why am I no longer tried in public?
Why all these private examinations
in my cell?

CAUCHON
            We have reached a new stage in
the proceedings.

JEHANNE (*contemptuously*)
                    And what is this new stage?

CAUCHON
Alter your tone of voice and I may tell you.

D'ESTIVET (*viciously*)
You are an insubordinate witch. Your
replies insult the Church.

CAUCHON
                    You reply too
boldly for your own good. Who is it bids
you treat the fathers and the theologians
of the Church as if they were mere children?

JEHANNE
But that is what you are. A little band
of children.

CAUCHON
　　　　It is your voices that
instruct you to reply like this?

JEHANNE
　　　　　　　　They
order me to make a bold reply.

CAUCHON
　　　　　　　　　So
they are not concerned with the impression
that you make?

JEHANNE (*looking towards* LEPARMENTIER)
　　　　　　I will not answer that. Who
is that man?

CAUCHON
　　　　You have not met him yet.
Your voices do not tell you who he is?

JEHANNE
He stands in too much darkness. His smell is
evil.

D'ESTIVET
　　His name is Leparmentier.
He is the public executioner.
Also the torturer to the Holy Inquisition.
He is an expert at his profession.
At the ordeal by water. At stretching
limbs by ropes.

JEHANNE
　　　　　　Poor man! To have to earn his
living by producing so much useless
evidence.

CAUCHON
I tend to agree. But it's
not always so. I have sad news to bring
you.

JEHANNE
Sad news?

CAUCHON
Your father is very ill.
The shock of hearing what men say of you
has hurt his heart.

JEHANNE
He knows that I am not
a sorceress. He knows you lie.

CAUCHON
He has
been informed that we have reached a new stage
in our proceedings. We have now attained
the ordinary hearing, the second
phase of the trial.

JEHANNE
I see. The second part.

CAUCHON
Remember how we read the other day
to the assessors the summary of
our findings?

JEHANNE
Who could remember that?
Seventy rambling and repetitive
clauses, all packed with lies, distortions. Not
once did you include one single word from
my responses. I deny everything
you say. I refer to my previous
examination at Poitiers. It
is all written there. Consult that if you wish

to know my answers.

CAUCHON
There is a certain
justness in the way that you reply.
D'Estivet was certainly verbose.
So we've drawn up a second act of
accusation.

JEHANNE
We? Name to me that *we*.

D'ESTIVET
Ourselves. Helped by the theologians from
the University of Paris.

JEHANNE
And what do the theologians of the
University of Paris have to say?

CAUCHON
They've reduced the act of accusation
to twelve articles. They have summarised
the principal points to present the
matter much more briefly so that our
deliberations may proceed far more
efficiently.

JEHANNE
Efficiently? You have
reduced all those months of questioning to
just twelve articles?

CAUCHON
Yes.

JEHANNE
Will you read them
out to me so I may have them checked?

D'ESTIVET

We've
wasted too much time on that already.

JEHANNE
You have eyes like frozen spawn. Gelatinous,
and grey. How do I know that you have not
corrupted all my answers?

CAUCHON

There is
also a message from your mother.
She who made your body in her womb,
who taught your paternoster and your creed,
demands that you submit yourself to truth.
That you obey the Holy Inquisition
for her sake and to save your father from
an increase in the suffering he feels.

JEHANNE
I hear you.

CAUCHON

So? What do you say to your
father and your mother?

JEHANNE

Bring them here.
Let me question them, then I'll believe you.

D'ESTIVET
You call us liars?

JEHANNE

God understands the
nature of your souls.

D'ESTIVET

Remember the
executioner.

JEHANNE
>Will you let me read
the twelve articles against me?

CAUCHON
>How can we?
You are illiterate.

JEHANNE
>While I've been shut
up here I've taught myself to read. To see
what you've been up to. I know what you've been
doing. You call your foreign doctors and
your jurists into consultation. Allow
all your assessors to deliberate
quite freely on the accusations brought
against me, but the text that they employ
has all been edited, truncated, and
falsified. You present them with a
travesty of truth. Remember the wrath
of God.

D'ESTIVET
>Shad-eating bitch!

BEAUPERE
>You are a major
theological problem for us, Jehanne.
And that problem is the nature of your
authority. You understand? Is it,
as you claim, transcendental, or is it
not? We are here to determine whether
that transcendental authority is
good, or whether it is evil. Whether
it issues from the Holy Spirit, or
from the Enemy of God. Possibly,
even a confusion of the two. The
charge of heresy is extremely grave.

JEHANNE
Then read what has been said at Poitiers.
I've been through this before.

BEAUPERE
                              But the fathers
at Poitiers were of the King's party.

JEHANNE
And you are not! A fine argument.
Theology is relative to one's
political opinion.

BEAUPERE
                    The Pope
is absolute arbiter on matters
of faith and morals.

JEHANNE
                         Which one of them?
You know my religious beliefs. My
ideology is the same as yours.
My religious practices are also
identical, except I spend more time
on them than you do. My religious
knowledge, that is the problem. Obviously
intellectually I know next to nothing.
I am a hollow hole, an empty well.
I have no training in the various schools
of theology. I know far more about,
well, sheep diseases, or castrating lambs
on the field-gate. Theology I leave
to the Pope in Rome, to the professors
at the University of Paris.
Where I differ from you is in my
actual religious experience,
the beings that I see and understand
and must obey. I differ in the
feelings that they bring into my heart,
the blinding joy, the orders that they give
and in the vast effects these bring about.

All of these discussions, all of these
relentless questions, scrupulous reports
are on one single point, one point alone.
The nature of my voices. And there is
one thing I know that I can never do
and that thing is to share what I now feel,
to give your hearts and individual minds
experience of their certainty and love.
Make me deny those, and I deny
the meaning of my essence, of my soul,
my individuality. Then I'm
a fallen ruin, ball of summer dung,
a river-bed, sucked empty by the sun.
Wonder is so private. But it is like
physical pain. It can't be shared. It
cannot be transferred. When your torturer
applies the thumbscrew, does he experience
his victim's pain? Of course he doesn't!
Neither can any of you take on my
visionary condition. You are too
evil, too corrupted, too absurd. How
could you be wrapped in bliss, become a child
that suckles at its mother? Joy would
poison you. Burn your throat like acid.
You'd say you were afflicted by the Fiend!
Bliss cannot be shared the way you hear
the noise of this my voice, the words it makes,
the sounds it leaves behind you on the wall
that echo from the mould. I pity you!
Believe me, I would teach you innocence.
Impress you with the lily on my seal,
teach to you that state of nothingness
that opens to the Spirit. But I can't.
There is no way my body can transfer
such golden information. None at all.
Pain as a sensation can't be shared.
Pain as an emotion, though, can move
a mild imagination, touch the heart.
So see my tears, and cease. Leave me alone
or get on with the sin that has to be.

D'ESTIVET
A very subtle woman.

CAUCHON
                    Very sly.

JEHANNE (*beginning to sound unreal*)
Of what do the Parisians accuse me?

BEAUPERE
Of relying on false revelations.
Of erring in your faith by claiming that
the articles of faith are less well-founded
than your personal disclosures. Of
being guilty of idolatry, of
schism, heresy, blasphemy and
immense vainglory.

D'ESTIVET
                    You have eaten shit.
But you have spat it out. And we must pick
it up.

CAUCHON
        Help us to share a little of
your experience of your voices. How old
were you when they first appeared?

JEHANNE
                            Thirteen.

CAUCHON
Were you a woman then?

JEHANNE
                    Yes.

CAUCHON
                    And where were
you at the time... (*Fingering papers*) Ah yes. In your father's
garden. Was there anybody there with

you at the time?

JEHANNE
        No.

BEAUPERE
        Did your face change?

JEHANNE
How should I know?

CAUCHON (*eagerly*)
        Did it look like St.
Catherine's?

JEHANNE
    St. Catherine's?

D'ESTIVET
        St. Michael's?

JEHANNE
No.

CAUCHON
  Did your voice alter?

JEHANNE
        No.

D'ESTIVET
        Speak like an
angel's?

JEHANNE
    No.

CAUCHON
    Sound like a man's as well as a woman's?

JEHANNE
No.

D'ESTIVET
Did you feel superhuman at the time?

BEAUPERE
That you could pull down trees? Dam the rivers.
Lift huge boulders?

JEHANNE
No.

CAUCHON
For how long did these
voices continue?

D'ESTIVET
One minute?

BEAUPERE
Two?

CAUCHON
Three?
Or longer?

D'ESTIVET
Did you lose consciousness?

JEHANNE
No.

BEAUPERE
Feel a spirit within your spirit?

JEHANNE
No.

CAUCHON
Did you struggle against it?

D'ESTIVET
                        Did you feel
unnaturally excited?

BEAUPERE
                Were you
having your periods at the time?

CAUCHON
                        Were you
quite lucid? Did you remain quite conscious
of yourself?

D'ESTIVET
                Or did you feel in sudden need
of exorcism?

BEAUPERE
                Purification?

CAUCHON
Tell us now.

D'ESTIVET
                Confess now.

BEAUPERE
                        Tell us everything.

CAUCHON
Woman swims in sin as a fish in water.

D'ESTIVET
These voices. Did they smell sweetly?

JEHANNE
                                They smelt
like paradise.

BEAUPERE
They left no stench behind?
Like dung, or burning sulphur?

JEHANNE
Theirs was the
sweetest scent that I have yet experienced.

CAUCHON
They left behind no howling sounds of grief or
desolation?

JEHANNE
I had never seen a
devil, until I saw you.

D'ESTIVET
Do you know
just how many devils are abroad
within the world? Seven and a half
million.

JEHANNE
I can quite believe it.

BEAUPERE
And you have never seen them? Never seen the
Fates? The poltergeists? The incubi and
succubi? The marching, raucous hosts of
noisy men? The nightmares? The demons sprung
from semen, from the black abyss of sleep?
Those who masquerade as women, or as men?
Those who make old women think they've flown
to witches' sabbats?

JEHANNE
I have seen those who
appear as holy men, and tantalise.

CAUCHON
Those flying heads you saw...

JEHANNE

                       I saw no

flying heads.

CAUCHON

        Did they have bloodshot eyes and
matted hair? Or did they look like skulls?

JEHANNE

Catherine's face is very beautiful.

D'ESTIVET

So is the face of Lilith. And she is
sexually insatiable.

BEAUPERE

            Are you
sexually insatiable? Have you
ever attacked men in their sleep? Seduced
their bodies? Drunk their blood?

CAUCHON

                    Drunk their blood?

JEHANNE

I have never even heard of such vile things.

D'ESTIVET

The English say you have. They say you've been
an acolyte at the Black Mass.

BEAUPERE

               That you
lie along the whole length of an altar.

CAUCHON

Draw your knees up.

D'ESTIVET

            Hold two candlesticks
with black candles.

BEAUPERE

Set a cross between your breasts.

CAUCHON
A chalice between your thighs.

D'ESTIVET

Make the priest
stand between your knees.

BEAUPERE

Then sacrifice
to Ashtoreth while killing a small child.

JEHANNE
I know nothing of such evil practices.
Ants must feed on fungus, I suppose. And
cockroaches will eat their parents' faeces.

CAUCHON
Yet you continually use magic.

JEHANNE

No!

D'ESTIVET
At Beaurevoir, for instance. You leapt down from
the tower. A fall of seventy feet.
Did devils bear you up? Answer us!

JEHANNE
I felt it was my duty to escape.

D'ESTIVET
By jumping seventy feet?

JEHANNE

I was wrong.
My saints were greatly troubled by my act.
You see, I knew the danger at Compiègne.
I'd heard the things that Burgundy had said.

That everyone above the age of seven
would be destroyed. Yes, all of them be killed
by fire or sword. You see, I loved those
people in my heart as God has loved them
in his own. I could not bear to think
that they would die. But since that jump my saints
have calmed my mind. And they are always right.
They told me that the town would be relieved
before the mid-November, and it was.
It came to pass exactly as they said.

BEAUPERE
The evidence for sorcery is strong.
Your knowledge of the battle at Rouvray.
The sign you gave the Dauphin and the way
you saw into his heart, his secret prayers.
The sword you found at Fierbois and the change
you fashioned in the wind at Orléans.
That leap from Beaurevoir. The Lagny child
your breath brought back to life. All these are strange
and must be more examined.

CAUCHON
                    We must read
the scenes beneath your eyelids. Enter in.
See the things that still obsess your brain.
What lies behind your strange transparent stare,
that different existence of those eyes
that look and know.

D'ESTIVET
                    Actions must be judged by
their effects. We look around. Charles is crowned.
The country's plunged in conflict, far and wide.
Our own exchequer's bankrupt, as you know.
France follows some degenerate murderer
who throws away the conquests he has won
to buy himself an idle, unjust truce
so he can lie in bed and fornicate.
Is this the will of God then? Answer me!
Your king won't lift a finger for you now.

Ingratitude's his essence, always was.

JEHANNE
You lie, for there are good men at the court
of probity and honour, whom I love.

BEAUPERE
Where are they then? What ransom do they pay?
And where's their aid? The point's important child!
My dear, you are deserted, cast away.
A failure and a problem for us all.
A deep embarrassment to everyone.
Your voices chose an idiot for a king.
Your friends are fighting for the English now.
If only you were less intransigent.
Remember that we do not wish to judge
but only to assess, evaluate,
to transfer information, so your soul
may grow to heaven far more easily.

CAUCHON
We wish to act as fathers in this case.
Communicate through loving, deep concern.
Remember, though a court seems firm and grave,
that underneath that mask it is your friend.
Some acts are good and other acts are bad.
Some acts are intermixed. We tease things out
and try to be objective, day by day,
to stay quite calm and neutral in our hearts.
You must not take our firmness for a frown.

JEHANNE
At least you will not frighten me with praise.
I always fear the flattery of friends.

D'ESTIVET
The fact, my child, is that we're on your side.

JEHANNE

Then you must ask my voices what they think.
You'll get a different answer. This trial is
vitiated, both in substance and in form.
It is tainted with fraud, with calumny,
with contradiction and iniquity,
has manifest errors in fact and law.
It will be made null, invalid, worthless,
without effect and annihilated.
Your articles of accusation will
be torn up in the marketplace and you,
you all will burn in hell, as you well know.

BEAUPERE

We could offer you an advocate.

JEHANNE

I have no need of any advocate.
Now that they are here I'm truly whole.

CAUCHON

Princes pass away. The Church remains.
Expediency is not her moral law.
The Church abhors all bloodshed. Nonetheless
those heresies that damn the human soul
must not go uncorrected. Everywhere,
on all sides, men and women stride the earth
who claim they hear the whispers of the Lord
and scandalise the people. Do you still
refuse to tell the truth about these things,
the revelations sent to you, you claim,
by God alone?

JEHANNE

                I do not lie. Such things
were told to me for my dear king alone.
Such things I'll never tell to any here,
not even should you cut my head away.
I've sworn to tell you I will speak the truth
about my parents and all my campaigns
and everything pertaining to the faith.

But not my revelations. (*Pause*)

CAUCHON (*rising, walking round her, examining her clothing*)
                    I am sad
to see you here like this, dressed in this way.
You feel no shame?

JEHANNE (*wearily*)
                    Shame? I feel no shame.

CAUCHON
You think such clothes appropriate to your sex?
You do not feel indecent dressed like this?
An outrage to the natural law of things?
An insult to the shape of womanhood
to sit there like a common man-at-arms,
your hair shorn from your head, just like a dog's?

JEHANNE
I am a soldier. As I've said before,
if I were a priest I'd wear a skirt.

CAUCHON
I quote to you from Deuteronomy.
The twenty-second chapter. Listen now.
Mark this carefully. I'll translate for you.
A woman shall not wear a garment that's
pertaining to a man. Nor shall a man
put on a woman's clothing. Those that do
become abominations to their God.
St. Paul condemns the practice. And I quote.
When any woman prays or
prophesies, her hair uncovered, she
dishonoureth her head. For it is just
the same as if her head were shaven.
And doth not even nature teach us that
it's shame to men to wear long flowing hair
but in woman it's a glory since her locks
are given for a covering. Corinthians.
Book One. Chapter Eleven. Well, my child?

JEHANNE
My Lord and all his angels order me.
And they are quite sufficient.

CAUCHON
                         The King and
Queen and others of your side did not
request it?

JEHANNE
                 That is irrelevant.

CAUCHON
You know you are forbidden to hear Mass
dressed as you are. Surely it's more fitting
to attend in woman's clothes? Which would you prefer?
To dress in woman's clothes and go to Mass
or stay in man's attire and keep away.

JEHANNE
Guarantee I'll hear it if I change
and then I'll give an answer.

CAUCHON
                              You have my pledge.

JEHANNE
But what if I'd promised Charles that I
would not remove this clothing?

CAUCHON
                              You made him
such a promise? I think you play with us.

JEHANNE
Make me a dress that stretches to the ground
without a train. I'll use it at the Mass
but afterwards resume these clothes I wear.

D'ESTIVET
The tailor of the Duchess brought a dress
but you refused to wear it.

JEHANNE
                    Indeed I did.
The tailor tried to stroke me on the breast.
The soldiers tried to rape me afterwards.
Had I been accoutred in a dress
they surely would have managed. Anyway
no man in battle ever fights in skirts.
The idea is ridiculous.

CAUCHON
                    One understands
you would not tempt the men. There's credit there.
But even when with women you dress so.

JEHANNE
Because I am a soldier. Passez outre!

D'ESTIVET
When did your voice last speak to you?

JEHANNE
                                        It came
this morning. It came yesterday as well.

D'ESTIVET
Yesterday as well.

JEHANNE
                    That's what I said.

D'ESTIVET
At what time did you hear it yesterday?

JEHANNE
In the morning. Then at Vespers. In the bell.
The third time was the evening Angelus.
It often comes more frequently than that.

D'ESTIVET
And what would you be doing at the time?

JEHANNE
I was asleep. Then the voice awoke me.

D'ESTIVET
On all three occasions?

JEHANNE
That is correct.

D'ESTIVET
Did the voice have a body? Did it touch you?

JEHANNE
It did not touch me.

D'ESTIVET
The voice was in the room?

JEHANNE
I do not know.

D'ESTIVET
But it was in the castle.
Did you thank it? Did you fall down on your knees?

JEHANNE
I thanked it. I was sitting up in bed.
I clasped my hands and asked for its advice.
It told me I should answer without fear.
Without one fear. One single fear at all.

CAUCHON
Before you prayed, the voice said certain things?

JEHANNE
I could not really understand them all.
But when the voice awoke me from my sleep
it told me I should answer without fear.

CAUCHON
And that you should not answer what we ask?

JEHANNE
I will not answer that.

BEAUPERE
                    But you have said
that you have revelations from that voice.

JEHANNE
About the king. I must not tell them you.

BEAUPERE
Because you are forbidden?

JEHANNE
                         I don't know.
I've had no clear instructions. Give me time.
Some fifteen days and then I'll answer you.
You question me for months, incessantly.

CAUCHON
Was there a face accompanying the voice?

JEHANNE
You know I'm not allowed to tell you that.
My oath does not apply to saying that.

CAUCHON
You heard the voice some seven years ago
for the first time, some seven years ago,
and you were very frightened, for a light
accompanied that sound. What exactly did
the voice tell you?

JEHANNE
                    I have told you that.
That I was destined for a different life.
That God had chosen me to aid the king.
To regain for him his kingdom.

D'ESTIVET

What else?

JEHANNE
That I should dress in masculine attire.
Bear arms and lead the army so the land
was guided by my counsel.

D'ESTIVET

And you, like
Deborah, obeyed. You have said it was
the voice of Michael. Of St. Michael.
How did you know that it was he?

JEHANNE

He used
the speech of angels.

D'ESTIVET

Ah! The speech of angels.
How could you understand how angels speak?

JEHANNE
I wanted to believe it, and I could.

D'ESTIVET
At first, though, you weren't totally convinced?

JEHANNE
I was most scared. I only was a child.
Later on he taught me many things
and in the end I knew that it was he.

D'ESTIVET
Supposing that the Enemy had come,
disguised himself by taking on that form,
how could you then have known if he was good
or evil?

JEHANNE
     It was quite obvious.
I knew quite well that angel was not bad.
He told me to be good. That God would help.
That Catherine and Margaret would appear
and that I should obey them, since their words
were sent me by the ordinance of God.

CAUCHON
You breathed no word of this to anyone?

JEHANNE
None at all.

CAUCHON
     Not even to your father?

JEHANNE
That is correct.

CAUCHON
     Together there were three?

JEHANNE
I told you so.

CAUCHON
     And you saw them clearly.

JEHANNE
I did.

CAUCHON
     As clearly as us?

JEHANNE
     The same.

CAUCHON
But in a cloud of light.

JEHANNE
                    But in a cloud
of light.

CAUCHON
          Did you touch them? Did you embrace them?

JEHANNE
Yes. I did.

CAUCHON
                    About the head? Or round the
lower parts?

JEHANNE
                The lower parts.

CAUCHON
                              You felt their warmth?

JEHANNE
Of course.

BEAUPERE
          And do so still?

JEHANNE
                         Of course I do.

BEAUPERE
You smell them too?

JEHANNE
                          Their perfumes are most
beautiful.

D'ESTIVET
          And was St. Michael naked?

JEHANNE
You think Our Lord's no clothes to dress him in?

CAUCHON (*growing angry*)
How was he accoutred when he came
the first time to the hillside. (*Wrenching her head towards him*)
Answer me!

JEHANNE
I saw a crown. I saw no other clothes.

CAUCHON
He wore hair?

JEHANNE
He was not bald, like you are.

CAUCHON
What colour was his hair?

JEHANNE
I cannot say.

BEAUPERE
In what style was it trimmed? The English or
the French?

JEHANNE
I must not say. Were I allowed
then I should tell you willingly. It's
written in the book at Poitiers.

CAUCHON
St. Catherine and St. Margaret. Are they tall?

JEHANNE
Sometimes they are taller than yourselves.
At others they're no more than finger-high.

CAUCHON
How do they speak? As loudly as I do?

JEHANNE (*ironically*)
More softly. With a calm and humble voice.

CAUCHON
And you've seen them many times? Several
hundred times in all?

JEHANNE
                    I have.

BEAUPERE
                         St. Margaret

speaks in English?

JEHANNE
                    Why should she, since she's not
upon their side?

BEAUPERE
                    Does she hate the English?
What about St. Catherine? Does she hate them too?

JEHANNE
She loves the men Our Blessed Saviour loves
and hates the men He hates.

CAUCHON
                    A clever girl.
Such sly simplicity! St. Margaret and
St. Catherine dress alike? Answer me!
How do you know your saints are who they are?
How do you know their names are as they claim?

JEHANNE
My saints are who they are.

CAUCHON
                    You have no proof.

JEHANNE
Believe me if you like. That's your affair.
My head goes round. I cannot tell you more.

BEAUPERE
Do they have arms?

D'ESTIVET
                    Or other members?

JEHANNE
Why do you keep asking me all this?
You know I am a poor and peasant girl
who scarcely reads and writes. So let me be.

CAUCHON
Do you believe you're in a state of grace?

JEHANNE
If I am not, then may God put me there.
If I am, then may He keep me in it! (*Silence*)

CAUCHON
Will you abide by the decision of
the Church, as is your duty, if it is
found that what you've said is contrary to
the faith?

JEHANNE
          Your clerks must read my answers.
If they find there's anything opposed
then I'll consult my voices. Afterwards
I'll tell you what my voices have declared.

CAUCHON
And if they are opposed, what will you do?

JEHANNE
I can't support a faith opposed by God.

D'ESTIVET
You set your private judgement over us?

JEHANNE
My voices tell the truth. They will not lie.
How can they disagree if you're correct?

D'ESTIVET
You'd contradict God's vicar here on earth?
The priesthood of the apostolic church
descended from St. Peter?

JEHANNE
                    Contradict?
I do not understand how that can be.

CAUCHON
You claim then to communicate with heaven?

JEHANNE
Heaven must claim its right to speak to me.
I do not have to write to bishops first
and ask for their permission.

CAUCHON
                    You love the Pope?

JEHANNE
I venerate his office.

CAUCHON
                    And his faith?

JEHANNE
Of course I do. But sometimes he can err.
The poor man's only human, isn't he?

BEAUPERE
Then God alone is your authority?

JEHANNE
The Pope of Rome, the bishops of the Church
are there to guide the faith and keep it pure.
I love the Church with all my heart and soul.

God, the Church, the bishops, all are one.
Why must you make things seem so difficult?

CAUCHON
But what if the Pope should ask you now
to change your dress at once. What would you say?

JEHANNE
Just take me there. I'll answer what I should.

D'ESTIVET
You realise your words are heresy?
That everything you've said to us today
creates a dangerous precedent? Is
wickedly subversive? Look at me!
Don't you perceive the dangers of these days?
How men and women rise on every side
and claim their revelations come from God,
Our Lady and the angels, spreading lies,
incest, murder, bestiality,
and all from holy motives, burning hearts,
that hosts of souls may feed the fires of Hell?
You realise that this must end in flame?
Chained up to a stake, your body cursed
and given to the judgement? (*Shouting*) Answer me!
Have you not thought your voices came from Hell?

JEHANNE
Were I to see the fire and feel its heat,
were I to feel my flesh burn on the bone,
I would not change one single word I've said,
not one small white iota.

D'ESTIVET
                         You have sinned!
Oh France! I fear that you are much abused!
And Charles, who calls himself your lawful king,
endorsing all the words and deeds of this
most useless, most abandoned, wicked girl,
heretical, dissenting as he is,
is just as bad as she. I tell you, girl,

your king is a schismatic. So are you!

JEHANNE
I dare to say, to swear upon my life,
that he's the noblest of all Christians.
He loves the Church and faith. You're telling lies.

CAUCHON
Submit your words and actions to the Church.

JEHANNE
As for my submission to the Church,
she has my answers. Go to Poitiers.
There you'll read my statements in her books.
I challenge you, the justice of your court.
Let all my deeds and words be sent to Rome
and set before the Pope, whom, after God,
I venerate most humbly. He will know
that what I've said and done has been through God.
I accuse none, least of all my king,
nor seek to charge his crown in any way.
If there's a fault, then it is mine alone.

CAUCHON
That won't suffice. The Pope is far away.
Our ordinaries are judges, each of them
sufficient to his office.

JEHANNE
                              So you say.
Again I must appeal to see the Pope.
You write the things against me, not the things
submitted in my favour.

BEAUPERE
                              Why not the
General Council? Why not submit her
case to Basle?

JEHANNE
> Basle? What is that?

I've never heard of that.

BEAUPERE
> It is a

congregation taken from the Church
comprising all its parties, yours as well.

JEHANNE
If some of ours are there, I'll go to Basle.

CAUCHON
Be silent. You, clerk, erase those words from
our report. And hold your tongue. If you don't
go quickly to your place again then I
shall lock you up from sunlight for a year.

JEHANNE
You, Bishop of Beauvais, I speak to you.
You say you are my judge. I do not know.
Be certain that your judgement is not wrong
for fear another judgement fall on you.
I have done my duty. You are warned.
I know the men you are! I read you all.

CAUCHON
You realise that I can torture you?

JEHANNE
Even if you tear my limbs apart
so that my soul spills from my body, I'll
not speak in any way that contradicts
the truth. Torture me, if you must. If I lie
I'll always claim that it was forced from me.

D'ESTIVET
But don't you fear for death, the flames of Hell?

JEHANNE
I am a Christian, properly baptised.
And as a proper Christian I shall die.

CAUCHON
The last time now we ask you here today.
Will you obey the dictates of your Church?

JEHANNE
And I'll repeat what I've already said.
I will obey the Church, and all her laws,
but never will I lie about my saints,
my visions and my voices. And again.
Never, not for anything on earth
will I obey the Church if what she says
in any way is contrary to God
and what my voices order. Furthermore,
I always shall refer myself to God,
The Church Triumphant, high in Paradise,
yes, even if the Church declare my words
are evil, diabolic and perverse.
God must come first.

CAUCHON
                    Take her out of here!
Executioner, show her the instruments
of torture. How we rip apart the lies
of heretics.   [*Exit* JEHANNE, *hauled by* LEPARMENTIER]
                    That it should come to this! (*Silence*)
Thank God she's gone! I'm drained of energy.
I understand how Maximilian felt
when arguing with her great St. Catherine.

BEAUPERE
It is most dangerous to mix with things
beyond one's understanding, to put one's faith
in novelties, inventions and the like
where devils can insinuate their thoughts,
pervert the mind, suggesting occult things,
or shine like golden angels.

D'ESTIVET (*triumphantly*)
                        She stands condemned!
Each phrase she utters chains her to the stake.
Each sentence pours fresh oil upon the fire.

CAUCHON
Were she a man, I think she'd be the Pope.
The last thing we require is punishment.
We do not look for vengeance, only truth -
to bring her to salvation. If we don't
proceed with mercy now, then later on
we also may be banished with the rest,
abandoned, like the Saracens, in Hell.
Tomorrow we'll resume our questioning.
This business of her secret with the king
should bring out contradictions. Strange the way
that she reveres him, almost worships him.
He, the one who plotted her betrayal.
Until tomorrow, brothers, eight o'clock.
Our business here is virtually done.
The judgement, then the burning, that is all.
The one runs from the other, naturally.
No space for a repentance set between.
No need for a suspension in a cage.
I leave you to your consciences and prayers.

[CURTAIN]

SCENE X

BEDFORD, WARWICK, CAUCHON.

WARWICK
We are very angry.

CAUCHON
That is very understandable.

BEDFORD
You frightened her too much.

CAUCHON
The Church abhors the shedding of her blood. It was our duty
to make her recant.

WARWICK
The square is in an uproar. The paving-stones are flying. You
bishops fight with one another.

CAUCHON
How could we foretell how she'd react? It must have been the
shock of excommunication. She collapsed. Became as nothing.
Stripped of grace. (*Slyly*) Now that she has signed the cedule of
abjuration, perhaps you should keep her in a secular prison.

BEDFORD
She has promised to resume woman's clothes.

CAUCHON
Exactly. And I have no doubt that she will. But what will
happen when we take them away from her? She will hardly
wish to walk round naked, even if it is the merry month of
May. Besides, once her anger gets to work, once her voices
turn against her and she realises she has betrayed herself, she
will soon want to be a man again. Believe me, my lords, she
will relapse, she will soon resume her male clothing, and then,
then you will have her. There will be no second chance for her
then. You must burn her up immediately, and turn her bones to
ashes in the Seine. Insight! That is all you need. A little insight.
Turn her against herself. Her pride and her ambition will
destroy her. Use your brains! A little patience, that is all you
need. A little patience. Then all will be done. The girl will be
forgotten, evermore.

[CURTAIN]

SCENE XI

The secular prison. CAUCHON, BEAUPERE, D'ESTIVET, LEPARMENTIER, BEDFORD, WARWICK. JEHANNE *stands naked in her cell, covering her body with her hands and staring intently at the suit of male clothing - tunic, hood and gipon - that has been laid out before her. Three* MEN-AT-ARMS *stand threateningly behind her, offering immediate execution, almost pricking her with the points of their weapons, trying to goad her into reassuming her male clothes.*

SOLDIER 1
Folk witch!

SOLDIER 2
Political witch!

SOLDIER 3
Heretic witch!

CAUCHON
Folk witch!

BEAUPERE
Political witch!

D'ESTIVET
Heretic witch!

BEDFORD
Folk witch!

WARWICK
Political witch!

LEPARMENTIER
Heretic witch!

OMNES
Folk witch! Political witch! Heretic witch!
Folk witch! Political witch! Heretic witch!
Folk witch! Political witch! Heretic witch!

JEHANNE
You do me wrong to expose my body,
to take away my woman's garments, so.

CAUCHON
Put on your male attire!

JEHANNE
                You have forbidden
it to me, on pain of execution.
I shall not wear it. How long then will you
keep me here in torment? I have stood for
many hours. All of you, you shame my body.
You also shame the future of your souls.

CAUCHON
You can stand there for the rest of your life.
It's up to you.

JEHANNE
             I signed the recantation
with a cross.

D'ESTIVET
           And smiled, as I remember.

JEHANNE
I fear that I was frightened by the fire.
My uncorrupted body felt the flames.
I'd rather be beheaded seven times
than burnt like that. It terrified my heart.
Culot took the paper from his sleeve.
He made me then repeat its words aloud.
I signed it with an O and then a cross.

CAUCHON
You see now what your spirits have achieved?
You acted on them far too willingly.
You should have turned to God in holy prayer
and asked him to reveal more certainty
about the things they said. You did not speak
to learned men to seek enlightenment,
consider your simplicity of state,
the lowliness of knowledge you possessed.
Those would have been the most essential acts
a peasant girl like you should have performed.
Our Blessed Lord in heaven, Jesu Christ,
when he ascended back upon his throne
entrusted all the government of things
to Peter and the rest, forbidding them
to take in their protection those who came
and claimed to be good Christians, but who brought
no other token but their empty words
to guarantee their statements. So, my child,
what then can you now say about yourself,
baptised into the faith by sacrament,
a long-established daughter of the Church,
if you do not obey Christ's officers,
that is to say, the prelates of the Church,
but answer to your own authority
and not that of your betters? Answer us!

JEHANNE
You forced me to deny my inward self,
proclaim aloud my life has been a lie,
so I disgraced my countrymen and king
and threw away my conscience and my soul
to save my flesh from burning.

D'ESTIVET
                              Whore of Lorraine!
Where are your voices now? Where were they when
you stood upon the scaffold, terrified?
The day that you were captured at Compiègne?
When you assaulted Paris? Answer us!

JEHANNE
I trusted in my own initiatives.
In that I was remiss. My conscience wronged.
I thought I saw the pattern of events
but that was far more devious than I knew.
You ask me where my voices are right now.
They're closer now than you will ever know.

D'ESTIVET
Your voices have returned? And when was that?

JEHANNE
They came back on the Feast of Pentecost.
They brought God's pity to me. Warned me that
when I'd abjured to save my flesh from fire
that I'd betrayed my God and put my soul
in danger of damnation. They revealed
when I was on the platform near the fire
I should have spoken boldly all they said
because the preacher uttered many lies
by saying I'd done things that I had not.
If I deny that God has set me here
my soul will be in peril of the fire
because the Lord has sent me. What I did
was only by his orders, his commands.

CAUCHON
The stake is in the square, heaped up with wood.
When you relapse you get no second chance. (*He signals to*
SOLDIERS *to assemble the people. Exeunt* SOLDIERS 1, 2, 3)

JEHANNE
Bishop, when I die, I die through you.
My death will set a curse upon your soul.

CAUCHON
You have brought your death upon yourself
by breaking all your promises to me.

JEHANNE
You promised me a prison of the Church,
not here, amid these English, in these irons.
You think you raise your fortune by these acts.
You smirch them by an infinite degree,
confine yourself far more than you can know
promoting this, my murder.

CAUCHON
                                You've sold your soul
for an imp of the devil. Through your acts
all France has been reduced into a state
of primitive brutality and vice.

JEHANNE
Look into a mirror, ugliness!
See your own reflection, what it is!
Mere barrels with no bottoms, all of you!
Yet all of you, you could have found your soul.
If only I could strip you of your sin's
imaginary divinity. But no!
(*Sadly*) They tell me I must dress now. So I must.
I hear them all. I hear the words they say.
That I must put it on, life's misery.
All time's unceasing dark necessity,
the burden of its penury and dearth
that grind all down. Yes, I must take it up,
must turn to the coercion and the pain,
must reassume these garments I so love.
(*Picking up her male clothing and examining its texture*)
They tell me all of these, each little stitch,
each warp and weft of each soft strand of wool
each in its way must constitute the same
warm clothing of the body of my God
and glimmer with a beatific joy.
The God of Love withdraws behind such forms,
these mean conditions, so that we can start
to purify our natures, find His love.
If we were once made naked for that love,
left lacking this soft cladding that we wear
of space and time and substance, then we all

would vaporise, like water on the sun.
Then there'd be nothing left to throw away
or yield to the necessity of love.
There! You see? I'm dressed now. Now my life
is yours to end, to mutilate at will,
and then possess as nothing. All we own
is what our souls renounce. I understand.
What we do not renounce soon flees from us.
I'm ready to be outraged and destroyed.
In life there are two moments, two alone,
two moments of unblemished innocence
and nakedness. When we arrive, and when
we depart. At those times we adore
in human form our transcendental God
without polluting His great holiness.
I am ready to be pure again. For
what is death? A quick, immediate state.
Futureless. No past, yet quite imperative
for entering eternity. For we
are not, of course. This we realise
through agony, by dying. So, kill me then.
I consent to be saved. To be transformed
and purified. Well, prelates, do your work.
My voices say my heart will fail to burn.
My entrails, though they hiss in burning oil,
will also be immortal. You will see.
Fetch me a crucifix, and hold it up
to burn like red-hot iron inside the fire!

                              [*Re-enter* SOLDIERS 1,2,3]

CAUCHON (*exultantly*)
Jehanne! You who call yourself *La Pucelle,*
you have gone back to your errors and your crimes
as dogs return to vomit. Therefore we
declare you excommunicate again,
abandoned to the mercy of the law,
a limb of Satan, severed from the Church,
to lie in Hell forever.

SOLDIER 1
                    Lift her up!

SOLDIER 2
Deceiver of the people!

SOLDIER 3

Sorceress!

CAUCHON
Blasphemer to her God!

D'ESTIVET

Presumptuous!

BEAUPERE
Disbeliever in the faith of Christ!

BEDFORD
Boastful and idolatrous and cruel!

WARWICK
Invoker of the devils! Dissolute!

CAUCHON
Liar and schismatic! Heretic!

D'ESTIVET
Apostate and a most pernicious liar!

JEHANNE (*to* LEPARMENTIER)
You, my executioner! Advance!
You who burn my body in the flames
and place your dunce's cap upon my head
with all its rampant devils, hear my words!
I do not lay this murder to your charge.
All of you, my judges and my guards, you Englishmen,
though soon my flesh must smoke across the fields,
my blood boil in a black fat on the stones,
be mixed with oil and sulphur, pray for me!
For I forgive you all this harm you do!
Tonight I shall be praying for your souls
in paradise! Note well these words I say!

WARWICK
Away, and chain her body to the stake.
Despatch her quickly. Read the sentence first.
Make sure that that is done before she burns.
To the stand, now. To the stand. Executioner,
make sure you part the flames to show she's dead.
Throw every scrap of ash into the Seine.
No further ghost of hers must trouble France!

[*Exeunt* OMNES *running, bearing* JEHANNE *on their shoulders like a rolled carpet.*]

OMNES
Folk witch! Political witch! Heretic witch!
Folk witch! Political witch! Heretic witch!
Folk witch! Political witch! Heretic witch!

(*Suddenly the stage is flooded with a red light.*)

JEHANNE (*off-stage, her voice growing louder with each cry*)
Jesu! Jesu! Jesu! Jesu! Jesu! (*With a final triumphant scream*)
Jesu! (*The red blaze from the fire is suddenly extinguished.
The* CURTAIN *falls.*)

THE COURTSHIP OF SOREN KIERKEGAARD

A VERSE PLAY IN EIGHT SCENES

DRAMATIS PERSONAE

SOREN KIERKEGAARD
PETER KIERKEGAARD, his brother
HENRIETTE KIERKEGAARD, Peter's second wife
ANDERS WESTERGAARD, Peter's manservant

REGINE OLSEN
CORNELIA, her sister
AUNT, their surrogate mother
COUNCILLOR OLSEN, their father

BISHOP MYNSTER

SCENE I

September 1840, in the library of PETER KIERKEGAARD, *overlooking Nytorv, Copenhagen. A painting of Michael Pedersen Kierkegaard overcomes one wall.* PETER *and his recent second wife* HENRIETTE *are standing by a window, pretending to be glass, watching* SOREN KIERKEGAARD, *who is behaving eccentrically at one side of the square, and drawing attention to himself by his exaggerated attempts to appear moral as he shadows Regine Olsen on her way to her music lesson.* PETER *is scanning his brother angrily through opera glasses.*

HENRIETTE (*gently, setting her hand on her husband's wrist*)
Peter. Peter.
Do try to see the funny side of things.

PETER
The funny side! (*He laughs, dryly.*) The funny side! See! My
brother. Making a fool of himself again.
Just look at him. The scourge of Hegel, the terror of Descartes,
out stalking some young schoolgirl through the streets.
Scuttling like a spider, here, then there,
yet still dressed up in mourning. Everyone
is watching. He is a disgrace to the
family. To the memory of our father.

HENRIETTE
He's in love.
Pass me the glasses. Well I must say
your brother has exquisite taste. Few aesthetes
could fault it. She's very beautiful you know.
Extremely luminous. Low-neck dress.
Ivory shoulders. Curls across high cheek bones.
The mouth is very liberal and kind.
The eyes are stunning. Utterly direct.
Roguish though. And slender with it too.
She really is a nymph. Yet vulnerable.
I wonder if she'll step upon his web.
Now she's turning off, down Vestergade,

to Vestervold. Here. Take another look.
She's late. She keeps on looking at the clock.
She's carrying her song-book. Obviously
she's going for her lesson. Now, she's gone.

PETER
How long has this been going on?

HENRIETTE
                                        Since his
return from Jutland. Since his visit to
Saeding, your father's former home. She
passes twice a week.

PETER
                    What happens next?

HENRIETTE
Just be patient. There. You see? He looks round
furtively, then steps into that pastry shop.
He takes a table - at the centre of the room.
Orders a cup of coffee. Extracts his
notebook, and starts to write again.
His whole life's one long novel. An experiment
with existential thought.

PETER
                    Do I know the girl?

HENRIETTE
Regine? Councillor Olsen's daughter.
He's a high official in the Ministry
of Finance. An Etatsraad. She's a first-rate
catch. If he doesn't move quickly, someone
else is sure to get her. Her former tutor
is in love with her, I hear. A decent and
God-fearing man. Her mother, alas, is
dead. Hallo! Something's happening. Your brother's
looking troubled. Now he's thrust aside
his coffee. Now he's walking out. Oh dear! I
think he may have seen us. The streets are hot.

He's shimmering in the heat. He looks
volatilised. Now he's beating his legs with
his cane. Now he's heading in this direction.
Tacking through the carriages and dogs.
He walks in such an odd unnatural way.
Mechanically, like some old marionette,
its limbs in all directions. Look at him!
Each foot has to remember where to step.
Nothing looks spontaneous at all.
Well. Are we at home? Are we going to
speak to him? I'll call Anders Westergaard.
(*She rings a bell.*) He'll know what to do.

[*Enter* ANDERS WESTERGAARD]

ANDERS
You rang, madam?

HENRIETTE
                    Soren Kierkegaard is
approaching. Are we at home to him
at the moment?

ANDERS
                    I believe so, madam.

HENRIETTE
Then you will lead him through the front door
and then guide him here, making sure that he
knocks nothing over.

ANDERS
                    I shall do my
very best, madam. Shall I serve refreshments?

HENRIETTE
                                        No.

He's looking too excited.

ANDERS
He is arriving now.
I shall deal with the crisis immediately.

[*Exit* ANDERS. SOREN KIERKEGAARD *hammers the door
with his cane. Re-enter* ANDERS *pursuing* SOREN
KIERKEGAARD *who strides into the room, and moves
immediately to the centre, vibrating with irony.* ANDERS
moves to leave.]

SOREN
No. Stay Anders. Stay exactly there.
Listen to what they have to say. I am
being watched. Did you know that, Anders? I
am being watched. Overlooked. Now it is
most difficult to think while one is
being watched. It interrupts one's processes
of inwardness. Another's soul disintegrates
the Spirit. Floods it with an alien
and negative becoming. Reflection
is destroyed. Confusion reinstated.
Inwardness, the instant, the now, all gone.
All gone, Peter. (*Shouting*) All gone! You understand?
I sit, the unconditioned Absolute,
then suddenly I find that I am watched,
am back in pain, a point of consciousness
inside this dreadful cliché, this poor fool,
this hideous compendium of a man,
its sum of concepts, feelings. Then I am
made flat again. A shadow.

PETER (*contemptuously turning his back*)
You think too much.
Exaggerated self-analysis
leads to madness. I have told you that
many times before. The act of thinking
occasions a secondary reflex
act. Its object is the primary act,
the subject that initiates. That
subject's made an object. Thence there
issues subjectivity. But think too much

and overstrain - well - the observer then
gets disconnected from his actions,
so things appear to happen of themselves.
One no longer feels a person. Feels a loss
of individual activity. That one
is altered, shifted, lived, moved. Spoken.
One is on the way to lunacy.
You must reduce thought. Stop all this thinking.

SOREN
Living separate, in my new flat, is difficult.
I am impractical. The practical
life is impossible to me. I loathe
its nonsense and confusion, all of its
inaccuracy. The world is filled with
petty annoyances. I am estranged
from it. I have a basic sense that it
is alien and infected. All existence
makes me anxious, from the smallest fly
to the mystery of the incarnation.
Nothing is intelligible to me.
Most of all myself. So I explore my
inwardness. It's no less infinite, no
less contradictory than what's without.
I'm weakening my hold on outer things.
I'm living in a world of fantasy.
I live through mere personae. I become
devitalised and unspontaneous.
The falseness of my masks reduces me
to clichés, into mere banalities.
I turn into quotations.

PETER
                              Obviously.

SOREN
You must send me Anders. To me he is
my Archimedean point, my own true Pole.
This man must come to me. I insist.
He must become my legs, my arms, my fingers.
Existence is too difficult without him.

He protects my subjectivity.
I'll buy him from you. No? Well then I'll hire
him. Monthly? Weekly? You could at least spare
him for an hour or two. In Jutland he was like
a father to me. A living father.
(*Picking up the opera glasses and squinting round the square*)
Well, what did you think of her? Egh? What did you think?
(*Putting down the opera glasses*)
I saw that you were watching her. Watching me.
Watching for the watcher as he watched.
How do you estimate her? Will she fit
into this sad dilapidated family,
or won't she? Not bad these glasses. Quite a
good magnification. Look! There's another
pretty one. There. And another. And
another. Everywhere, in every female face
are memories of her beauty. But I should have
to marry each in turn before I held
a charm and splendour half so fine as hers.
I should have to sail right round the world,
collect, say, here an eye, and there a nose,
a fingernail, a tooth, a wisp of hair
before I could assemble anything
as luminous as she is, half so pure.
Oh I admire her, Peter! I admire her!
I find in her the being that I seek.
The goal of my eccentric premisses.
An order from my God to go beyond.
I march around, swell, pregnant with ideas.
Oh yes. I am in love with an ideal.
But nothing else can image my desires
but she. Am I in love, Henriette?
It is all most interesting. Watching
what is happening to me. The growing
expectations. All the complex hopes.
Fantasies of meetings and response.
Reveries of passionate delight,
of sudden comprehensions. Mutual
correspondences. Most wonderful
strange masquerades. Sudden glorious dreams
where everything's in shadow, but herself.

Regine pounds and pounds across my brain.
Am I in love, Henriette? Tell me. Now!

HENRIETTE
Quite possibly. What other symptoms have you been
experiencing? What about loss
of appetite?

SOREN
        I starve.

HENRIETTE
          Breathlessness?

SOREN (*wheezing, deliberately*)
I spit blood.

HENRIETTE
        What about sleeplessness?

SOREN
Definitely. Each night I burn in Hell.
My legs. My thighs. My stomach and my head.
I wake, and find I'm feverish with fear.
Everything is contradictory.
Wild excitement. Dark anxiety.
I am, at times, completely horrified.
To fall in love! To open! To reveal
the essence of one's being! Every hour
I praise her to the skies, then worry that
illusion may have chosen what's unreal.
I'm driven like a ship before the wind.
God knows where I am headed. Anywhere.
I would not have it otherwise. It is
the greatest pleasure, most delightful pain.
I feel the greatest freedom I have known.
The prison door has opened, finally,
and I can walk outside, and bathe in air.
Even here! In common Copenhagen! It
is a grand obsession, brother. The very
grandest of obsessions. I think of her,

then think, and think again, and then again.
Each second that I hear upon the clock
recalls me to her image, as all day
I circle and recircle round the dial
to gaze in at her lovely painted face.
Such blissful repetitions. Round and round.
Eternity made patent, here in time.
I spin round very slowly, till I fall. (*He spins and falls into a chair.*)

PETER
You are infatuated. Can you give
yourself to work?

SOREN
                    With an unprecedented
abandon. Such pathos. Such passion.
Such a faith. A church of two. A duple
creed. A perpetual communion. Bread of heaven!

PETER
It makes a change, this state of ecstasy.
And all this for a schoolgirl, for a child.
Your visit to Jutland has certainly
transformed you. Your three-week pilgrimage.
What was it like, at Saeding? How was our
family hovel?

SOREN
                    Beautifully ugly.
Gloriously mean. Hideously humble.
Full of terror. Full of human dignity.
So different from this sick necropolis.
I watched the women harvesting the fields.
Their bodies seemed to blend in with their acts.
Such earth-brown skin, the hair as blonde as straw.
They merged in with the landscape, finished it
with perfect human features. Brother, the primitive
reveals our deepest being. All seemed
a golden garden. Holy. Numinous.
Near Haeld I met a vagabond.
(*Rising again, walking slowly round the room*)

He lay there on the heathland on his back
with just his stick beside him. Then we walked.
To Non Mill. There we met the Koldbaek Stream.
The tramp explained its water was the best
in all the district. He went down to it
flat-out upon his stomach. How he drank!
So unconcerned! He quickly fell asleep.
Just lay there on the heather once again.
So simple. So straightforward. Such a life
reminds us of our time in paradise.
Of where we should be. Where we all belong.
He possessed nothing. He was wholly innocent.
Yet I, who was a city millionaire,
felt lonely as a stone upon the coast,
had nothing that could start to satisfy.
For he, a living paradox, had all. Yes,
he was a good man, that tramp. He did not
refuse to understand that there was
something that he could not understand. He
clearly understood that he could not
understand. And so he was not confused.
He roamed around with faith in earth and
water. No labouring to assimilate
yet more material, more. For him the
paradox was not a surrender. No, but
a category. An ontological
definition. One that expressed a live
relationship between his existing
comprehending spirit and eternal truth,
which he had personally assimilated.

PETER
You visited our father's house?

SOREN
                              Of course.
Such a strange nostalgia filled my soul!
For he was dead, yet I was there, alive.
A bone grown from his body. Flesh from flesh.
A spirit from his spirit. With his eyes
I saw his father's cottage, watched his flocks,

the hearth where he had watched his brothers die
and seen his sisters suffer. I went out on the heath.
I saw him scan the steel plate of the sky,
climb up on that terrifying mound
then curse the living God with all his soul
for what He had inflicted on the world
to make His loved ones suffer. Oh yes.
I saw my father's face in everything.
It wept from every melancholy tree.
It billowed on each transitory cloud.
He stared round every corner, by each beck,
his knickerbockers tucked into his boots,
his long drab coat, its colours faded out,
disintegrating slowly in the wind.
Those eyes that saw a sheep a league away
were blank and glazed and lifeless as the air.
He lingered long in life, and loathed it all.
I felt so dark. My veins were thick with guilt.
I heard his voice quite clearly on the mound.
"Marry her!" it murmured. *"Marry her!"*
That man destroyed my childhood out of love.
Now, out of love, he visits me again,
to turn me into spirit, painfully –
this wing-shot, incapacitated bird.

PETER
Our dead father ordered you to marry?

SOREN
Quite clearly. I heard his voice. As close as your own.
I felt his wish becoming my desire.
Stealthily. Insistently. As always.
Altering my radical estrangement.
Finding consummation in her Self.
You must have noticed, since our father's death,
I've altered, been a most obedient son.
Continued his experience carefully.
I'd do that anyway, of course. That would be
quite inescapable. You see he needed
an oblation. Something he could set
upon his altar. Offer up. Some very

minor Isaac. After all I was his
confidant. His friend. Even his confessor. I
must obey him. For I owe everything
to him. My life itself. My pain. My
financial independence. I could tell
that he was very worried. Afraid that I should be
sexually degraded. As he was by our mother.

PETER
Soren!

SOREN
   But it's the truth, isn't it? It's
the truth. We mustn't hide it, must we?
I loved him. I would always bear his
melancholia. I was the keeper
of his being. He taught me everything.
So I must enlarge his studies. Throw light on man.
On human consciousness. For that is all
that really matters, isn't it? Throwing
light on human consciousness. Testing out
the truth of Christianity. He
knew I knew he knew of my intention.
He'd seen me starting out. Probing. Wooing her
for months. Now off. Now on.
Passing books to her. Sermons she should read
and inwardly digest and criticise.

PETER
But she is still a child.

SOREN
     But innocent,
I think, quite innocent. I shall teach her
virtue. I shall open up her depths.
Disclose to her her deepest suffering.
Her Self. Her soul. At times I really think
she's unaware, completely unaware
of having an eternal soul at all.
But it is there. It is there. She simply
has not been turned towards it. She is like

a Philistine, without the courage to be
Spirit. Living in the cellar of her being.
Not on the top floor. Not where there's the best
most brilliant view. But I shall show her it.
I shall reveal it. She has no fear of
ignorance. No fear at all. So light her
heart is. Like a feather. But I shall show
that error is a thing that she should fear,
most deeply. I know, you see, that she is
not within the very best of health.
Nobody has told her yet, but she is
suffering from consumption. Why should they tell?
The unawareness of the sickness of despair
is most common. It is the commonest
thing in the whole world. Oh yes. She is too
light. Too separate from her God. Too opposed
to him. She lives a disrelation I
shall change. She is a silly, gay young pagan.
And still she does not know it. I shall bring
her Spirit. Alter her aesthetic standpoint.
She lives in such obscurity about
herself. In deepest darkness. I see
her virtues are but splendid vices -
as St. Augustine says. I'll alter that
and teach her all the benefits of dread,
a different class of darkness her gay songs
could never dream of. You are right. She's young.
She has an undistinguished inwardness.
One that's mainly imitation. Mimicry's
a low form of mimesis. Soon she'll
understand reality, the real. No, don't
move Anders. I'll leave by way of the window.
Time flies. The old grey heron must resume
his pale invigilation. There is still
so much to learn about her, and her soul.
Her lesson will be ending. I must go.
Your glasses, brother. Take a good deep look
and see how she reacts. I mean to speak.
[*Exit* SOREN KIERKEGAARD *by the window. The others,
lost for words, watch him tacking off in his characteristic
erratic style of walking.* CURTAIN]

SCENE II

COUNCILLOR OLSEN's *house, one of 'The Six Sisters',
Borsgade.* REGINE OLSEN *is drawing her elder sister*
CORNELIA. CORNELIA *is drawing her maternal* AUNT,
now her surrogate mother. Her AUNT *is drawing*
COUNCILLOR OLSEN *who alternately reads a newspaper
and falls asleep. As he does so, ash drops from his
extinguished pipe onto his trousers. Across the sparkling
Slotsholmgade Canal lies the old island of Gammelholm.
Barquentines and three-masted schooners prod against the
wharf before the house, and attempt to thrust their bowsprits
into the drawing-room. There is a fragrant scent of Baltic
timber, cutch and Stockholm tar. The room smells of the sea.*

AUNT
So you caught young Master Kierkegaard.

REGINE
I did exactly what you suggested.
I stepped into a side-street. I paused for a
moment, and then walked in front of him. We collided.
Marguerite's spinning-song was struck into the
gutter. He was covered with confusion.

AUNT
And did you ask him why he followed you?

REGINE
No. But I let him know I knew he had been
watching me.

AUNT
             And what did he say to that?

REGINE
That he had been conducting a literary
experiment. He quoted the *Phormio*
of Terence. In it, apparently, Phaedrio
falls in love with a cithern-player.

The only way that he can gratify his passion
is by following the young girl to and from
her music school. While she plays and practises
he sits inside a barber's shop and waits
for her return. *"Dum rediret."* The use
of the subjunctive showed the lover's
wistful passion, so he said.

AUNT
I see. So he offered you a grammar lesson.
What happened then?

REGINE
He picked up my hands, dusted them, and walked them home.

AUNT
And what did you discuss on your way home?

REGINE
We spoke of Mozart.

AUNT
                    Mozart?

REGINE
                    Soren has
attended *Don Giovanni* every night this week.

AUNT
Don Giovanni? And what did he
have to say about that libertine?

REGINE
He spoke of the immediate sensual
genius. Immediate in the
Hegelian sense of the word - with no
intellectual, cognitive mediation.
He spoke of music's power. Its vital
sensuousness that sweeps one like a leaf
before the wind, with no pause for reflection.
A power nothing human can withstand.

Don Juan is the life of the idea,
the magic, living impulse of all love.

AUNT
The man is a seducer.

REGINE
                    Not by will.
Not by guile and cunning, but by life.
By wonder. By vitality. Desire.
Desire is the seduction.

AUNT
                    So I
see. And what else did you discuss?

REGINE
He recited the list of popes.

AUNT
                              That's
no proof of virtue.

REGINE
                    And their dates.

AUNT
And mistresses no doubt. Well, I don't know.
(*Putting down her sketch and staring at the ceiling*)
He really is a most peculiar man.
That strange, unruly dress. That dreadful tie!
That hair, brushed like a coxcomb, in a tuft!
It stands up over half a foot in height.
That Spanish cane he carries! Like a rule.
He looks like an assistant in a shop.
Some half-demented draper. And his walk!
The way he always zigzags down the street.
His trouser-legs hang half-way up his calves.
He skips off like some wounded kangaroo.
One moment he is tripping on a kerb,
the next he's stumbling down some cellar-hole.

The poor man is a cripple, obviously. (*Pause*)
There's something in the way he looks at you.
He goads you from a distance, all the time.
With just one little movement of an eye
he gets beneath your skin, and irritates.
(*Scratching with her pencil*)
He always seems to read your secret thoughts.
(*Re-examining her sketch*)

REGINE
There's something very gentle in his look.
So calm, and very loving. Oh I know
his back's a bit deformed. He laughs at it.
He fell down from a tree when he was young.
His hair is high, but blond and very fine.
His face is strong, intelligent, refined.
Soft with sorrow, then with tenderness.
Defiant, bold, then rich with irony.
Such soulful eyes! They shine like glinting stars.
A dialogue of diamonds. Oh I know -
his clothes are too quixotic - quite bizarre -
but you should hear the way he dressed at school -
such dark, old-fashioned, melancholy rags.
They nicknamed him *The Choirboy*.

AUNT
Well, now the choirboy sings a different tune.
Regine - he's a most eccentric man.
Everybody says so, everywhere.
He's wanton, and a spendthrift. Drinks too much.
He lives within the lap of luxury.
He's indolent, indulgent, self-obsessed,
and quite unlike dear Schlegel.

REGINE
                              I agree.
His presence, though, his presence, Auntie dear!
When he is here I really come alive.
Everything about me catches fire.

AUNT
Exactly dear. And you are far too young!
Too young, by far. Too inexperienced.
I knew his father. What a man! Those eyes,
those peasant's orbs, so round, so wide, so dead,
half-blackened out with madness. And those lips.
Like petals. Red and sensuous. Hanging down
and drooping like a bloodhound's. Oh my dear,
to marry into misery like that!

REGINE
You're prejudiced. Like all old women are.
Once you get to know him you will change.
He has a way of altering things at will.
I love him and I want him. He'll be mine.
Marriages like ours were planned in heaven.

OLSEN (*awakening, dusting his trousers*)
There's very little yet she has not got.
Thank God the young know nothing. If they did
we'd have no talk of weddings any more. (*A bell rings.*)
Well, that's your visitor no doubt. [*Enter* MAID] Yes. Show him in.
(MAID *curtseys and shows* SOREN KIERKEGAARD *through
the door. He moves towards the centre of the room, bowing
elaborately, kissing in turn the fingers of the ladies, then
finally the bowl of the Councillor's pipe.* EXIT MAID.)

SOREN
Good tobacco! Frau Olsen, Cornelia Olsen, Councillor Olsen.
And Regine Olsen, henceforth to be called Regina. Queen of
heaven. Queen of hearts. Of diamonds, clubs and spades. No.
Do not move. Not to the distance of the half part of a hair! This
room, this afternoon, are perfect. I have found my soul again.
Its purest, clear existence. I am now a Vermeer interior. How I
have had to purchase this transcendence! Those moments,
minutes, hours of my life. How dearly this is bought! But now
it's come! It's here! I am ecstatic! Entangled by transparency!
All existence seems poetic, so distended, so open to my
contemplation that even the most workaday, most vulgar truths
on offer on those quays are pulsing with profundity. Sails swell
with their most pregnant allegories! My visual perception's so

144

refined that I can see the air. It's palpable. Like water on the
surface of a dream. I kiss its softest surface. I am totally
absorbed. I find finality, within, without. This place I have
been brought and lived towards. My life's ironic myth is
finished. Cancelled. Utterly forgiven. Set at nought. Its plot
resolved. I too am now transmuted into dream. Am I awake?
Or do I sleep? This cannot be a fiction. It is real. Am I inside
my body, or without? I'm wafted through the aether with the
gulls. I'm blown down the canal, on soft October gossamers.
Past Holmen's church. Bells celebrate my joy. The fragrance of
the hour! I drift into the sweet Norwegian pines. The pungent
scents of cutch. Of Stockholm tar.

AUNT
Whatever was all that about, young man?
Do pull a chair up. Now if you sit quite
still we can all begin to draw you. From all
directions. You'd like that, wouldn't you?
You'll be the complete centre of attention.
Three women will pretend you're beautiful.
The Councillor will also try his hand.
We'll try to catch your essence with our leads.
Well? Did you take a carriage here, or did you waltz?

SOREN (*ignoring the offered chair, waltzing round the room,
frustrating the women's attempts to sketch him*)
I waltzed.

AUNT
How very sensible. You look as if
you need to exercise. It's quite a distance
to our house. The barometer has promised rain.
It might get in your library. Have you
considered that?

SOREN
                    My man-servant, Anders,
I can assure you, is a first-rate closer
of windows. He is also excellent
at mopping up all types of fallen water.

AUNT
I'm glad to hear it. We get too much rain
in Denmark. Thunderstorms are forecast, I
believe. I should hate you to be drowned.
Your home, I believe, is some sort of witch-
house, or mausoleum. People die there
rather frequently.

REGINE
                    That's cruel of you.

SOREN
Not at all. It's seen a lot of death.
My mother died in 1834.
My father four years later. As for my
sisters, well Maren died aged twenty-four.
And Nicoline - her age was thirty-three,
the same as dear Petrea. Peter's wife
died recently. Singing hymns. I could hear
them through the walls, down all the darkened
passageways. She sang so beautifully.
We buried her three years ago. As for the boys,
the other Soren died when he was twelve.
A blow upon the head, received at school.
My dear, dear brother Niels was 24.
He died in Patterson, America.
Which leaves my elder brother, Peter,
and myself. Peter now has managed
35. While I am 27.

AUNT
And did your dead brother have a career?

SOREN
My father wished that all his sons should have
a different profession. Peter, the
church. Niels. A business man. He loathed it.
His mind was set on books, on literature.
It cast a constant sorrow on his life.
His time was very short. My father thought
his family would die before himself.

He thought it was a punishment from God.
He had a most prodigious sense of sin.
I proved him wrong. As Peter did, as well.

OLSEN
And what were you consigned to?

SOREN

To
philosophy. Or a country parsonage.
The girls required no formal tutoring.
They waited on their brothers, served their needs
and lent a ready hand about the house.
My mother was quite small. She couldn't write.
She signed things with a carefully guided pen.
She longed to keep us limed up to the nest.
Every day she tried to clip our wings!

OLSEN
Your father's death left you a rich man.

SOREN
Thirty-three thousand, five hundred and
ninety-four rigsdaler. One quarter of
my father's estate. I live off the capital.
I receive no interest. The Bible
forbids it. The bank's perplexed, of course.
My father was a first-rate business man.
He also had the shrewdest of advice.
When war arrived his bonds remained untouched -
in deference to foreigners. Most shares
tumbled. Many rich were beggared. But not us.
We rose in value as the others fell.
A rising market did it all for us.
My father just did nothing. Sat and watched.
Held fast to what he had. At forty he
retired, and took to books. He started
reading Wolfe. When I arrived, his last,
he'd nothing more to do than spend his time
examining his conscience, warping mine.

AUNT
A most unusual family. Your father
died, then all your broken pieces came together.
So I hear.

SOREN
Very quickly. Death is a great healer.
Now I am reliable and wise. I have
even gathered a degree. Divinity.
The fourth best on the list. Ask me anything.
Church history. Canon law. It's all
stacked up in here. (*Tapping his temple*) When my father died
there was no one left to argue with. So
I was forced to take his part. And as I
argued better, well, he won. So now I am
a graduate.

OLSEN
   But what next?

SOREN
        One carries on.
For lack of better things. I'll have to write
a thesis.

OLSEN
   Upon what subject?

SOREN
       Irony.

OLSEN
And how long will that take you?

SOREN
        A few days.
A month perhaps. I'll spin it out a year or so.
There are so many other things to do.

AUNT
You must have some ambition?

SOREN

          Well, perhaps
the University. It has an empty chair.
Moral philosophy. I think that I could fit it.
But first I must obtain my next degree.
The myth of Faust keeps running through my mind.
Müller kept on urging Socrates.
Both were rebels. Individualists.
But acting in a different sort of way.
Shall I go on?

OLSEN

      Of course. I'm interested.

SOREN (*sitting*)
Tragedy will lead you into death.
Madness, to a world of fantasy.
Yet both are an advance into the world.
The ironist is different. Not for him
that total grand commitment to his fate.
He stands apart, and lets things co-exist.
He contemplates their tensions with a smile
of secret non-involvement.

REGINE

       Do go on.

SOREN
Irony's a basic attitude.
A problem of existence, of all life,
the terrible ambivalence of things.
The ironist's a melancholy man.
His greatest love's to jest at suffering,
to set it at some distance from himself
and make it something he can contemplate -
the echo and the empty parody
of all we think substantial. He kills
all spontaneity, all life, while claiming he's
the master of experience. But instead
he's actually its victim.

AUNT
                    That's serious. Well
I cannot really see you as a country parson.
The country can be bracing, for an hour.
But then there is so little going on.
You'd soon get bored with sheep and clouds and seas
or reading prayers to pastures. The cow's
unskilled at dialectic, I believe.
Well, my sketch is finished. So is yours
Cordelia. And yours as well, I see,
Councillor. No doubt Regine will wish
to discuss her own with our visitor.
I see it's far more flattering than ours.
The young judge on appearance, don't you think?
No? We shall go. All three of us. One
moment more, and all *three* of us will begin
to drift towards real tediousness. And so
I leave you, at the summit of my wit.
My portrait's quite appalling.

[*Exeunt* AUNT, CORNELIA, OLSEN. *Silence falls.* SOREN
*stands, then sits again. He adjusts his trousers, then stands
once more. He coughs nervously.*]

SOREN
I have the sense of an occasion.

REGINE
                    Yes.

SOREN
Of the *kairos*. The predestined time.

REGINE
                              Yes

SOREN
Of fate.

REGINE
          Yes. (*Silence*)

SOREN
>Butterflies. September
butterflies. Outside the window. They chase
each other for miles.

REGINE
>So I believe.

SOREN
Can you feel it too?

REGINE
>Feel what?

SOREN
>The presence
of our ancestors. Dread.

REGINE
>I think so.

SOREN
>The sick
sheep wanders off and leaves the flock. It
stands beneath a side-hedge or a wall
and coughs. Sometimes it grazes on its
elbows. The ewes come on heat twice a month.
Did you know that? Stand to take the impact of the ram.
The impact of the ram. I have been walking
in the park.

REGINE
>Did you meet anyone you knew?

SOREN
Only an hypothesis.

REGINE
>You met it
this morning?

SOREN

        This afternoon. He was a
fairly young hypothesis. Much the same
age as myself, to think about it.

REGINE

                              Was

he well?

SOREN

        No. He seemed to be suffering from *Angst*.

REGINE

                                       Angst?

SOREN

Yes. *Angst*. It's a common enough condition among
the young. You can see it in this drawing
that your aunt has recently completed.
There is no sign of it in yours. Nor your
sister's. And a little perhaps in this picture
by your father. A hint of darkness. See?
You do know what I mean, don't you? *Angst*. It is
a faculty in human nature. *Angst*.
A presupposition of original sin.
It is a foreboding. A sense of something
imminent, of something yet unknown.
Unconscious. What is it? It is tomorrow.
It is the day to come. It is connected
with our freedom. Like a steeplejack
high up upon his spire, fearing a gust,
that sudden unexpected wind when his
attention is elsewhere. You follow me?
It is a form of dread. A terrible
attraction to the thing one fears the most
yet cannot name. A sort of sympathetic
antipathy. Do you follow?

REGINE

        I think so.

SOREN
Good.

REGINE
      What sort of life had this young hypothesis
been leading?

SOREN
A disconnected one. He was an aesthete.
He sought a life of pleasure. Of happiness.
Of joy. He was, in fact, something of a
philanderer. He would not work. He would not
plan ahead. His sole thought was enjoyment.
As much as possible. In the most refined
way, of course. He kept independent, as far
as he could. Not tied down by commitments.
Unbound by social obligations. Those he had
he'd break whenever he required to.
He had no close friends. Kept clear, of course,
from marriage. His sexual relations thus
were trivial and superficial.
He could not consider any real vocation.

REGINE
Do continue.

SOREN
Well, this young hypothesis was close to
despair. The aesthete, you see, while seeking
independence from others at the same time
makes his pleasures contingent upon them.
The aesthetic comes and goes. It is fickle,
and gives no lasting satisfaction.
Once a sweet is eaten, that is that.
The aesthete's led inexorably towards
despair.

REGINE
      I understand. So what did you say?

SOREN
I pointed out to him how very
unsatisfactory and crippling his
attitude was.

REGINE
                    And what did he say to that?

SOREN
Oh, he agreed completely.

REGINE
                            What treatment
did you recommend?

SOREN
                    Marriage.

REGINE
                        Marriage?

SOREN
Marriage. The ideal of social life.
Any man who wishes to rise higher
must find his place *inside* the community.
He must develop his powers and must
exercise them where he finds himself.
Grow in harmony with his surroundings.
Assume the ethical mode of existence.
Which, of course, is best exercised in
matrimony, its ideal condition.
The aesthete lives on mood. Everything
must fit into his moment. All that won't
is rapidly discarded. The ethicist
is different. He does not suppress
the aesthetic. He simply provides the
proper sphere in which it may be exercised.
The aesthete is forever looking outwards
for his pleasure. The ethicist
looks inward. Into the decisive instant
which is nonetheless an atom of

eternity. It demands he live
for duty, that he surrender to
obligation. Yet the ethico-
religious instant does not discard the
aesthetic moment. There is no basic
opposition between them. The art of
mastering pleasure lies not in its total
annihilation or renunciation.
One must simply determine the instant.
Effectuate it. Yield to its demands.
The aesthete howls in absolute despair
as Time devours his children. But the
ethicist grows clearer. Every day
he polishes his crystal. Each *Weltanschauung*
that hangs on some condition that's external
is just a mode of ultimate despair.

REGINE
So your theorem chooses the ethical life.
He chooses marriage. What then is his problem?

SOREN
His problem lies with the ethical.
What are its two main characteristics?
One. Its universality. Two. Its openness.
To live an ethical life he has to
reveal himself, to practise disclosure.
Disclosure. And that is very difficult.
It sends an Arctic chill straight down his spine.
You see, that is the purpose of life. That
a man, or a woman, become revealed.
Both to him- or to herself. And to others.
Whatever we are has a deep inner urge
to present itself, to show its true nature.
So ethics is uneasy. Hence its
imperative mode. Nothing must be hidden.

REGINE
I agree that nothing should be hidden.
Marriage is most intimate.

SOREN

Exactly.

Thus, problems must arise.

REGINE

Of course they must.

SOREN

The ethical conception of life
is realised in marriage. But it must
be under ideal conditions. Where there
are hindrances, a marriage should not occur.

REGINE

Hindrances? What sort of hindrances?

SOREN

Where there are secrets. Secrets in the life
of either party, you understand? Things
that cannot be revealed to the other.
Secrecy creates an atmosphere
of mystery, reserve. Lack of total
frankness stops real unity of heart.
Creates a spirit of distrust, a
dissonance.

REGINE

One should tell everything.

SOREN

Exactly. But other problems arise.

REGINE

Other problems?

SOREN

Other problems. Problems
concerning one or other's fitness
to receive such intimate disclosures.
What, for the sake of illustration, if
the woman proved unworthy of a secret?

What if she were to prove too fickle, too
shallow, too given to the life of pleasure?
A woman and a man are different.
A girl does not develop like a boy.
She wakens like a summer butterfly,
emerges from her chrysalis, twice-born,
but born a finished product, fully grown,
substantial, and corporeal, yet a dream.
Enchanting in her soft unconsciousness
but useless for the life of paradox.
What then?

REGINE

        How does he feel towards this woman?

SOREN
He really feels he loves her. He is most
attracted to her. But every approach
seems to entail a melting together with
her. A fusion. A personal disintegration.
Her body is so very beautiful.
So proud, so upright, desperately desired.
But feared like death. He wants her statuesque.
Yet passionate. Quite perfect. Several times
at her approach, he's feared that he'd go mad.

REGINE (*laughing, yet uneasy*)
You say such funny things. He would not
damage her, would he? Not if he loved her?

SOREN
That is another of his fears. You see
disclosure is ongoing. Together
they must find the Self. The *Self.* That most
abstract of all things. And yet the most
concrete. True liberty. Real freedom.
Ethics wants the Absolute Self. It will have
none other.

REGINE
So how would they approach it
together?

SOREN
By terror. Only terror,
to the point of absolute despair,
takes woman to her full development.
And man.

REGINE
Is there no other way?

SOREN
No. None at all.

REGINE
During the cure, do many girls succumb?

SOREN
Many go quite mad. Or die from *Angst*.
We are handled roughly. And that is
very, very useful.

REGINE
Well. I see his problem.
Not much of a proposition is it, for
a young girl? The certainty of terror.
The possibility of lunacy.
The misery of despair. I think that
must be the most original hypothetical
proposal I have ever heard. (*Turning away*)

SOREN
It leads
to freedom. Bliss. To heaven. (*Impulsively*) Join in
my salvation! Salvation is endeavour.
Endeavouring to choose the Self that's true.
Choose the objective uncertainty.
Choose it with the passion of the infinite.
Leap, leap into the darkness, here and now!

See if we shall float on the abyss
or fall a million fathoms! Leap, dear! Leap!
Appropriate. There is no other truth.
The Self, the *Self*'s the Absolute. So choose.
Yes, choose yourself, and be the one you are!

REGINE
Are you proposing marriage?

SOREN
                              Of course
I am. Marry me. Give me my reply.
Immediately. I am the hypothesis.

REGINE
I need time. Give me time. As you say
I know so little of your nature, of
your *Angst*. Your arguments are just the same
for me. I need to know your hindrances.

SOREN (*visibly shaken*)
Of course. You are quite correct. You must
visit my brother. Our house. You must know
more of our father. The various shapes
parading through our brains. The thoughts I am.
You must have that disclosure. Tomorrow, then.
A visit to my brother and his house.
Then you can choose. Or choose provisionally,
at least. After all, choice is the only
way we acquire personality. The
exercise of will. Of human will.
May I keep your sketch? I have a rosewood
cabinet at home. In it I shall keep
all of our mementos. Everything.
Letters, tickets, trifles. Every one.
Just in case you will not be my wife.
Just in case you will not be my bride.
Tomorrow afternoon, then. I'll call at
Two. You will arrange a chaperone, no
doubt. Will do what is reasonable. I'll
see myself out. I shall find the way.   [*Exit* SOREN *looking*

bewildered by what he has proposed. REGINE *crosses to the*
window to watch him leave. She does not wave farewell, but
stands looking serious, hence sad, as the CURTAIN *falls.*]

SCENE III

PETER KIERKEGAARD *is performing a Dance of*
Melancholia, accompanied by a plaintive, one-finger piano
melody, with many wrong notes. He is dressed in black
trousers and a white unbuttoned shirt. His hair is awry. His
father's unframed portrait has been removed from the wall to
stand on a chair close to the front of the stage. In one hand
PETER *is holding a long knife. The weird dance reaches its*
climax as PETER *lifts the knife to plunge it into his father's*
face, only for him to become arrested in catatonic paralysis, at
the apex of dread, like an Abraham on Mount Moriah. His
face is a masterpiece of agony as he starts to turn the blade
slowly towards himself. Enter ANDERS, *taking in the*
situation at a glance, and proceeding to deal with it
imperturbably.

ANDERS
Mr. Kierkegaard and Miss Olsen, sir.

PETER (*agonised*)
My brother!

ANDERS
Exactly sir. And his proleptic fiancée. They are as I explained
to you, half-engaged to be married.

PETER
Half-engaged?

ANDERS
Mr Kierkegaard has told me that he hopes to be fully engaged
by the time of the conclusion of this visit.

PETER
Fully engaged?

ANDERS (*removing the painting from the chair and returning it to the wall*) Yes, sir, fully engaged to be married. (*Reaching up to remove the knife from his master's hand*) Just a little looser, sir. That's right. Now if you will allow me to comb your hair and straighten your cravat. That's right, sir. Sit down on the chair. You're feeling better already, aren't you?

PETER (*sitting where his father's face had been*)
Henriette? Where is Henriette?

ANDERS
Talking to Miss Olsen. She is showing her round the house. Your brother has been accompanying them. They are waiting to visit the library.

PETER
How are they getting along together?

ANDERS
Very well, sir. Quite famously. There, sir. All over now, isn't it? Another nice warm day. I'll put the knife away inside the drawer. Ready? This is how to greet her. *"Ah! My dear! How very nice of you to come and see me so quickly. You are looking quite radiant today. Quite radiant. I do hope that we shall all pass your inspection."* Repeat what I have just said, sir.

PETER
Ah! My dear! How very nice of you to come and see me so quickly. You are looking quite radiant today. Quite radiant. I do hope that we shall all pass your inspection.

ANDERS
Excellent, sir. Word perfect. I shall now show them in.

(*He crosses to the door and shows in* SOREN, REGINE *and* HENRIETTE. REGINA *is dressed in white from head to foot,* SOREN *in colourful riding attire.*)

PETER
Ah! My dear! How very nice of you to come and see me so
very quickly. You are looking quite radiant today. Quite
radiant. I do hope that we shall all pass your inspection. May I
kiss your hand? And my brother. What's this? Riding dress?

SOREN
Exactly so, my brother. Exactly
so. I still smell of the horse. Of sweat and
leather and the crushed grass. I have become a
man of action. I have regained a fresh sense
of personal duration. I have a
new being. One that has discarded the
subjunctive mood. Now I live in the
indicative, all day long. I have been
exercising, preparing for marriage.

PETER
I'm glad to hear it.

HENRIETTE
                    Was the exercise
successful?

SOREN
My riding-master was, unfortunately,
unimpressed.

HENRIETTE
            Oh? Why?

SOREN
                    Apparently my
posture is all wrong. I sit too
rigidly. Am far too tense. And I lack
confidence. The man is right. I'm always
trying to remember my instructions.
The horse, of course, well knows what's on its back
and soon plays up, so things get quickly worse.
I am advised that I should give it up.
For my own safety. It's no fun, none at

all, being at the mercy of an
animal! I shall go back to my coach.
I like the action of a coach. I sit
right in the centre, searching left and right,
observing men and women. I prefer
the state of general idleness induced.
Riding's far too violent for me.
A coach relaxes, makes one very calm.
One glides along at ease. Things come and go.
One's shaken very gently, to and fro.
If something very beautiful occurs
one stops the wheels and contemplates its state
in indolence and languor, peacefully.

PETER
Perhaps, Henriette, we should leave the two
young people together for a little time.
There is much that they will want to discuss.

HENRIETTE
Of course. So, we'll see you later then.
If there's anything you want, just give a ring.

[*Exeunt* PETER, HENRIETTE, ANDERS]

REGINE
Together again.

SOREN
                    Yes.

REGINE
                    The library.

SOREN
Of course. It's not too chill for you?

REGINE
                                        No. Not at all.

SOREN
Not too stale, too frowsty? Many of these books
are very dirty. They have been through
unusual hands.

REGINE
    I quite like the room.

SOREN
You do?

REGINE
   So many books. Hundreds. Thousands.
Have you read them all?

SOREN
       Most of them. The best
are at my flat. Books are living things.
Some illuminate. Most are very dangerous.
Some enlighten, just a little. Most pollute.
Not that you would know about that.

REGINE (*approaching the portrait*)
         He must
be your father. Frameless.

SOREN
     I was his frame.

REGINE
You also worked in here?

SOREN
      A great deal of the time.
Yes. I would come back here. Back from my strolls
among humanity. Straight to my desk
to write things down. I work standing upright.
On guard.

REGINE
   What would you do on your walks?

SOREN

Oh, I carried out psychological
experiments. On passers-by. I put
myself in complete rapport with those that
I have selected. Well, some of the time.
I greet them at a distance with a look.
Just that minor movement of the eye
that means so much. Gentle. Goading. Loving.
Irritating. People are attracted
or repelled. Embarrassed. Made uncertain. Or afraid.
I use two sorts of conversations. One
is for reporting. It is meant to rouse
and stimulate. The second is ironic
questioning. You understand? That is why I have
acquaintances in crowds, but scarce one friend.
I am not that loveable, I fear. My
disciples do not like me. I can be
sarcastic, and I tend to bear a grudge.
I am a strange man. "The peculiar one".
That's what they all say. And I agree with them.
I am more suited to the world of children.
I prefer magic. I delight in fantasy.
I enter into children's worlds at will.
I am, you see, a child deep underneath.
A wounded, crippled, infant. That man did
the wounding. Out of love. From deepest love.

REGINE

They say your father kept the strictest house.

SOREN

Everything was ordered well ahead.
Cakes were bought two weeks before a feast.
The next child's suit of confirmation clothes
was cut and bought before the older child
had finished with the priest. Yes. All was planned.
Meticulously ordered, night and day. (*Changing tone*)
I don't know what you think about our house.
The chemist's to the left. Law courts on the right.
Our windows have a fine view of the square.
I'd watch them as they rode the Diet in.

At times it seemed the whole show was for me.
Heralds in their gorgeous velvet capes
on horseback in the middle of the square.
Around them rode the Life-Guards in an arc.
They read the proclamation straight to me.
Then next day came the King. A golden coach
with all its grand procession! Up it rolled.
It seemed that he was coming to our door.
Alas, he never entered. Afterwards
I felt absurd, ridiculous, unreal,
as if I'd lost my true identity.
Slighted by a parent I should own,
I'd ended being visited by death.

REGINE
Why was your father so meticulous?

SOREN
Guilt. It cemented everything. Held
us all together. Moral Law. That's what
we all called him. Old Moral Law.

REGINE
                                How old was he
when you were born?

SOREN
                    Fifty-seven. My mother
was forty-five. She was gay. Flighty.
Fickle. Illiterate. Ridiculous.
My father had great mental powers.
He was no mere hosier. He overwhelmed
me with his gifts, both for philosophy
and for theology. He gathered round
himself an intellectual circle. He
could hold his own with all of them. Churchmen
and professors. I listened to his
arguments with wonder. Thunderstruck.

REGINE
He seems unsuited to your mother.

SOREN

He was.

REGINE
Yet he must have loved her. He married her.

SOREN
Yes.

REGINE
Were they happy together?

SOREN

No.

REGINE
Why?

SOREN
There are some questions it is better
not to ask.

REGINE
But we have an agreement that
we will teach the truth to one another,
practise total disclosure. It was your
idea.

SOREN
My father was a deep and separate sea.
He possessed great energy at times. Great
energy. That energy was blocked.
I had no childhood. No child companions.
I had an injury, you see. A special wound
from infancy. It made me alien.
I took no part in normal exercise.
If I wished to go outside to play
my father used to walk me round the room.
He talked to me of things we would have met
outdoors. The trips that we would take! The scenes
his eager mind would paint, the quays, the docks,

the people in the palace, on the streets,
the markets and the churches, on and on!
Fantasy you see was primary.
I lived in an imaginary world.
Became old-fashioned. A precocious child.
A ten-year imitation of a man
bent double by a melancholy guilt,
where everything meant sin, the fires of Hell.
Religion was a serious affair.
All melancholia. Just an old man's view
of life and its attractions. At school
I was alone, a solitary boy.
I could not ask companions to my house.
So nobody would ask me in return.
I was thin. Awkward. Peculiarly dressed.
The others laughed at me. But they soon found
the way my tongue could sting them, lash them back.

REGINE
What was his guilt?

SOREN
                        Don't ask me that.

REGINE
                                    I have to.

SOREN
In time, perhaps.

REGINE
                        Was it a civil crime?

SOREN
                                    No.

REGINE
More personal? Intimate?

SOREN
                        Yes.

REGINE

You said
that he possessed great energy.

SOREN

I did.

REGINE
What sort of energy. Physical?

SOREN

Yes.

REGINE
Sexual?

SOREN

Sex was never mentioned in this house.
It was suppressed. Both by look and by gesture.
Both by day and night. It was considered to be
a mortal sin.

REGINE

For which you had to pay.

SOREN
He harnessed me to haul his cart of shame.
If only he had been a simpleton.
Free-thinking and absurd, a hypocrite.
But no. The man was pious, feared his God,
was deeper than the ocean. Constantly
a dark unrest was seething in his soul.
Nothing gave him peace, and all made dread.
I became an old man while a child.
I loved him and his love half-crippled me.

REGINE
What do you mean "his love half-crippled me"?
In what sense of the words?

SOREN
>   I bore his pain.
I lived with all his boulders on my back.
What could have been a transient, passing thing,
repressed, left unrepented, soon became
his quintessential feature, tore my soul
with lusts such as the pagans never knew.
I knew quite soon that I myself was born
to contradict the good of Providence.
I knew that I was born a victim-soul,
an Isaac for his Abraham, a life
laid out on Mount Moriah for the knife.
From him I learned the mercy of God's love.

REGINE
What sin did he confess to you? Was it to
do with his marriage?

SOREN (*annoyed*)
>   Yes.

REGINE
>   Another woman?
Other women?

SOREN
>   He went with whores.

REGINE
>   I see.
And he believed he was diseased.

SOREN
>   Yes.

REGINE
He watched his children die. He thought he was
the cause.

SOREN
      There was also the question of
the curse. In Jutland.

REGINE
              But that was not all?

SOREN
No.

REGINE
   Well?

SOREN
       He confessed he had seduced my mother
while he was still in mourning for his wife.
She was a servant maid. She worked inside
the house. One night he lost control. He - raped her.
He married her when she was five months gone.
He went through every detail of the act.
He raped the second, praying for the first.
He made the maid the mother. She was
a second cousin. He believed the
union was incestuous. A mind like his
would seize on anything.

REGINE
            Is there more?

SOREN
Yes.

REGINE
   Have you had carnal knowledge of
other women?

SOREN
        When I was younger.

REGINE
Prostitutes?

SOREN
                    Yes. It seemed necessary
at the time.

REGINE
                    To prove that you could do it?

SOREN
Yes. This is very dangerous.

REGINE
                                        You
began it. Are you going to break faith
already? Did you enjoy it?

SOREN
                                        It was
useful.

REGINE
        Useful?

SOREN
                    Sometimes a man must test
himself.

REGINE
            Are you clean?

SOREN
                                    Clean?

REGINE
                                Have you suffered
from the symptoms of syphilis?

SOREN
                                    No.

REGINE
But you spit blood?

SOREN
>I have sensitive lungs.
A snuffed candle will excite them. I need
to exercise each day. To take my air-baths.
Fully clothed, that is. Do I fit with your
requirements for a husband?

REGINE
>There are
other things you have not told me?

SOREN
Of course. There is a whole life of lies.

REGINE
>Lies?

SOREN (*slightly dissociated*)
Of lies. Fleeces are deceptive. Like my own,
they look absorbent, soft, seem very fine.
Possess a bright white lustre. Yes, they glint
and shine, first diamond. Very clear. Spring back
with a strong elastic crimp. Never hang
exhausted. But when you get closer the
quality alters. Much has been discoloured.
It is full of stains. Needs sorting. There are
spines of brambles. Bits of straw. The wool
is dirty, thick with grease. (*Approaching* REGINE*'s head*)
How nice to pull a fleece's locks apart
and find there are no briars and bits of dirt
embedded in the curls. No signs of weakness.
No second cuts, made by the clumsy shears.
It's nice to feel a britch-end, roll it in,
then tuck it in the woolsack. Then you see
it leaves a golden feeling on the skin.
Do I disgust you?

REGINE
>Not at all.

SOREN

I have

brought much back from Jutland. Many thoughts.
The land's ill-drained. It's soaked through by the rains.
I stepped upon infection, everywhere.
I brought back poisons. Sensed them anywhere.
In the cracked bricks. In the dirty crevices
of farm-walls and old buildings. Black disease.
Tetanus and struck. Dormant and unbreathing.
Ready to grow active, spread again
like sudden maledictions. The best beasts
stiffen. Tail to head. The sickness strikes at
random. Runs amok. The strong lambs lie there dead,
or foaming at the mouth, in dreadful pain,
their kidneys turned to pulp. You understand?
I have a thorn embedded in my flesh.
I've told the truth to no one, not one soul.
I may still tell you more, dear, even more.
But later on, much later, if I dare.
Much later on. (*Changing mood*) Well, then, how do rate
your putative fiancé? Egh? What an
education in dread! Our father's life
was not a blessing. It was a curse.
Our intellectual gifts were given us
to punish us. That we might lacerate
each other. Tear ourselves to pieces.
I watched my sisters dying, one by one
and realised I too was going to die.
Another cross upon that granite tomb
of all his hopes. A guilt lay on us all.
The punishment of God. We had to be
quite wiped away by God's almighty hand,
swept aside, like any sick mistake,
all memory erased, no trace of us,
with no one left behind to walk the earth.
One curse for another. That was all.
My father was a type of wandering Jew.
I too was being punished for his sin.
I saw myself a human sacrifice.

174

REGINE
But now he's dead. *He* has been the sacrifice.
Now you can come alive.

SOREN
                                    I live, pursued
by dread. My inwardness is constant fear
and trembling. I have a catastrophic
consciousness. I am a dirty old
theologian. A disgusting old man.
You will be well rid of me.

REGINE
                          What would you teach me?

SOREN
Inwardness.

REGINE
                  What is inwardness?

SOREN
                                         It is
a deepening. Yes. A deepening.
It goes beyond the soul into the spirit.
Beneath becoming, into being. It is
the religion of the essence. That Which Is.
The Unconditioned. The Eternal. Am I
already boring you with clichés?

REGINE
Not at all.

SOREN
                  Inwardness and the instant
and the now are of the same eternal
order. The trouble is that there are no
short-cuts into one's essence, into
eternal life. Would that there were! Instead
one has to accept one's conditions. Accede
to the limitations of time. Mortal life!

Mortal time! We glimpse things through the lattice
of the flesh. How very brief it is,
the instant! How temporal! Gone before
the thought can master it. Like all instants.
Like all the following instants. And yet it
is decisive. Full of eternity. I call
that instant *the fullness of time*. It is
completion. It is perfection. But it
involves a leap of faith. One must believe
in that experience. Accept it.
And acceptance implies paradox. Why?
Because it is filled with emptiness.
It is overflowing with nothingness.
What fills it with eternity is the
apprehension of the incarnation.
It is then the decisive instant of
faith. Later it may be different.
It is the instant of repetition.
Past, present, future, all are fixed in that
immortal moment. One must work in that
instant. Transcend. Incorporate
the peace that passes understanding.
Let transcendence be the immanent.

REGINE
Then you are a mystic.

SOREN
                    Not at all.
Mysticism is a short-cut to
salvation. Christianity gives it
no warrant. I preach no mystical
revelation. With me, everything is
dialectical. I experience
no momentary unity. No ecstasy.
All spiritual experience is
rigidly conditioned. It is subject
to a divinely appointed dualism.
To tension. To dialectic. To
paradox. To dread, and to despair.
I will show you dread. I will explain

the meaning and the purpose of despair.
Or could do, should we marry. That is now
impossible, I fear.

REGINE
                    Not at all.
I see you need me. As much as I need
myself. In fact you are myself. I shall
be your pupil, and your governess. Your
mistress, and your child.

SOREN (*shaken*)
You mean that you will marry me? Enter
all this wilderness?

REGINE
                    I accept your proposal.

SOREN
Why?

REGINE
        Because I love you.

SOREN (*bewildered*)
                    Love? But what about
Schlegel?

REGINE
        Well, I love him too, I suppose.
But a little less than you. A little less.
Do you have a ring?

SOREN
            No.

REGINE
                    Then you will have
to purchase one. We shall go together.
But you must be careful. When a woman loves
she gives everything. It is for her a

total gift of body and of soul
without reserve, without regard for
anything. It is her faith. Her life. Be
gentle with me, Soren, be very gentle.
Now we shall have a real engagement party.
For the King and the Queen and the whole court.
And you must show how wonderful you are.
Your glory must be seen before the world
more clearly. I have plans to make you great!

[CURTAIN]

SCENE IV

The Olsens' drawing-room, as before. AUNT *and* OLSEN.

AUNT
Well, Councillor Olsen.

OLSEN (*playing with her*)
                    My dear?

AUNT
                                        I am
waiting.

OLSEN
          Ah! Who's coming then?

AUNT
                                        I am
waiting for an apology.

OLSEN
                    I see.
When is the apology going to
arrive?

AUNT
That is what I'm waiting to see.

OLSEN (*turns the newspaper*)
Ah! Shares are falling again. Third day in
a row.

AUNT
You've no idea, have you?

OLSEN
On shares?

AUNT
No. Not on shares. (*Removing his paper*)
Not on shares. On etiquette.

OLSEN
Etiquette?

AUNT
Yes. Etiquette.

OLSEN
In what area?

AUNT
Social obligation. Good manners.

OLSEN
Good
manners? Have I offended anyone?

AUNT
You have.

OLSEN
Oh! What a pity. Well, send him
or her along and I'll sort it out with them.

AUNT
She is here now. She is standing beside you.

OLSEN
Oh? Where?

AUNT
       Here.

OLSEN
                Here? I can't see anyone.

AUNT
Sometimes I think you are the blindest man
I've ever met.

OLSEN
           Oh! You mean you? I've
offended you!

AUNT
         Exactly.

OLSEN
             Surely not.

AUNT
I fear you have disgraced me, Councillor.

OLSEN
Disgraced you? When did I disgrace you?

AUNT
I plan a glittering reception, to
celebrate the betrothal of your
daughter. I invite the King of Denmark.
I invite the Queen of Denmark. I
invite Prince Friederich. The Princess Marianne.
It is a sparkling occasion. To
glorify Regine. To introduce
her brilliant future husband. All the lords

and ladies of the court are longing to
see Soren Kierkegaard. To watch his wit
run flickering through the room like bright white wires
of lightning. To hear his intellect outshine
the tongue-tied Prince. Regine looks around.
Where is her fiancé? In the room?
Walking up and down, the cynosure,
delighting all society? Not he!
He runs off down the street into a wood
with you absconding with him. It's a scandal.
An humiliation. An absolute
disgrace.

OLSEN
        I thought it was quite funny.
Everyone was looking round for us
and there we were together in the wood.

AUNT
And what were you doing in that wood?

OLSEN
Listening to a starling. A starling is
a very clever bird. The way its throat
was labouring! It's an excellent mimic.
It looks as if it's choking. Soren tried
to make it imitate the King.

AUNT
                          Was he
successful?

OLSEN
        Not really. It was more like
a thrush.

AUNT
        At times I quite despair of you.

OLSEN
Well, marriages involve a lot of show.
It's all so artificial, isn't it?
It's all too like a battle. Everyone
must show himself superior, mustn't he?
You know how I abhor the social crowd,
especially the women. As for Soren,
I sympathise. I know just how he feels.
Walking up and down those smiling rows,
entering their purposeless intrigues.
The man is far too serious for all that.

AUNT
We must all act, Councillor. How else is
life to continue? How could we
tolerate it, if we did not cultivate
appearance? It was your duty, Councillor,
to smile and be polite, pass pleasantries.
Instead I had to say that you were ill.

OLSEN
Well that was true enough.

AUNT
                              Oh you are all
so unreliable. You men are all
the same. What isn't yours, you want. And when
you've got it, you lose interest, and go.
That Kierkegaard's no different. You will see.
He winks at her, and says he longs for her,
but all he is is curious, playing games.
Later on he'll simply sit and grin.
That sort of man's soon altering everything.
He changes his companions like his clothes.
The same with his fiancées and his wives.
He spins round like a weathervane. His moods
are variable as moonlight. Your poor child
would really be much happier with a dog.
A man like him will finish on the stage.
Now Fritz is such a diplomat. So calm.
He sees all round an argument. Besides

he'll make a lovely father. So well-bred!
So decent. Such a perfect gentleman.
He'll make an ideal husband. Watch Kierkegaard.
His heart just isn't in it. This business
with the jaunt into the wood. It's not the
only thing, you know. The man is proving
an eccentric sort of suitor. Not that
you'd notice anything. These papers he keeps
sending her. On really amorous topics.
Like *Original Sin. The Fall of Adam.*
Lessons in Dread. In *Dread!* I mean, they're
hardly that engaging for a lively
seventeen-year-old, are they? And the looks he
gives her sometimes. So insulting. Full of
scorn, almost. No visits to the opera.
None to the stage. No concerts. No sabbath
walks along Bredgade, or upon the
Esplanade. Oh, he's chaste enough, in an
arctic sort of way. But there's no flame
between them. No passion. No desire.
Not that you'd have noticed. One would think
the poor girl was in training for a nun.
She won't find peace in needlework and prayers.

OLSEN
He's busy on his dissertation.
Still, I suppose he has been looking
rather gaunt, now you mention it, under
strain, as it were. He's started wearing black.
Black coats. Black suits. Black ties. Black everything.
He looks more like an undertaker's man,
a most unusual lover. Anyway,
I think he's shy.

AUNT
                Do you? You know he keeps
on watching us?

OLSEN
                Watching us? Where?

AUNT

                              Here. In this house.
All day, sometimes. Through a telescope.
He's probably at it now.

OLSEN

                    Now why would he
do that? Do you think he's jealous?

AUNT

                       No. I
think he'd be delighted if she jilted him.
It would fit in exactly with his
intentions.

OLSEN

        Of jilting her?

AUNT

                  That's right. Only
he wants her to do it.

OLSEN

            Why?

AUNT

                  To save her
reputation.

OLSEN

        Chivalry?

AUNT

              Or to
reduce his guilt. I know there's something wrong
with him. Something physical. His family's
quite dubious, you know. His father was
a peasant. God knows what he got up to
with those sheep. A horrifying man!
All those deaths! He stares at us so urgently.
It seems he wants to check we're still alive.

OLSEN
Well, I'm not dead yet.

AUNT

No, my dear. Not quite.

OLSEN
And what does poor Regine think of this?

AUNT
Oh, she thinks he's testing her. That it's a trial
of her sincerity. Some sort of rite
of initiation.

OLSEN

Ah! A test.

AUNT

To see
if she's inconstant. Or too young.
To teach her desperation. Anxiety.
To see if she is fit to be his bride,
can weep enough to counterpoint his sighs.

OLSEN
Well I never. What an unusual man.
I'll have to talk with her. Does she want
to break the whole thing off?

AUNT

No. Not at all.
The worse he gets, the more she seems to love him,
the more deeply attached she becomes. She thinks
it shows how much he needs her. She really thinks
her love is going to cure him, change his life.
That she'll be his redemption! What a thought!
I think, dear man, you'll have to chat with her.

OLSEN
I shall, my dear, I shall. And straight away!
Once I have read my paper. Straight away.   [CURTAIN]

SCENE V

SOREN KIERKEGAARD's *flat, Norregade 35.* ANDERS WESTERGAARD *opens the door* to REGINE OLSEN *who is tense, pale, and unchaperoned.*

ANDERS
Miss Olsen!

REGINE
                    Your new master. Is he in?

ANDERS
                                        Of course.
But is it wise to enter?

REGINE
                    He is working?

ANDERS
Naturally.

REGINE
                    Then please tell him I am here.

ANDERS
I shall, madam. [*Exit* ANDERS. *He returns with* SOREN KIERKEGAARD, *distraught.*]

SOREN (*anxiously*)
You! In here? Stay there, Anders. Do not move.
Is no one with her?

REGINE
                    I am unaccompanied,
sir.

SOREN
    Unchaperoned? Well. What is it then?
Get to the point. I am in the middle
of a complex thought.

REGINE
                        When were you otherwise?

SOREN
Sarcasm's the crudest form of irony.
Unpolished. Unrefined. And obvious.
Characteristically female, I believe.

REGINE (*pushing past him*)
So this is your new existence. This is
where you plan my next humiliation.
It's not what I expected.

SOREN
                        And what *did*
you expect?

REGINE
                Something unwelcoming. An
austere chamber. A cold monastic cell.
Something like an ancient praying-room.

SOREN
Ah! I see. Then I must disappoint you.
I mortify the soul, but not the body.
You find it uninspiring? Bourgeois? Yes?
I must surround myself with entities.
With solid, comfortable objects. I live,
you see, inside a spirit-world. I float
off freely. I often leave my body.
I'm frequently outside myself, whole yards
away. My body's just an object. It
exists with other objects. Something
that's a living inconvenience,
and *here*. Discomforting at times. A
genuine impediment, I fear.

You might inhale me. Draw me in with one
quick breath, then blow me right away. And so
I need things round me, firm particulars
that tell me I have limbs, real bones, and skin.
Let me present you with one such object.
Here, hold this skull! (*Thrusting a skull towards her*)

REGINE (*shrinking back*)
                    It's horrible!

SOREN
                              To me it is
an emblem of the Spirit. The Spirit is
a death's-head in appearance. Obviously
a skull's its fittest symbol. Put it to
your ear. Listen to its chuckles. Hear what
it is telling you. That Kierkegaard is useless
as a tin of piss. A wintertime latrine.
His name's his soul. There is a cemetery
inside his personality. He guards
a graveyard. He has no Self. It's buried
somewhere else. Smell him. He is like
an undertaker's man. A coffin-rose.
Darkness glows around him. His emotions
are inverted. Those he loves he'll savage. (*Withdrawing the skull*)
Well, then, now you're here, I'll show you round.
You'll have to learn the way I like to live.
I always like my room to be arranged
with delicate precision. Its creates
the right mood for my work. The heating for
example.

REGINE
          It feels quite cold in here.

SOREN
                              Tell her the
exact temperature, Anders.

ANDERS

                              Thirteen degrees
centigrade, sir. And three quarters.

SOREN

                              If he
exceeds, then I'm all rage. When I go out,
all windows must be opened, flung out wide.
When I come back, I check each room. I flap
my handkerchief, checking that the heat's
precisely as it should be. In wintertime
the stove is sprayed, thus, with eau de Cologne.
The flasks are always ready, stand prepared.

REGINE
Do you always live on the first floor?

SOREN

                              I do.
I cannot bear to see men's passing eyes
and faces. One suffers much less sunlight
than higher up. One must shut out the sun.
Subdue the windows, both inner and the outer,
with white curtains, heavy tapestries. I
cannot bear one single beam of sunlight.
Like a dwarf, I always walk in shadow.

REGINE
It helps you concentrate.

SOREN

                              Exactly.
But there's always something irritating.
Disturbing. A light, stabbing across the
street. The stench from the tanner's. Howling dogs.
Still, at least I can control what I perceive
a little. I must have room. Feel free.
My flats have many chambers. Six or seven.
Eight is the ideal. All nicely warmed
and lighted. Oh yes, it costs a lot,
I know. But there we are. At night

the walkers stare in wonder at the blaze.
They think I hold a soirée. You like my
furniture? Neo-classical. Flowing
female shapes.

REGINE
    It feels expensive.

SOREN
       It is.
Mahogany and rosewood. Sombre grains.
Like veins and arteries. In every room
there have to be flat surfaces at hand
with paper, pen and ink.

REGINE
      Why is that?

SOREN
So I can catch ideas. And fix them to
the sheets. Ready for analysis. When
I think, I stand. When I reason, I walk.

REGINE
What a huge desk.

SOREN
     Also in mahogany.
I head for it whenever I return.
Then write. My top-hat, mounted, so. My cane
or my umbrella underneath my arm.
And by the desk's my rosewood cabinet,
in which I keep two copies of my works.
Not many yet, but soon they'll fill each shelf.
Exquisitely printed. Gold-edged vellum.
And all bound by my own book-binder,
N.C. Møller.

REGINE
    And what's in those tin boxes?

SOREN
They hold my manuscripts. If there's a fire
they only must be saved. The rest's insured.
That's my china cabinet. Over fifty
cups and saucers. Each pair its own design.
Which one would you like? Choose one.

REGINE
There are so many. This one.

SOREN
                              Why? Because
it's pretty? Or because it's large?

REGINE
                              Both reasons.

SOREN
I thought as much. It is a test I give
to all my visitors. People choose. Their choice
reveals their characters and motives.

REGINE
I see. And what does my large cup signify?
Generosity?

SOREN
             No. Greed. You should not
be here, Regina. Consider your reputation.

REGINE (*laughing*)
My reputation? What reputation?
You destroyed my reputation long ago.
Or have you forgotten already that
you've sent me straight to Hell?

SOREN (*looking straight into her eyes*)
Good. The more Spirit, the more dread.
The greater one's desire for heaven,
the more one must experience of Hell. I
am glad to hear it. It accelerates

the red speed of the blood. I welcome such
examples of your darkness. You're growing
deeper now. Much fuller. And correspondingly
attractive. Your sins proliferate.
Grace is now abounding. More and more.
Your despair is extremely delightful
to the angels. And it is anguish to
the demons down below. Tell me what you see
now of the damned. Do they appear in the
images of their real evil? Are their interiors
one with their exteriors? The face, the
body, the filthy speech, the dirty
gestures? Do they menace you? Are they full
of hatred, crimson angers? What happens
when you venerate them? Egh? When you
commend and worship them? Egh? Do their
bodies recompose? Show gladness and
delight? Do they alter, change their features?
Are their faces dreadful? Void of life?
Like those of corpses? Black? Like graveyard
ghosts? Or are they glistening with pimples?
Warts? Suppurating ulcers? Bleeding
chancres? Just as Swedenborg describes them?
Or does no face appear, no face at all?
Just something hirsute, bony, wet with blood,
with grinding, broken teeth? Or do they appear
like me? Like men, and not so odious to each
other as they appear before the angels?
But you see, such aspects are delusive.
As soon as just one ray of heavenly light
has entered, all their forms turn monstrous once
again. Just as they really are. They flee
the beams of heaven. Cast themselves back down
to their own light, that burns like glowing
charcoal, heated sulphur.

REGINE
                    You are ill.

SOREN

                              Do you like
Hell's entrance? Is it pleasing to you?
The introduction's fine enough. Quite
welcoming. One is greeted well. One feels
among compatriots. That does not last
for long. No. The new inmate, you see, the
new guest is being checked. Explored
for her wisdom. Her type of consciousness.
Later she's examined zealously.
The further she advances into hell
the more malicious grow the spirits.
They fall on her with savage chastenings.
Reduce her to a state of slavery.
Uprisings continually occur.
Everyone desires to be in charge.
To subjugate the ones that were their friends.
The lesser hells are filled with filthy dens.
They stretch away and fill the lanes and streets
with robberies and acts of violence.
Some hells hold only brothels that are stacked
door-high with different kinds of excrement.
Forests where men roam like animals.
Sterile deserts full of rocks and caves.
Or are you different? Are you an angel
sent from heaven? Full of bright white wisdom
and intelligence? Do you turn away
from evil? Turn right away? Become
invisible, as all good angels are
to demons? I must sit now. Start to feel. (*Appearing tranced*)
Feeling's the most basic part of mind
and corresponds, of course, to purest thought.
Feelings form their corresponding thoughts.
I've watched them. There's great holiness when you
are imaged. Great sanctity indeed.
I know that you're not trying to deceive.
Your words are always suited to your thoughts.
Your face too is your feelings, inwardness.
Dreams, you see, are feelings. Your speech and face
are fashioned like an angel's, correspond
more closely than mere beings' on this earth.

Three words, that's all I utter, just three words
and you can tell exactly what I am
and read my inward nature, each of my
essentials, so pure you are, so clear.
A loving person sees a loving world.
You only see the holy. What you are.
If we were correspondents, you and I.
Grounded, both, in pure transparency...
Dear Regina, my Regina, dear.
Are you there?

REGINE
        Of course I am.

SOREN (*distantly*)
                        Have you come
for your lesson?

REGINE
        I have.

SOREN
                What did I teach
you last, when we were walking in the park? Kneel, my child!

REGINE (*kneeling, speaking automatically, having learned by
rote the answers to this erratic catechism*)
Despair is glorious. Dread transfigures us.

SOREN
And from where does one commence?

REGINE (*stumbling slightly*)
                         From sin.
Sin is the only base from which one can
attempt the leap of faith. *"Behold, I will
enter into judgement with thee, because
though sayest, 'I have not sinned.'"* Jeremiah.
2.35. Sin is the decisive
expression for the religious mode
of existence.

SOREN
        So true.

REGINE
                To say that a
child is born in sin expresses its
profoundest dignity. Inwardness, our
eternal happiness, is first perceived
through sin. *Continue*. We must not discuss
sin in a disinterested way. In a
mood of dialectical indifference,
as if sin can be examined thoroughly.
Sin is something that resists analysis.
(*Relieved to have finished the quotation*)
That resists analysis.

SOREN
                Continue.
And sin is for the ethical consciousness...

REGINE
Sin is for the ethical consciousness...er...
what ignorance is for knowledge. Sin is not
a category of aesthetics, though...though...though
it affects aesthetics.

SOREN (*sighing*)
              Exactly. Well, come
along then. Let me walk you round the flat.

REGINE
Will we be living here?

SOREN
                Quite possibly.
You see Regina, what I am slowly
teaching you is this. The Absolute
Paradox.

REGINE
>The Absolute Paradox?
I am trying to understand. Trying hard.

SOREN
The Absolute Paradox. You see, what
the reason is forever doing, with
infinite passion, is trying to
destroy itself.

REGINE
>To destroy itself?

SOREN
>Yes.
All the conflicts of dialectic have
one sole purpose. They are designed to end
in such a state where all their efforts are
unnecessary. But, alas, reason
never quite achieves its self-destruction.
It always finds a limit. Beyond that
it cannot go. *"Canst thou by searching find
out God?"* Job.11.7. You must know it well.
One comes to the Unknown. The Absolutely
Other. Defined thus, its seems to be
right on the point of disclosure. But it's
not. The reason can't even imagine
an absolute difference. It cannot
negate itself absolutely. It uses
itself for the project. Therefore it only
finds such dissimilarity in itself
as it conceives by way of what it is.
The reason, you see my dear, cannot go
completely beyond itself. Therefore
it shapes only that form of transcendence
above itself as it can conceive by
itself. Eternal Truth is the final
paradox to the reason because it
is the opposite of what reason expects.
It is not contradiction. It is a concept.
Not merely a negation but a

definite positive category.
Kant's thesis of radical evil has
one fault only. It does not make clear
that the Unfathomable is in fact
a real class. Don't you see, Regina?
The whole of philosophy turns on this.
Are you listening to me?

REGINE

                         Listening
to you?

SOREN

      Yes. Listening to me. What I said
is quite crucial.

REGINE

               Ah. Yes.

SOREN

                    Repeat what I
just said to you.

REGINE

          Repeat?

SOREN

                   What I just said
to you.

REGINE

   Ah!

SOREN

        Have you forgotten already?
Or were you refusing to listen?

REGINE

                   Oh. No.
My mind was distracted. By your furniture.

SOREN
My furniture.

REGINE
             Its quality is
excellent.

SOREN (*bending, stroking her chin*)
             The fact is, Regina, that you
are not really interested in the
positive category of the
Absolute Paradox.

REGINE
             Oh I am, my
dear. I am. Everything that concerns
you is of interest to me.

SOREN
             Of interest.
Only of interest?

REGINE
             No. Of real concern.

SOREN
Of real concern. I practise self-disclosure
and you admire my furniture. Is that good?

REGINE
No.

SOREN
    No. It is not good. Not good at all.
I try to save your soul. I really do.
I cannot try to shield you from the world.
I set you right against it, face to face. (*Lifting her*)
It has to be, my dear, it has to be!
Remember how King Abner kept his son.
He set him from the instant of his birth
inside a stately castle, gave commands

that he be kept in ignorance of the world.
Nothing sad or wretched was allowed
to scald his calm awareness. Everything
was youthfulness and beauty, utter joy
and nothing else was mentioned. How absurd!
His life itself became an open door
through which his pain invaded. Don't you see?
Pleasure turned distasteful, joy to grief.
He longed to quit his black felicity.
Everyone desires the beautiful.
But individual beauty fades with time.
The five-day blossom drops into the mould.
Temporal things are subject to decay.
Aesthetics in itself can't satisfy.
Its pain impels us towards a higher state -
the ethical. Remember? Understand?
Your world is discontinuous. All it is
is separate fleeting moments as it flits
from one flower to another. Underneath
there's nothing firm, no inner unity.
And so the world is turned into a void.
You stick your thumb in, thus, then pull it out,
and sniff. It stinks of nothing. So, you see,
that nothing grows, develops, but despair,
the underlying suffering of the world.
Such attitudes can lead to suicide.

REGINE
To suicide. I hoped to find my joy in
married love.

SOREN
               Of course you did. And we are still
discovering ourselves. The task is
difficult. We must not marry lies,
things spurious and pseudonymous. Outlines
glimpsed in mist, shadows on the scrim-scene
of a stage. We keep ourselves unsullied,
frank, sincere. Hide nothing. Utter all things.
Seek them out. My arm is not a grappling hook.
My wife's mind must be accurate, refined

and not stuffed full of samplers. If you feel
the project is too difficult, then you
must use your will, and cut the whole thing off.
I could be delusion in your way.
At times I fear I understand your mind.
My mother was a woman, like the rest.
As simple, straight and even as a street.
No bend, no turn, no corner. I could see
from one end to the other at a glance.
You'd walk me on your arm across the world
as if I were some pet that you possessed,
a figure to support you on your stage,
colluding with your acting, its pretence
of self-sufficient being. I will not.
Perhaps you're wrong to find the thing you seek
in me. Life's paradoxical. Perhaps
your eyes would cloud, and you would wish to die.

REGINE
In you I find my life, my everything.
I long to live beside you, be your aid.
I need you, need your spirit to endure.
Without you I should fall apart and die.
Nothing must be hidden from our love.

SOREN
Nothing is a hideous abyss.
Nothing is an everlasting pit.
Nothing there can enter and remain.
Nothing's like a vortex in a void.
A sort of cornucopia in reverse.
Nothing can't devour, yet must destroy.
Nothing would consume you, limb by limb,
tear apart your being, piece by piece,
take you in its belly, immolate
all parts of you, each tiny particle.
Nothingness alone would then remain
while you descend through terror, as you drop
through nothingness forever. Stay away.
You know I do not fit inside my skin.
I wear this broken body like a cloak.

I enter it and leave it as I will.
I put it in a wardrobe or a drawer,
fling it on a bed, across a chair
according to my wishes. Poor young girl.
Why marry me? A dummy would be best.
A posture in the window of a shop.
Don't touch me. Keep your distance. Stay away.
I rub off black upon you.

REGINE
                    I don't care.
Treat me as your slut, your common whore.
Already they are sniggering in the streets.
The crueller you become, the more I know
your need for me is growing desperate.
You know I'm good. I won't retaliate.
Hatred makes my virtues multiply.
Nothing will destroy my trust in you
or doubt that you are loving, underneath.

SOREN
You do not wish your ring to be returned?

REGINE
Never. Never. Never.

SOREN
                    I live next to
catastrophe and death.

REGINE
                    So be it, then,
so be it. I won't imprison you, or
kill your mind.

SOREN
                    I am not worth your passion.
Not one jot.

REGINE
     You are. You are. You cannot
cast me off. No more than you can throw
away your body.

SOREN
     So I see. So we are
one flesh. Already.

REGINE
          At any time. You
only have to ask.

SOREN (*shocked*)
          I am too harsh.
I utter challenges. Statements that will
get a hearing. Not cautious and considered
judgements. I must plan a radical
Christian revolution. I knew that years
ago. That my task in life was self-
examination. Self-understanding.
To find the real idea by which to live
and die.

REGINE
     What do you call your philosophy?

SOREN
The philosophy of existence.
Existentialism.

REGINE
          What is this
existentialism?

SOREN
          The conflict of
becoming, not the calmness of being.
Conditioned human life, lived in the
tension of reality, not life passed
in the abstract. You see, the existing

202

individual exists upon the
borderline between eternity and
time. The finite and the infinite. He is
the gate that swings between the world he sees
and Unseen Spirit. Existential truth
is paradoxical. Addresses my
subjective suffering. My conflicts. My
despair. The extremity of inner
division.

REGINE
  It sounds dangerous.

SOREN
      It is.
Paradox can drive a person mad,
when wrongly approached. Then it keeps on
sliding backwards, straight into absurdity.
Into the irrational. It needs
an antinomian mode of thinking.
A simultaneous yes and no. I stride
the streets. I release my shining cries.
I call with passionate intensity
that I'm radically concerned. "Look within!"
I shout. "Your religion is inwardness!"
Spirit is inwardness. Inwardness is
subjectivity. Subjectivity
is passion at its maximum. It is
a personal and violent concern
about your own eternal happiness. I am
the microcosm. My private
happiness and pain are those of the world
in general. My inner drama is
universal. I am concerned with man,
rather than myself. But I know that
in the analysis of myself I can
best know the one outside me. I am a
passionate man. A passionate man
is a suffering man. I have an
infinite receptivity for
suffering. To act in inwardness is

to suffer. For suffering is the crowning form
of inwardness. As inwardness increases,
suffering intensifies. The inner
life is no quiet harbour. It is a sea
of storms. Of shipwrecks. Death. Of suffering
embraced right to its utmost, to the
centre of existence, to the quick,
the living diamond point of consciousness.
Look out there, Regina. Copenhagen
is a safe port of probability.
I offer an ocean of uncertainty.
Spiritual. Intellectual. Moral.
We must abandon probability.
Inwardness brings terror. It brings evil.
The highest and the lowest. We enter
the Unknown. Hear the voice of inwardness.
What it brings at first so near to us
is evil, the Appalling. Nothing good.
The greatest truth beside the hideous lie.
A chaos. An abyss. Deception and despair.
Two premisses exist to help us on.
The first is the existence of the soul.
The second that of God. Incarnate God.
A crisis now is facing consciousness.
It must change, or it will break itself.
Our culture, our morality, our faith
are now too old, too sterile, and the fire's
already lit beneath them. Europe's ill
and dying. It will soon be torn apart
by demons wearing human uniforms.
The Christian ethic only can control
and regiment that chaos. One that has
the boldness to oppose that inner world.
But it can only tame that inward world
by altering its methods and techniques.
I must test it out. I, an idiot of
the Spirit, I must take the cross into the
new emerging underworld. Do you
desire to come?

REGINE
> I do. With all my heart!

SOREN (*taking her hand*)
Then we must visit Hell. And love what comes!
Must love what comes! Together!

[CURTAIN]

SCENE VI

PETER's *library. He sits, slumped up in a chair, staring at his untied shoelaces.* BISHOP MYNSTER *is advising him on how to deal with his depression.*

PETER
Bishop Mynster, I am a great burden to you.

MYNSTER
Not at all.

PETER
Just look at me. I cannot find the energy to tie my shoelaces. I am the most wretched of sinners. I am unfit to speak the name of God.

MYNSTER
We all fail to live our ideals. It is the common human condition. Your vitality is low. It makes you exaggerate a situation that is entirely normal for any educated conscience.

PETER
I am a danger to my family.

MYNSTER
So am I to mine.

PETER
Inadequate.

MYNSTER
Who isn't? That insight is an accomplishment of your spirit.
You should be proud of your humility.

PETER
I worry over money.

MYNSTER
You are a rich man. You overflow with grace.

PETER
I am unrighteous.

MYNSTER
I shall make you a bishop. Very soon.

PETER
Impossible. I live my life in reverse. I am always in the past,
questioning. Wondering. My dear wife, dead and buried. Dead
and buried. My brothers and my sisters, perished too. And all
through me, for my fault.

MYNSTER
Your father was the same. The hours I spent with him,
listening to the bleeding of his grief.

PETER
I have sinned against the Holy Ghost. Somewhere, somehow, I
have committed the unforgiveable sin.

MYNSTER
The times I've heard those words. From so many lips. The only
sin that cannot be forgiven is the one that believes that it
cannot be forgiven. Time has not run out for you. There *is* a
future. Life *will* be renewed. Contemplate the resurrection.

PETER

I see the world upon its death-day. All are dying. The young
and the old, the new-born child, the ailing grandfather. All of
them are weary, racked with pain. All waiting for the
Judgement.

MYNSTER

And how is God going to reward you, egh?

PETER

With Eternal Hell.

MYNSTER

I see. For what sins?

PETER

I do not know. They are buried in my conscience. They will not
be disinterred. My guilt is in my essence. My birth was just a
criminal mistake. I came here from a rape. From an incestuous
seduction.

MYNSTER

You are rich with gifts. You sin by blinding yourself towards
them. You must let go. Stop trying to earn forgiveness. It is a
free gift. Forgiveness obliterates sin. Completely. It no longer
exists, not even in the mind of God. It is rubbed right off the
board. No trace of it remains. No sign of it at all. Not one black
consonant.

PETER

To wake up, cleansed of darkness, be alive. Each morning I'm
awake before the dawn, and mourning, always mourning.

MYNSTER

Oh, you'll survive. Most melancholia passes. In a month. A
year perhaps. Though whether poor Regine will endure...
(*Pause*) It worries me, the suffering that your brother still
inflicts. There is nothing in it that is Christian. His mind! His
mind! It is as if he starts a game of cards then sets himself to
lose it, trick by trick, so he can be the winner. Why does he do
it, though? What reason is there for it? Each day there's some

new insult for the girl. You'd think his mind was set to drive
her mad, or force her to some other.

PETER
His mind is like a labyrinth. Where you see an exit there's a
hole. You're always falling further. He's always been a law unto
himself. There is a disproportion in his life between his soul
and body.

MYNSTER
It's widening. He looks more like a puppet than a man. An
effigy of pipes and sticks and rags. His eyelids blink
continuously. His lips are flickering and restless, muttering
words he spits at every corner of himself. Both legs jerk and
quiver, like his arms. His nostrils twitch and shiver like a rat's.
I know I must confront him, face to face. Demand some
explanation of his ways.

[*Enter* SOREN KIERKEGAARD]

SOREN (*casually, his back to them*)
Just come here for a book. Right, Brother
Melancholia? Just come here for a book.

MYNSTER
I wish to speak to you.

SOREN
                                    Speak away.
I might even choose to listen. Speak away.

MYNSTER
Our toleration...

SOREN (*turning*)
                                    Yes. What about your
toleration?

MYNSTER
                        Our toleration is
almost at an end.

SOREN

     Our? What is this *our*?
This personal impersonal dual form.
Or do you simply use a royal *we*?

MYNSTER
All of Copenhagen's scandalised
by what you do. Listen to me, now.
Too long we've stood aside and watched you fall,
the ways you court your individual quirks,
abusing the Eternal. Oh yes, we know.
You wish to build a palace from your thoughts,
desire to be its owner and its lord,
determine what it is, where it will stand,
the contents on display inside its walls.
I warn you, though, the real world says the same.
You're built on false foundations.

SOREN (*yawning*)
        Continue.

MYNSTER
You like to think you're special, that God's will
has marked you out profoundly from the rest
and let you know you're one of the elect,
a real Hegelian hero. But I say
such concepts soon reveal they bear a curse.
Their glamour may appeal, but they will change,
will turn into a way to hate the world,
a dark excuse to turn your back on God
and kiss your grim affliction. You are proud,
determined at all costs to be yourself,
a total individual, free, alone,
accountable to no one, but I say
that, gradually at first, then stage by stage,
you'll turn your back on man and then on God.
You'll scorn all possibility of help,
invest yourself with black demonic rage
preferring all the agonies of Hell
to cling to your position, its excuse,
your greatest fear that vast eternity

requires that you should let your suffering go,
should lose it in the depths of God Himself
through self-humiliation. Change your ways!
You stand before me now, exhausted, weak,
tormented by a desperate inner pain
that knows that it must let its torment go
but daren't for fear your whole identity
collapses with its idol. God alone
must make an individual what he is.
All else is sin, despairing vanity.
That special pain you say that you possess
can only cure itself through someone else.
To turn your back on marriage is a sin.
Marriage is the school of natural love.
Without it you are stunted, half a man
and half of your humanity is gone.

SOREN
Wind straight from the Infinite. A gas
from far beyond the planets. Your concern
enunciates my thought of years ago.
The rational adolescence of a mind.
I reason from existence, not towards.
You, Mynster, know the head, but not the heart.
Man is not a concept in a book,
a theory or a static apothegm
to illustrate a passage from a text.
Man is an existence on the move.
He strives to be ahead, before his thought,
reducible to nothing but himself,
unable to be analysed, beyond
all categories of nature. Humankind's
a process of becoming and a flux,
a passion unsusceptible to thought,
a feeling that at best can be described
but never be explained, a mystery
that moves towards a possibility,
a pulse in the becoming that is free
to exercise a liberty of choice
and be an individual. Passion, yes,
not wild, unshaved emotion, bloody rage,

nor sentimental loving that destroys,
obliterates the aspects of the world,
but something deep, quite infinite, a force
relating to the highest things in man,
that validates each action, every thought
according to its interest.

MYNSTER (*contemptuously*)
                    You say this,
you who alter every passion into thought
and kill the very life you claim to seek.
Passion, from a man as pale as you!

SOREN
Existence does not move on logically
from one step to another, stage by stage.
It's not a philosophic argument.
It leaps at the Uncertain as it makes
a basic change in quality and kind
and not in static quantity. Consciousness
when entering on an existential choice
is always in a mood of active dread,
for things are unpredictable and choice
is always quite inseparable from risk.
Progress is a leap in the unknown.
One stands above an ocean ten miles deep
uncertain if one's going to sink or swim.
What matters is the earnestness of choice,
the energy, the pathos of the act,
and not so much the need for being right.
Life is ever freedom, therefore life
is choosing, on and on, eternal dread,
eternally becoming more and more,
a movement to religion. Thus we leap
from pleasure to the ethical and then
at last into religion, where a man
can stand, an individual, face his God.

PETER
Hegel does not say so.

SOREN (*scornfully*)

            Hegel? Him?
This Hegel. Who is Hegel? What is he?
A man who builds a palace then exists
alongside in a hovel. What is thought
must have an existential inwardness.
All else is mere chimera.

PETER

            Socrates...

SOREN

Socrates was midwife to his truth.
It lay there deep within him, like a child
his ironies uncovered. Ignorance
was all that really needed to be thought.
With me it's wholly different. Here and now
the temporal meets eternity. Right now
two orders co-exist, or fall apart,
or simply lie alongside in the mind.
The choice is in our will, what we decide.
Socrates could recollect a soul
that I renounce for paradox. Yes, paradox.
The pathos of the intellectual life!
The more the proof, the less the certitude.
My answer is my infinite concern.
The more the love, the further it must grow
to contradict all mere mortality
within its own experience. I believe
with passionate sincerity. Oh,
I know you all, I know you very well.
You Christians are just pagans in disguise.
Your thoughts are on your livings and your tithes,
your patterns of promotion. All's a play!
The parson's game of Christianity!
You live in fear, and so you must attack!
Believers fear disorder in their lives.
Demoniacs live in dread of waking up,
of finding a sobriety that brings
the terror of the nightmare.

PETER (*rising*)

          Heresy!
God and man are different, and the gap
is absolute. There is no chain between.
God alone can bridge it with his grace.
The choice is fundamental. Have belief
or be repelled. Reject God. Take offence -
until you reach the last stage of despair -
declaring all religion is untruth,
the ultimate condition of your sin,
the crime against the Spirit.

SOREN

          As you know
the Spirit lives through warfare, not by peace.

MYNSTER

I see in you three stages of descent.
First there is indifference, your neglect
avoids the case in hand. Secondly
you simply stand your ground, refuse to move,
decline to make the effort to be free
but hold on to the state of passive sin.
Then, thirdly, you move out on the attack,
proclaiming Christianity's a lie.
At such a stage my vision sees you now.
Each stage is an expression of despair.
Regine is a victim of your war.
You do to her the things you do to God,
you crucify her daily.

SOREN

          So you think.
She needs to feel an infinite of pain,
then she will be perfected.

MYNSTER

          Poor, poor child.

PETER

There seems to be much more for me to pay.

SOREN
The single individual stands alone.
He stands alone. Alone too, he will fall.
I am here, and I attack your Church.
I am here, have come to disabuse
your simple congregations. Understand?
That will be my life's task, and my death's.
That will be my leap into the dark.
My one, decisive, existential act.
Official Christianity's absurd.
Ludicrous aesthetically. And
intellectually. I reject it! It's
a scandal. I accuse Hegelian
idealism. I attack Cartesian
logic. I reject nationalism.
I condemn all liberal constitutions.
They are intolerable. I detest
Romanticism. It overflows all
limits. I renounce all humanism.
What is it but a vague, vain, vaporised
Christianity? Its ultimate lees.
I revile all evolutionary
gradualism. I proscribe all marriage.
I offer life. I offer liberation.
The freedom of the individual choice
in spite of all that's psychic that denies.
I hate all Copenhagen. All the court.
Its senseless, mean and predatory lives.
I leave it all. I flee to Germany.
Berlin. To being. Quality of thought!

[*Exit* SOREN. PETER *moves as if to restrain him.* MYNSTER
holds him back.]

MYNSTER
Let him go. The man begins to rave.
He is possessed.
First one loses balance, then one falls.

[CURTAIN]

SCENE VII

The Olsens' apartments. REGINE *stares out of the window.*
From now onwards she is dressed in black. A letter is beside
her on a sidetable. Enter OLSEN, *a book in his hand.*

OLSEN
What is the matter, child? What is this? (*Picking up the letter*)
I recognise that handwriting.

REGINE
                        You may
read it.

OLSEN
    It is addressed to you.

REGINE
                        It
concerns you.

OLSEN (*sadly*)
                Ah. The ring again.
How many times is that? I suppose you
have lost all count by now. Well, what is it
to be? He returns your ring. You fly round
to his apartments. Tears saturate
the carpet, and back you come again,
the ring back on his finger. To and fro.
To and fro. One day we're engaged, the next
it's off. And your face grows paler, paler.

REGINE
He has been very busy. First there was
the thesis to defend. And then the
dissertation. I think that he is
counting on the chair. No one thinks like him.
He is engaged on many projects. Many
thoughts. He is founding a completely new
philosophy. Once he settles down,

becomes an academic...

OLSEN

                    He's due for
disappointment.

REGINE

          Disappointment?

OLSEN
I have it - quite unofficially, of course -
that Rasmus Nielsen is preferred.

REGINE

                         Rasmus
Nielsen?

OLSEN
          Rasmus Nielsen. He is thought to
be, well, how shall I put it, less erratic.

REGINE
Less erratic! Less erratic! But Soren
has the finest brain in Scandinavia.

OLSEN
Great brains make great enemies. It's time
he learnt that simple lesson. Let him go.
Your love is an imprisonment for him.
Some men can never marry.

REGINE

                              He must try.
I tell him all he needs is faith, real faith
in love. He so lacks confidence. For
everything he does reveals his need.
He thinks I'm simple-minded, that my brain
can't understand his deep complexities.
He always speaks of life's uncertainties.
Why then should I be different from the rest?
I know the risks. I've weighed up all I can -

his temperament, his sicknesses, his fears.
I love him, and to me that's everything.
I'll hold him to his contract. We'll be wed.

OLSEN
And so it will go on, until you break.
First one way, then the other, till you're dead.
You used to be so gay, so full of life.
A brilliance seemed to follow you around.
Now it's turned to shadow, utterly.

REGINE
Despair is the condition of my life.
He's taught that me. I now know it is true.
Only when one's truly willed despair
has one selected what despair desires,
one's true, eternal, fixed validity.
Then one's at peace in freedom. Only thus
can one aspire to win the Absolute.

OLSEN
And that is what he's taught you - to despair?

REGINE
I thought that I was happy, since my life
was beautiful as blossom, full of joy.
He showed me that the opposite was true.
That happiness is just illusory
and just the outward sign of inward loss,
an emblem of my spiritual disease.
He understood my beauty, what it meant.
He watched my easeful tragedy of life,
its love of bliss, of music, merriment
and mourned that the deceptive joys of time
had kept me from my deep identity
to alienate my being from its God.
He knew it was the best thing he could do -
to open up the depths of my despair
and show to me the sufferings of love,
the madness of believing in a man
and not his holy maker. He knew well

his cruelty would bring me to my God.

OLSEN
And has it?

REGINE
             I am stripped of joy. I am
at peace. I understand his aims. I know
his mission was to help me be my age.

OLSEN
Seventeen. Seventeen. Not fifty-seven.
He did all this to you.

REGINE
             I did it to
myself. I chose. He simply showed to me
the choices. It all was for my good.
He yearned to be the guardian of my soul,
to order me exactly what to do,
admonish and rebuke and give advice.
But that would cause deception on both sides.
He said he was a signpost on the way.

OLSEN
I've been too easy on the man. Too lax.

REGINE
Not at all.

OLSEN
             He confuses love with hatred.
This misery must end, for all our sakes.
Address the thing you dread, and see it home.
This failure at the University
will mortify his pride. So, go to him
and end it all. Renounce him. Do it! Finally!

[CURTAIN]

SCENE VIII

SOREN KIERKEGAARD's *apartment. Books stand in piles, dusted, ready for packing and a journey to Berlin. SOREN is picking through them, agitatedly. Enter ANDERS.*

ANDERS
Miss Olsen, sir.

SOREN
   I am unwell.

ANDERS
      Exactly, sir.
So I have informed her. She says that she will
wait till you recover.

SOREN
     Then she will wait
forever.

ANDERS
  Yes, sir.

SOREN
   What is the time?

ANDERS
Five, sir. More or less.

SOREN
     And when must I expect
my next crisis?

ANDERS
   Half the day has
elapsed since the last one. It should occur
at any time now.

SOREN

How does she appear?

ANDERS
Deathly, sir.

SOREN (*guilt-stricken*)

Deathly! Does she look as if she's dying?

ANDERS
Definitely, sir. If you see her now
it may well relieve you of the necessity
for a further attack. At least for today.

SOREN
Do I look like a murderer to you?

ANDERS
Yes, sir. Indubitably.

SOREN

Do I?

ANDERS

You look the very
picture of guilt. Of dark foreboding. As if
divine retribution were at hand.
The basis of morality is guilt,
as you have often told me, many times.

SOREN
Divine retribution! Oh my God!
What sort of retribution?

ANDERS

Death, sir. As
I said.

SOREN

     I seduced her, you know. There is a
higher form of seduction. Much worse than
that of lust. Much worse than that of lust.

ANDERS

Of course, sir. Perhaps it would be better
to see the lady, sir. There is still some time
before your train. You will see no more of her
once we are safely in Berlin. A kind word
now, and you may well be saved whole months of
anguish later. Should you wish it, of course.

SOREN

Should I spit on her? Or treat her kindly?

ANDERS

Remember Goethe, sir. Treat people as they are
and you make them worse. Treat them as if
they were exactly as they ought to be
and you will help them rise to the ideal.

SOREN

Right then. Show her in. But hang around. There's
bound to be great ructions.

ANDERS

     I shall, sir.   [*Exit* ANDERS *who
returns quickly with* REGINE *and stands behind her.*]
Miss Olsen, sir. Your fiancée.

REGINE

     You're packing!

SOREN (*sorting books*)

What about Descartes? Creative doubt!
I think, therefore I am. A curious thought.
A thought proves its existence by a thought!
A facile contradiction. Book on book!
This Leibnitz is the dullest of the lot.
Arid and pedantic, tedious.

Worse than his disciple, sombre Wolfe.
My father used to read him, night and day.
His grease is all across it, and his tears.
Pluralist or monist? Well, who cares?
The attributes of single substances.
A dreadful smell of decadence, decay.
And yet those men could think. No women there.

REGINE
Why are you leaving me? Please answer me.
Are you going far away?

SOREN
     Far, far away.
This is more to the point. Aristotle.
He tells us of the groom who left his bride
precisely at the moment of his vow.

REGINE
Why?

SOREN
   The augurs. They warned him off the act.
It would end, they said, in disaster. So.
Should the man explain himself, or not?
Three possibilities arise. One.
That he continue with his marriage. Stitch his lips.
But that was wrong, since it involved his wife.
Two. That he stop the marriage. But what then?
That would have brought great suffering to the girl,
destroying his relationship with her
and all it might have led to. Number three.
Speak out. Explain the meaning of his act.
That would have caused no problem, since the Greeks
well understood the force of prophecies
and must have known what ethics would require.
But if the prohibition had been made
in quite a private manner to the groom
then things would be quite different. The command
would place him right before the paradox,
beyond the reach of ethics - where a man

must stand alone, before the Absolute
in absolute relationship. Hence the doubt.
Was it inhibition, or pure faith?
Was there some inward motive for withdrawal
or was it an especial act of God,
a summons to encounter? Which was it then?
No principles could justify the act.
An Abraham in anguish kills his child
believing that by dint of the Absurd
another Isaac's going to return
to vindicate his act. But will he though?
Therein lies the torment. There's the rub.
He either stands uniquely with his God
in absolute relationship with him,
or Abraham, the relative, is lost.

REGINE
Horrible!

SOREN
      I agree. It is horrible.
Unthinkable. Yet sometimes we are commanded
to do the unthinkable. God instructs.
Man, before the Absolute, obeys.

REGINE
                      And
what has God commanded you to do?

SOREN
                          That is between
ourselves.

REGINE
      To let me go? To break your vow,
just like the bridegroom did?

SOREN
                   Like the bridegroom could
have done.

REGINE
>You torment me.

SOREN
>Perhaps God is
protecting you. *The outward is the
inward and the inward is the outward.*
My Hegelian thesis. Look what nature's
done to me. She stopped at every turn.
Come now. Look at me. Observe my arms.
From shoulder to the elbow they are long.
Immensely long. From the elbow to the hand -
truncated. Chopped. Cut off. The same is true
when analysing how my face is shaped,
the structure of my fingers. All is odd.
Misshapen. Listen to my speech. Just the same.
All my speeches start off promising,
seem full of hope and interest. Everyone
sits up in expectation. Then, you see
the whole thing ends in nothing. So, my dear,
I'm full of power, then - total impotence -
a slave, whose freedom seems unlimited,
but all he says and does is fantasy.
You will be better off without him. He lives
at a second remove. Watch him. Now. See?
He forms an idea of you. He
idealises. Then he destroys. Understand?
Always there's a concept set between.
An intellect. Nothing is spontaneous.
He is distanced from reality. And
he knows it.

REGINE
>You try me to the end. It is a
very dangerous test. A nasty trial.
You make me walk the tight-rope. Do you feel
no anguish I may slip, begin to fall?

SOREN
Oh, you won't fall. You're far too skilled for that.
I can feel cunning and deceit through
countless layers of clothing.

REGINE
                                    Where are you
going?

SOREN
        To Berlin.

REGINE
                    To Berlin? Because
the University has snubbed you?

SOREN
It has chosen. I abide by its decision.
My future lies in exile, I believe.

REGINE
Don't you love me any more? Please answer me.

SOREN
You drew me in your world with skilful art.
The first love is the true love, so they say.
The wonder of its soft unconsciousness,
that melting into being, all that warmth
of infantile endearment, that sweet swoon
that kills the thinking spirit! Yes. I loved.
At school I was promiscuous. I would mix
with everything. I poured myself in all.
In every type of strange receptacle,
each pot and bottle, vial and glass retort.
I soon assumed the shape of any form.
But no fixed contour ever held me long.
I went off like a vapour, in a cloud!
Evaporated promptly. So with girls!
One melts away. I move on to the next.
The Don Juan of the north. The very man.
Novelty in love is everything.

REGINE
If you want me, I am yours. At any time.

SOREN (*contemptuously*)
For that I'd go to downtown Copenhagen.
Times are I look at you and see the very
purpose and the meaning of my life.

REGINE
And what is that?

SOREN
                    To be brought to the highest
measure of disgust for it.

REGINE
                    Disgust?

SOREN
Through a crime I came into existence.
Against God's will. Giving life. That was the
offence that made of me a criminal.
His giving life. The punishment must accord
with the offence. To lose all wish for life
in all its forms. At the centre stands the Fall.
Human self-centredness, focussed in
the act of coitus. In giving being.
In the continuation of the species.
God demands that all of us renounce
such vanity, so that all may love Him. (*Moving closer*)
Believe me, dear Regina. Hear my words.
God wants to call a halt, to stop the Fall.
Its constant repetition. The return
of time. Stay a virgin, my dear. Untampered with.
Untouched. A sheet of snow that bears no
footprints. No. No darker mark of man.
Stay celibate, my dear. You see this whole
existence is opposed to God. It is
a false step, a mistake, a lapse from grace.
All the time His love is pitying men
yet wants to pick a quarrel. For the race

is finished. God has had too much. We must
be rescued from the flesh. We must begin
to kill the future. Kill all future births.
Sexual relations are a sin.
A sin against divine omnipotence.
And woman is the problem. Woman is
self-centredness incarnate. The whole sad
history between the sexes is
a huge net, yes, a black web of intrigue
that's aimed at killing Spirit in a man.
One has to learn contempt for all this world.
One must die off, my dear. The senses are
antagonists of Spirit - all this flesh -
this warm subhuman beauty. "What is
Spirit?" you may ask. I'll answer you.
It's being free. Yes. Free to will that thing
that flesh and blood must shrink from. Understand
that dying off entails more agony
than dying. To die is just to suffer.
The act is fairly short. Does not last long.
But dying off continues all your life.
To be a Christian - I speak truly now -
to be a genuine Christian is the most
appalling of all torments. Has to be.
To have your Hell around you, here on earth.

REGINE
I can't believe these words.

SOREN
                              Answer me.
What do you most shudder from, my dear?
From dying. From the future throes of death.
To be a Christian means that you must live
for forty years or more within that state
experiencing one long death-agony.
One screams out like the shrieking animal
that suffers vivisection. Yet that is
a minor form of agony compared
to that known by the Christian. Loving God
means loathing all that's human. Hate yourself.

Leave everything. Mortify the flesh.
Assume your cross. Despise your family.
This land is morally corrupt. All
eventually receive their punishment.
Just look at you - so healthy, plump and fine.
To lead a truly spiritual life
while you are living here in such a state
is totally impossible. We need
more cholera to teach you you're a real
free individual. The slums of Ripengade,
of Christianshavn. Pray for syphilis,
for much more gonorrhoea to drip its
spiritual benefits. Our natural home
is pain, disease and death. (*Presenting the skull once more*)
                          Touch this skull
again. (*She touches it gently.*) Again. She was a woman once.

REGINE
I do not wish to.

SOREN
                  She was beautiful.
But Beauty is Herself anathema.
She lives the outward. Binds you to the world.
The Christian man must turn to ugliness.
The death's-head is the symbol he most loves,
the skull that underlies the lovely flesh.
Learn to love the ugly, to rejoice
in what is disproportionate and vile.
Be the Holy Ghost, the Head of Death.
To humankind, immersed in flesh and bone,
the Spirit is most terrible of all.
Listen to the skull. You hear its speech?
I used to think disgust was just the
province of the aesthete. Now I see
disgust's in fact a moral absolute.
God requires disgust from Christian men.
Existence is a crime, and sex the Fall.
One's born into a prison-house, a jail.
Our punishment, of course, is to exist,
so pray for Death, for God to send release

then thank him for the blessing that he sends.
We're foreigners, mere strangers in this land.
Fixtures in its still-life of despair.
I honour it. Our constant ennui.
It's central to all Christian suffering.
I kiss with joy the tedium that I flee.
Our essence is hypocrisy, you see,
a battleground where opposites collide.
The world is unendurable and I,
in time, at last will turn my back on it,
and willingly, with great alacrity.
Be fanatical, Regina. A zealot
eager for her death. Pray for me, daily.
Once you reach the summit of disgust
the grace of God enables you to know
He did it all for love. You'll understand
in every dirty corner of your soul
that God is love. Then you'll be ripe to die,
to pass into eternity. Why cling to life?
Why hold on to this rot, this nothingness?
Hold fast to dread. Your dread will show the way.
Follow it along, right to the end.
Follow it, in burning agony.
Cultivate a melancholy search,
seek in all directions till you meet
the dreadful. Let it grip you with its
terror. Do not flee. Endure it. Then
you'll find religious calm, composure there,
at last be free and happy, spiritual!
In temporal existence one's prepared
to suffer all things, be receptive, yes,
to open up. Don't stop half-way. Be led into
the infinite security of love.

REGINE
Then it seems that I must bid you farewell.

SOREN
Don't worry about me. I shall endure.
I shall build a fortress for my sorrow.
High up. Like the nest of an eagle. Mixed

with mist. Where no one can attack it.
I'll dart down to this dull sublunar world
from time to time, then seize my fleeting prey,
some thought, some quick sensation I can grip
to weave into my palace tapestries.
And there I'll sit, as if within a dream,
immersing all my sufferings within
a baptism of sweet forgetfulness.
All temporal and contingent things must die.
And there I'll wait, a dotard, day by day.
Grey-haired, yet always thoughtful, I'll explain
the sequences of pictures of my past,
my voice soft as a quiver of the wind,
the whisper of an ice-sheet, as it spreads
its cold film down the surface of a pool.
A child will sit and listen at my side.
So close, attentive, filled with care and awe
remembering in his mind each thing I see
before my voice can form them from the air.

REGINE
Forgive me for the things I've done to you.
What shall I become, I wonder? A
governess, perhaps. There's nothing else.
My reputation's lost. All nudge and grin.
No other man will want me.

SOREN
                              Excellent.

REGINE
Here's your ring. Set it in the cabinet.
With all the rest. May I shake your hand?

SOREN
Only if you glove it.

REGINE (*withdrawing her hand*)
                    Well, farewell then.
My eyes are wet.

SOREN
               They shine like morning dew
beneath the rising sun. So off you go.
Like Clytie deserted by her God.   [*Exit* REGINE]
I'll watch you, step by step, make memory.
Engrave my dark perception with your light.
(*He crosses to the window, a book held in his hand.*)
Like Clytie deserted by her God.
Like Clytie deserted by her God!
(*He hurls the book to the floor with a scream and falls on a couch, arching backwards in a sudden quasi-epileptic fit. ANDERS leans over him quietly, gags his mouth, brushes the book he has taken from SOREN's hand, then sits down peacefully, proceeding to read it.*)

[CURTAIN]

BESS AND BOB

A VERSE PLAY IN FIFTEEN SCENES

DRAMATIS PERSONAE

BESS, ELIZABETH I
LADY MARY, a Maid of Honour
EDMUND SPENSER
LORD BURGHLEY
ROBERT CECIL
his SECRETARY

BOB, ROBERT DEVEREUX, 2ND EARL OF ESSEX
LADY ESSEX
FRANCIS BACON
ANTONY BACON
UNTON
PEREZ
BLOUNT
LORD HOWARD

BISHOP, CHAPLAINS 1, 2
GAOLER, CAPTAIN, GENTLEMEN 1, 2

SCENE I

Whitehall Palace, London. EDMUND SPENSER, *discomforted, is about to read the latest verses from his 'Faerie Queene' to* BESS, *Queen Elizabeth I.* LADY MARY, *a Maid of Honour, works petit point as Dr. Lopez, the Queen's physician, is being tortured at the instigation of Bob, Robert Devereux, the Earl of Essex, in The Tower. On a table beside* BESS *is a series of masks on sticks, which she is playing with, holding each in front of her in turn.*

BESS
You suffer, Mr. Spenser?

SPENSER
                        I do,
Your Majesty.

BESS (*holding before her the mask of a wise philosopher, through which she views her poet*)
                        Directly, or empathically,
or vicariously, dear friend?

SPENSER
                        Empathically.

BESS
But to a minor degree, Mr Spenser.
A tremor, now and then. Odd shoots of sweat.
Nothing uncontrollable. Dew on manna. (*Pause*)
These are dark days, Mr. Spenser. Dark-black
days indeed. All England croaks with omens,
rots with prophecies. So, what do we do?
Shadow-battles everywhere. All around
things rise to challenge our inertia.
We have to face ourselves in a new way.
Unknown events, yet strangely intimate.
Humour and calmness, Mr. Spenser.
Humour and calmness. The Eternal Thought
comes to fulfilment through order, and through

order alone a man lives up to his being
the image of God. But one can over-
emphasise that state. You have touched your ruff
twenty-three times in the last six minutes.

SPENSER
Have I? My apologies. May I sip a glass
of wine?

BESS
                If you don't spill it.

SPENSER
                                That may
not be possible. (*As he tries to pour a glassful, the jug rattles.
The wine spills.*)

BESS
                        Don't worry, Mr.
Spenser. It has not turned to blood.

SPENSER
                                No. Not blood.

BESS (*walking slowly, setting aside the mask of the philosopher*)
You wonder why we're torturing the Jew.
Set my Spanish doctor on the rack.
The reason is that Essex is convinced
the man has turned a traitor. That is why.
Of course it makes no sense, no sense at all.
Why should Lopez plot for Catholics
when all they'll do is burn him at the stake?
A house in Holborn, son at Winchester.
Both adore the Holy Trinity.
What higher post in England could he hold? (*Musing*)
And yet, some say, he worked for Walsingham.
Some men are drawn by instinct to intrigue
and find what they desire in guile alone
and in deceiving a deceiver.

SPENSER
He's far too old to torture.

BESS
                    I agree.
The process of our justice, though, demands
his statements should be tested by the rack.
He knows the mystic Qubalah, all through.
What's life and death to him? A trick, a wink.
The opening and the closing of an eye.
Divert me, Spenser. Fill my brain with verse.
And stop this pointless suffering. Poor young man.
You Platonists despise the actual. You
should use it for your freedom, not your jail.
(*Overlooking his shoulder*)
The Seventh Book. You have it? Excellent.
On social and subjective virtue.
Constancy. Diana is in Ireland.
Faunus is about to tempt her maid
with cherries. I'm listening. Do get on with it. (*She assumes a
mask with the face of Diana, chaste, idealised and beautiful.*)

SPENSER (*clearing his throat*)
The simple maid did yield to him anone;
and eft him placed where he close might view
that neuer any saw, saue onely one;
who, for his hire to so foole-hardy dew,
was of his hounds devour'd in Hunters hew.
Tho, as her manner was on sunny day,
Diana, with her Nymphes about her, drew
to this sweet spring; where, doffing her array,
she bath'd her louely limbes, for Ioue a likely pray.

There Faunus saw that pleased much his eye,
and made his hart to tickle in his brest,
that for great ioy of some-what he did spy,
he could him not containe in silent rest;
but breaking forth in laughter, loud profest
his foolish thought. A foolish Faune indeed,
that couldst not hold thy selfe so hidden blest,
but wouldest needs thine owne conceit areed.

Babblers vnworthy been of so diuine a meed.

BESS (*with quiet anger, taking up a mask of wrath*)
Stop!

SPENSER
 Your Majesty?

BESS
      What are you doing,
Mr. Spenser?

SPENSER
   Reading *The Faerie Queene*.

BESS
Don't be facetious, Mr Spenser. It does not
become you. When I asked you what you were doing
I did not expect a literal
reply, not from such an experienced
allegorist as you are. What were
you doing?

SPENSER
    Depicting Diana, Your
Majesty. And the god Faunus.

BESS
        Yes?

SPENSER
He was staring at the goddess Diana.

BESS (*growing angrier*)
Who was naked.
The goddess of virginity was naked.
You see what you are doing? You ogle
her nudity. You gawp at her perfection.
Then what do you do? You find the act so
ludicrous you burst out into laughter.
(*Thundering*) Who is Diana?

SPENSER

You are, Your Majesty.

BESS

And who is Faunus? You are. You the poet.
Leering at divinity. You, peering at her flesh.
Dribbling on her skin, then grinning like a
pander. Am I tickling your heart then, Mr.
Spenser? I tell you this. Your work no
longer pleases me. I do not find it
apposite. You are passé, out of date,
outmoded, obsolescent. You are just like
all the others. You celebrate a woman's
beauty, but underneath you are repulsed
by the very fact of her existence.
Next you will show me as a butcher. A
woman of intolerable cruelty.
You will be covered with a deer-skin
and torn in pieces by my hounds. Is that
so? You will luxuriate in that most
hideous spectacle and claim you love the
world through art, though underneath of course
you find it miserable and evil. I
tell you, Mr Spenser, I feel sullied
by your eyes. By their secret contemplation.
Your thoughts leave filthy imprints on my soul.
They pollute me, until I start to feel
intolerable. What are you doing,
egh? Contemplating very lovingly those
very torments that your blessedness
consists in so avoiding! You are
like all the others! Watching the Queen's
body. Flattering her form with metaphors
in which you wholly disbelieve.

SPENSER

Your Majesty,
for aesthetic contemplation one has to be
equally free from the desire to possess
as from abstract thinking. If what you say
is true then I have been betrayed by my

imagination, nothing more. It was not
my wish to mock you bathing naked.

BESS
Unconsciously it was.

SPENSER
                    If that was so
it was unconscious and therefore not my
will's responsibility. The Queen can
be appreciated for her beauty
in itself.

BESS
        But Faunus laughed.

SPENSER
                            I was careless,
perhaps. A poet is easily led
astray.

BESS (*satisfied, reassuming her first mask, the philosopher's*)
        Poor Spenser. You have been caught out
by polarity. Still you have not learnt
the opposite is always present. You
are no politician, my friend. Like Essex,
would never make a king. You shudder
once again. Dear Dr. Lopez suffers,
suffers still. Poor man. He also saw me
naked. Now look what's happening to him.
He is dissected by the rack. Quite
vivisected, stretched out twice his length,
like old dull-yellow vellum. Poor old man!
(*Pause. She tilts her head and listens.*)
Ah! You recognise the knocking of that stick?
That limping syncopation? That must mean
my Burghley's on the way, and Cecil too
still leading him, still propping up his bones.
Open the door, Mary! (LADY MARY *scuttles across.*
BURGHLEY *totters in, supported by* CECIL.)
                My burly Burghley!

Our stable instability. What news
of Lopez? His patients grow impatient,
breathe my breath. You've seen the application
of the torture?

BURGHLEY
                    Unfortunately. The rack
still tightens.

BESS
                    That's no news. No news at all.

BURGHLEY
Exactly. There are moans, of course, and groans
that mix in with the screams of the machine,
but nothing that's substantial. As we know,
justice is the victim of the rack.

BESS
The torturer is adept at his trade?

BURGHLEY
Yes. Quite an artist. Anticipation's
everything. And knowing when to stop.
(*He gives her a penetrating glance.*)

BESS
Is there a plot against me?

BURGHLEY
                    Plots are everywhere.
All history's a dark conspiracy.
Will always be so. There's a plot of sorts.
It is not aimed at you. May I sit down? (*He sits, painfully.*)
I feel that I've been dislocated too.
Nowadays each bone is on the rack.

CECIL (*looking more than usually crippled*)
We searched his house at Holborn. It was clean,
from the attic to the cellars. Nothing there.
We asked him questions, both examined him

and found he was a sober, decent man.
Each question was replied to honestly. (*Shaking his head*)
Then Essex had him taken to the tower.

BESS

My Essex is all charm. Just like a boy!
My heart burns in the auburns of his hair
each time my eyes are turned towards his head.
So feminine those hands! So exquisite!
Such fingertips should never grip a spear
but only gather roses.

CECIL

He's like your son.

BESS

He is my sun. My most impetuous son!
Poor Essex, so unable to deceive!
Always in a hurry, in a dream!
He never knows which food is in his mouth,
no, let alone what clothing he has on.
Even when he's dressing he donates
his body to his servants, lets them clad
its beauty in whatever lies around.
He simply wears whatever they decide,
then off he goes, head forwards, into wind,
on long wide strides. Fighting. Always fighting.
How I admire the passions of the young!
How deeply I mistrust them. Their bad faith. (*Growing serious*)
He's warm and young, and I am old and cold,
as lonely as a lampless labyrinth
whose atmosphere's as frozen as its stone.
A poor half-buried thing, a shell of air.
A corpse, mere carrion, just mere nothingness. (*Whimsically*)
They tell me that our earnest Spanish saint,
our Philip, with his body stuffed with worms,
all writhing like a desert anchorite's,
has tried to have me murdered fifteen times.
He plots to turn this beauty to a ghost's.
And yet I think he loves me underneath.
With Spain I have a most ambiguous war.

It crawls on by inertia, like a snake
just glutted with the body of a deer.
No battles can occur. We lack the cash.
We're both too weak. The fight has ruined us.
A war that is no war! Precisely what
most pleases me. Yet dangers still abound.
Doctors, poisons, drugs, a world of them!
And Essex has a plotter's cast of mind.
Essex must have enemies abroad.
Essex must have enemies at home.
His shadow speaks in Spanish. When he coughs
its echo always forms some foreign oath.
His eyes bore into keyholes, corners, doors.
Conspirators and agents everywhere!
Always he is spoiling for a fight.
How else can our great flower of chivalry
unfurl the coloured buds of his romance
and gain the golden glory he desires
except by wondrous acts of derring-do?
How long before the verdict of the trial?

BURGHLEY
An hour perhaps. Or two. It may take more.

BESS
And Essex gathers evidence, no doubt.

CECIL
The evidence of terror, hate and fear.
An intercepted letter has appeared.
A secret bribe of fifty thousand crowns
for Don Antonio's son, who undertakes
that he'll remove his father's standing threat
to Portugal.

BESS
        His threat to Portugal!
Antonio is a miserable cur
who treats his men like slaves. What else is there?

CECIL
There is a man, Ferreira, who's confessed
that Lopez once approached the King of Spain
and offered to perform what he desired...
Tinoco has supported what he said -
that Lopez plotted treason. The victim,
Your Majesty. The executioner,
the doctor himself. The method, poison.

BURGHLEY
Mere fantasy, of course. Just Essex's mind.
A plot from the physician of the Queen?
What else but an attempt to murder her?
Once that quick conclusion has been reached
it soon becomes a statement in the mouths
of the accused. The rack arranges that.
Then comes the mass of details, such as which
slow poison was employed to bind the bowels
and where and when such poison had been used
and who had been accomplice to the act
till all's as clear as noonday, lucid
as a new dream. Alehouse conversation!
Altered by the twists and shifts of time.
Nothingness, to stuff into men's ears,
until they follow every lie they hear.

BESS
And yet I am the essence of the state.
Without me all the rest of you are dead.
That's obvious to all our enemies.
Assassinate the Queen and that will bring
success without the misery of war.
One act, one drop of poison will transform
the whole of Europe. This is known too well.
I do not like the justice of the world.
When it involves the safety of the Queen
there is no hope of equity at all.

BURGHLEY
No one is acquitted on that charge.
The allegation is the punishment,
the charge itself as potent as the crime.
Expediency must rule at such a time!
Better that one thousand innocents
be slaughtered than one murderer should live.
The crime is in a special category
where none can show compassion, not one word.

BESS
The process of the law must take its course.
You yourselves acknowledge it is so.
So be all eyes and ears! God follows all.
A foolish thing it is, to sin against
omniscience! And yet our follies grow!
To live in death, abandoned, all alone!
To feel the damp damnation of the ground
that rots imagination, watch the worms
that bore in through the mortcloth of the skin,
the mask of grease and paint that clads the bones,
yet sin and sin and sin continuously!
How ugly is our folly, day by day!
My head aches! I need music for my ears.
This process will continue, come what may! (*Turning angry*)
To poison me, his long, most constant friend!
I ought to fling the rat into the sea!
All this is on your conscience! See to it!
You bear the whole responsibility!
Hanged, and drawn, and quartered, what a death!
Singer, sing to me. Come, mourn with me.
Re-enter me, let grieving fill my soul!
It's ill and old and fears what has to be.

[*Exit* BESS, *looking the picture of self-pity*. CURTAIN]

SCENE II

An anti-chamber. BOB, 2ND EARL OF ESSEX, *is pacing the floor.* FRANCIS BACON *stands centrally, attempting to integrate him, alarmed at the possibility of their being overheard.*

BOB
The woman keeps me waiting. Hour on hour.

BACON
You press too hard. Be patient! Use your head!

BOB
Her heart's a flameless grate. Yes, she's as
savage as a kern! My life does not develop.
I cannot find the mind I try to read.
It falls like dirty water through my hands.

BACON
Ships cannot navigate by black Electra.

BOB
She never shows the slightest gratitude!
I labour for her, morning, noon and night,
I chase the Spanish round and round the globe
and all she does is frown, prevaricate,
and keep me here, her vassal, hour by hour!

BACON
You must not expect great constancy.
A woman's not the equal of a man.
Her mind is frail, and quickly pulled apart.

BOB
I've hanged the traitors, lopped them into bits.
I burned them. All of London cheered me on.
But still the Queen says nothing. Answer me.
Have I not done all things that you advised?
Shown myself the perfect diplomat?

Filled my house with educated spies
to seek out information for the Queen?
Played the sober statesman, well-informed,
given up my former youthful tricks,
acted with all honour, gravity?
I've even started paying off my debts.

BACON
You must not weave your soul into your sleeve.
You must be more evasive with the Queen.
Flatter, like a vacant sycophant.
Dissimulate like priests. Use a reserve
that puts a theologian in the shade.
Imitate your father and his style.
The Earl of Leicester knew just what to do.
But don't assume your mother's forthright ways.
Try to be more careful with your looks -
they must not seem too formal, otherwise
the Queen will wonder what lies underneath.
Always have some business well in hand
pursuing it with all due earnestness
and evident affection. If you learn
Her Majesty observes it with dislike
be ready then to drop it. Understand?
Pretend that you must go away to Wales
to visit your estate and when you learn
the Queen does not feel pleased to see you go
relinquish it. Take good care that nothing
is remiss. Dress, clothing, different gestures,
everything. You understand my meaning?
Make sure you keep your popularity.
Guard your reputation. Let her see it so
but be quite sure that nothing that you do
can alter you at all in any way.
Underneath remain the thing you are.

BOB
I lack your calm phlegmatic temperament.

BACON
Each stage of education must repeat
the lessons of the last. But with more guile,
a content that's more complex than before.
Men repeat their cycles of ideas,
and each time far more substance is revealed
to those who know the thing they're looking for.
You need to know far more to learn the Queen.
She owns a perfect mastery of Greek,
of Latin, Music, Pure Philosophy,
of Logic and Arithmetic. Hebrew, too,
as well as fine Italian, Portuguese
and Spanish. The Friend of Scholars. The
Patroness of Literature.

BOB
                        Nonetheless
her prose style is unbearably obscure.

BACON
The style flows from the subject, naturally.
Thank God she's the exception to the rule.
Women are quite dangerous enough.
We do not need to swell their subtlety
by training them in craft and eloquence
until they match the orators of Rome.
Women are still women nonetheless.
All daughters of the whore, our primal Eve.

BOB
You make my back as twisted as your brother's.
How shrewd you are. As cunning as a snake!
If I could only change my nature! I've
embarked on the attempt. Have grown this beard.
An excellent excrescence, is it not?
To terrify the Spaniard in our war.
Lopez is dead, but still the Queen delays.
I found all out, but now she seems so cold.

BACON
Be cautious in your military ways.
My lord, can't you see the sort of danger
you must pose towards Her Majesty?
Why else this sudden coldness, this delay?
Any *king* would see you as a threat.
How then should a woman look on you?
Act the way your father would have done.
Or Hatton. Flatter her. And nod your head.
Praise her male opinions. When you do,
make sure your voice and language seem sincere.
Ask favours to renounce them when her mind
decides it will oppose you. Understand?
Keep full control of military affairs
but do not seem to do so, for, you see,
most people grow suspicious when they see
a military following. They
fear a revolution, coup d'état.
And seek for different duties. Renounce
the Master of the Ordnance. Take instead
the office of Lord Privy Seal, sedentary
and peaceful. And always take good guard to
use each chance to warn yourself against
a cheap, unthinking popularity.
That way you will remain her favourite.
If you should show compliance and respond,
her goodness will be endless. But if not,
why, then you stand in peril, for the Queen
will look on you as someone she must fear
because she will not know just where she stands.
Our Monarch's coming. Think on what I've said.

[*Enter* BESS, CECIL, MAIDS OF HONOUR]

BOB (*bowing stiffly*) My Queen!

BESS (*speaking to* CECIL *about Spenser, whom she has just dismissed.*)
I do not wish to see him. He can go!

CECIL
Poor Spenser is exceptionally distraught.

BESS
I know just what he's thinking. Keep at her!
Women are but women. They will change.
Invariably they alter in the end.
His artifice no longer holds its charm.
His idyll of the Holy Fairy Queen
grows gross and vulgar, quite ridiculous.
Belphoebe's face is haggard, cracked and thin.
For thirty years now she's been thirty-five.
Time was stopped by edict aeons ago.
Her teeth are black and broken and her head
ferments beneath a red blood-coloured wig
that writhes like the Medusa's. I hate the moon!
Her luminous manoeuvres. On and on.
I'll hear no more of Spenser in this court
encouraging my knights to go to war
to bankrupt my affairs with Spanish blood!
These men. They make me angry. Make me reek!
I'm stinking like a soil-pipe. Like a farm!
I'm poorer than a carter hauling dung
yet still the young bloods clamour. War! War! War!
Oh, who would choose to live here in the court?
To leave! Find peace. A pure tranquillity!
Exist, just like a beast, a peasant's pig,
on acorns, wasted barley and old bread.
I'd sit and keep two weaners, happily.
Rear half-wild hens that dust-bath in the yard.
Drink nettle soup. Spread dripping on my crusts.
Would starve, then net the sparrows in the eaves.
Catch thrushes, crows and finches by the week,
then stand for casual hiring at the fairs. (*to* CECIL)
Come, sweet pygmy, Monsieur le Bossu.
My hunchback fights Adonis? Which will win?
If only I could blend the two of you
and make of you one nature, that would be
a wonder to remember, would it not?

CECIL
Your Majesty. Poor Spenser does deserve...

BESS (*ignoring him*)
I fear now that the last years of my reign
will be too like the first. A challenge
for ambition. You, Essex, are the worst.
I hear you've painted Tyburn with fresh blood.
A poor old Jew who never did me harm.
I hear his ghost. His squeaking Jewish speech.
"The whole of physic turns upon two laws.
Sympathy. Antipathy. That's all.
The doctor who ignores this basic truth's
as useless as a door that's off its hooks."
My doctor. Hingeless! How I trusted him!
One sip from him, one poisoned medicine
and I, too, would be spirit, just a ghost,
a tiny minor movement of the air
that buzzes like an insect. There's a thought!
Then war would burn all corners of the land.

CECIL
They say that Leicester often used his arts.
That he distilled him poisons.

BESS
                              What of that?
Malicious men will whisper anything.
"Good for cracking lice and dosing pox!"
That's what their rumours murmured, what they said.
His voice was never sweet inside my ear.
His tongue would not deceive with flatteries.
This business stinks of Bacon, does it not? (*to* BACON)
You, Bacon, are profound in everything
apart from human nature. There you're a fool!
Tread warily, or one day you may find
I'll stick you on a gibbet where your bones
can rattle with the scraps of rusted chains.
I'll market out your carcase, sell your skull:
lop your head and pickle it in brine,
dry it till it stiffens, hard as iron,

then sell it, stuck with candles from your fat,
from dead-man's fat that lulls the world to sleep,
then vexes it with nightmares. Poor old horse!
If only you could rest your head each night.
Despite your labours, there's no great reward.
A bed of straw, a stable, and some oats.
Bran mash in the morning, then a field
to stand in all the day, and graze the grass. (*to* BOB)
Well then, my youngest mongrel. How's the world?
Who else have you been murdering today?

BOB
The traitor's dead.

BESS
                   I hear it entertained
my people.

BOB
               A most exemplary thrill.
He tried in vain to make a dying speech.
He said he loved you more than Jesus Christ.
The crowd was in an uproar, yelled and jeered,
and cried for them to hurry him away
and string him up. They cut him down half-hanged.
Castrated him, unwound his bleeding bowels,
then chopped him into quarters. The blood
ran everywhere. His guts stank in the fire.
Ferreira was the next, his shrieks and groans
made music for your loyal patriots.
Tinoco died the last. His death was best.
Cut down too soon, he leapt up to his feet
and fell upon his hangman. How they howled!
All gathered round, encouraging the blows
he rained on his tormentor - guards as well -
all made a ring to watch him. In the end,
perceiving that the victim gave the best,
they felled him with a blow upon the head
then hauled him to the scaffold. Like the rest
they severed off his organs, tore his bowels,
and quartered him to hideous yells and groans.

The spectacle was nauseous.

BESS
So it sounds.
He was innocent you know. Quite innocent.
There was something on his conscience, I know well,
but not the crime of treason. Anyway
Spain would not confirm it, or deny.
I waited for some sign. I did my best.
And now he's burned to ashes. Nothing more.
Poor Lopez. Such a very gentle man.
No part of me his hands did not explore.
No part of me he did not touch or probe.
He soothed my yelling joints, my hollow bones,
and cooled all the infections of my skin
so skilfully. And now he's lopped and gone!
Sawn up by the hangman, thrown in flames,
then scattered to the wind as casual ash.
See these precious stones he gave to me.
Crimson rubies, brilliant diamonds.
They burn into my heart like sacred rays.
I'll wear his ring until the day I die.
How cold life is today! How miserable!
The wind blows its midwinter instruments
and darkens all. Musicians, come!
Make different rhythms ripple down my spine.
Make me delight in tears and golden sighs,
and hurt me with your beauty. Let me ring
like virginals, dance bourrées and gavottes.
Today we'll hear no melancholy dumps.
I'll make these skinny ribs Love's sounding-box
and drown the jumps and bumpings of my heart.
(*She dances, alone.*)
I dance well, do I not? Most charmingly!
My figure's slim and fit, just like a boy's,
so pliant, so melodious! I feel
my body turn to honey! That's enough.
The room is filled with perfume. Quite enough.
It does not sound so sweet now as it was. (*She coughs.*)
Not speaking, Bob? No stream of quick conceits?
I'll book you for a lesson with young Donne.

BOB

I stand and watch the movements of your arms
and feel again the meaning of the sea.
I watch, and feel a liberated soul
whose time has come to pass into the stars,
to lift up from his body, willingly,
and greet the glittering spirits. Oh my love!
So still! So full! I feel the whole of life,
yet know no praise, but silence.

BESS

                    Do you now?
Then I must try to slap you back to time.
I'll dance again. Now join me if you dare! (*They dance, quietly.*)

BOB

Such sweet Italian hands. So supple, smooth.
They spread your inward soul, your character.
I think such hands were fashioned by a god
who loved dissimulation and delay.
At times they almost shine, so clear they seem
as if they turned transparent, made your nails
bright lights of changing opal I must kiss. (*He kisses her hand.*)

BESS

And now they're shrunken and rheumatic, hinged with skin.
But flatter on.

BOB

                It is no flattery.
Every word you utter is a shock
of wonder or of terror. Your beauty
still intimidates, and always will.

BESS

How long is it since we first danced like this?

BOB

Ten years ago. I still recall those days.
We talked and walked and rode the parks and woods.
Each evening brimmed with laughter, musical,

until these rooms of Whitehall were left bare
of all but us. Then we would sit at cards.
All night we'd play, play on till morning came,
each capturing the other, till at last
the moonlight left your silver furniture
and May became an earnest, burning June.

BESS
How rapidly my Essex climbed the sky.
He lifted like a rocket till he shone
like noon at night, a bright nocturnal sun.

BOB
I walked off through the summer dawns alone
and took your beauty with me through the world.
I trailed it through creation. Life was joy
dilating all around me. Flowers appeared
where thoughts of you went walking, spread as if
they left the feet of Venus.

BESS
                              They're older now.

BOB
To me they look much younger, quite renewed.
With love, things live forever, stay unchanged.
(*The dance stops.* BOB *bows profoundly.*)

BESS
Per molto variar la natura e bella.
I suffer, though. Hens brood. They incubate.
I grieve I have no child to call my own.
I'm sterile now. Have been so many years.
And yet I hatch out England, do I not?
Artists, playwrights, strong philosophers.
I sit upon my nest and keep them warm.
I let them come and go beneath my skirts
then bristle like a grebe inside my ruff.
These hooks, these swelling sleeves, they puff me up
like an old owl.

BOB

        I love you.

BESS

              Of course you do.
Like all of those who loved me down the years.
Your father, with his virile flashing smile.
Hatton that could dance the galliard.
De Vere, the tiltyard king. And handsome Bland
who lit up like a lamp each time my eyes
would drop upon his body. All of them
I loved with a Platonic dignity
that you now share.

BOB

        Elizabeth! My Queen!

BESS (*looking aside, through the window*)
Birds are more observable in snow.
The winds blow unresisted through the trees.
You did my Doctor wrong. I'm sure of that.
England, my dear England, is unwell.
I wish to be a blessing, not a curse,
but look now at the crisis we are in.
The harvests have all failed. The wheat went black.
The rains all fought for Spain and drowned the corn.
People now lie starving in the streets,
their ribs like rungs of ladders, every bone
thrusts sharply from their bodies. I have seen
small children walk like corpses, skeletons.
My beauty charms the land, but grace alone
won't fill their wasting entrails. Time is ill.
Dunghills spill the stables through the streets.
The channels from the houses stink with filth.
Prices rise. They now reach record heights.
Our God is much displeased to see the way
we sin against the old and innocent.

BACON
Lopez confessed. Little torture was used.
One hour upon the rack was force enough.

BOB
I need to say what all of England knows.
Our land is weak and very vulnerable.
Philip bides his time, awaits his hour.
He builds a new armada in Cadiz
expressly to attack the English throne.
I urge you, make a quick pre-emptive strike.
Annihilate his ships while still you can.

BESS
And naturally you'd wish to be in charge
of such an enterprise. Is that so?
And what a first-rate leader you would make!
You cannot tell the blunt end of a boat
from what sticks out in front. Well, can you now?
I don't like war. The cost of it's immense.
Thirty thousand pounds in aid of France.
Half a million on the Netherlands.
Naval expeditions. Irish wars.
This chivalry costs money. Four short years
have cost nigh on a million. All's been sold.
I've mortgaged almost everything I own.
Your military campaigns devour my cash.
They cause great discontent. The toll of life
is heavy, and the people do not like
to die for shallow fops like your Navarre.
I much prefer the art of piracy,
a form of warfare suited to our needs.
Commercial raiding, that's by far the best.
It swells out our exchequer and of course
it dislocates all Spain's economy.
Her fleets are stuffed with silks and gold and jewels
but Englishmen are masters of the sea.

BOB
My pirate queen! I beg you, let me go!
I'll spread my golden plunder at your feet!

BESS
What lessons do we learn from history?
What does the past record about our Earl?
What happened when I sent you off to Rouen?
When you arrived, the king of course was gone.
He'd changed his mind, so off you rode away
one hundred miles through hostile territory,
left your soldiers idling in their base
to meet him at Compiègne. And there he stood,
preceded by six pages dressed in gold,
the rest in orange velvet. Huguenots
besprinkled with a glaze of precious stones.
Six trumpeters announced him, while behind
stood twelve esquires and sixty gentlemen
from England. And how then did you fight?
You held a leaping match!

BOB
They challenged me. I trounced them, every one.
I overleapt them all.

BESS
                    No doubt you did.
With legs like yours you'd jump right off the globe.
I had to send the infantry to get
your body back unbroken. Look at you!
Although I was your Queen and General
you never told me anything you did -
your purposes, your daily whereabouts.
You're wholly irresponsible. You lack
all sense of duty, how one should command.
You play at war as if you coursed the hare
or sniffed out musty otters from a ditch.
You're like some untrained puppy that as yet
has never found the bone set in the tray,
a feckless hound, that slips off from the fox,
that slinks away, head downwards, running low
to mix in with the sheep, the milling flock.

BOB
When all this is accomplished, you will see
your eyes will be the fixed poles of my sphere -
as long as you will choose to keep me there.
I'll be to you your centre evermore.
Nothing else shall move me from that place.
Set me as an arras, some design
that shines in rusted gold against your dress,
a background to your throne and furniture.
And if you think that heaven too good for me
I'll vanish like a vapour in the sun.
My fortune's the affection of my love.
Deny to me the holy liberty
of loving you, then I must lose my life.
Your rage will never shake my constancy.
If all your sweetness turned to bitter gall,
it could not, great as that dislike might be,
affect my love, or make me love you less.

BESS
Your rhetoric's as flawed as your conceits.
You flatter, grow more frog-like than the French.
You make me look a fool before the world.
You're wholly unpredictable. Ignore
my orders at your whim, will trail a pike
like any common soldier. You're ordered home,
and then we see your sorrow's sweet enough,
a model of contrition, fogged with sighs.
The button of your doublet breaks away
as if it had been severed by a knife.
Your tears run dark as ink, they flood regrets,
but still your indiscretions grow and grow.
Before you left, you dubbed two dozen men.
What reason did you give for knighting them,
for honouring such rash adventurers,
those youths with scarce a beard upon their cheeks,
whose bodies were all feathers, lace and gold?
Because they'd had bad luck and missed the chance
to gain those honours that they might have won.
Since they had shown you such a great good will
you gave to them in fact what they'd have gained

in fantasy alone when in a fight.
You cheapen honour, make it mockery,
rewarding men for wars they never fought!
I'm sickened by your fatuous campaigns.
Oh yes, commanders have that privilege
but only where real bravery's concerned.
I do not like what flows from all of this.
The people say you've made a clientele
that holds itself beholden unto you
and not to me. Such men are dangerous.
Your ways are rash, intemperate and strange.
I don't know what your life will come to be.

BOB (*stung to anger*)
History won't change because you're mad.
Philip won't stop stocking up his fleet.
The galleons won't evaporate like clouds.
The Queen inclines to anger when she fears.

BESS
Go! Go! I tell you. Clear out everyone.
Leave me, every one of you, at once
but Cecil only. Cecil, you remain.
I need a time of silence. Need to think.
                    [*Exeunt* BOB *and* BACON]
Cecil, you will guide me. Clarify.
Although you bend, you see straight into things
and strike right at the centre. Stay with me.
There's much we need to ponder, to design.

[CURTAIN]

SCENE III

Essex House feels conspiratorial. LADY ESSEX *enters, trailed by* ANTONY BACON. PEREZ *and* UNTON *linger to the rear, uneasily.*

LADY ESSEX
And who's that latest madman, Antony?

ANTONY
His name is Perez, my lady.

LADY ESSEX
What sort of man is he?

ANTONY
A man of miracles, my lady.

LADY ESSEX
Of miracles? What sorts of miracles? Illustrate your answer.

ANTONY
He once escaped the Spanish Inquisition, after he had been charged with heresy.

LADY ESSEX
Heresy? What sort of heresy?

ANTONY
Apparently he had alleged that God the Father slept. That he had no care for mere mankind. Even worse things followed. He said that if the person who had caused his king to treat him with such deep disloyalty were God the Father, then he, Perez, would tug at God the Father's nose.

LADY ESSEX
Tug at God the Father's nose?

262

ANTONY
A proposition that the Inquisition found both scandalous and blasphemous, wholly offensive to their truly pious ears. It savoured of the Vaudois heresy.

LADY ESSEX
And what is the Vaudois heresy?

ANTONY
That God possesses a human body, human members too. Two ears, two eyes, two hands, two legs, two feet. And all the rest.

LADY ESSEX
But Jesus has a nose, and he is God. If Christ is God, then God must have a nose. The Sistine Chapel also shows a God who has a nose.

ANTONY
But that is art. Mere metaphor. The Infinite cannot be limited by ears and eyes and noses like the rest of us. The stake alone was deemed fit punishment for such a ghastly thought.

LADY ESSEX
But how did he escape?

ANTONY
The people rose in arms. They said their rights of jurisdiction were infringed, both by the Holy Office and by the throne. They poured into the prison, kicked the governor to death, then set at large our stormbird. The army of the king at last arrived and changed the constitution. Sealed it by burning Spaniards in the marketplace. The ceremony started with the dawn and went on till the evening. A smelly, rather dirty business, from what I hear.

LADY ESSEX
Where did this take place?

ANTONY
At Saragossa, Lady Essex. It was a long and vile performance.
So perish those

affirming God the Father has a nose.
We all could, too. We all could burn, you know. The Spanish
take religion seriously. The Pope himself has ordered Catholics
to murder our dear Queen. He says it is their holy Christian
duty. Is he right? He claims to be infallible.

LADY ESSEX
This Perez looks like a criminal.

ANTONY
No doubt of that. Full of Latin criminality. Delightful tropes of
rhetoric he owns.

LADY ESSEX
And French as well.

ANTONY
His French is excellent. He also reads Greek most fluently.

LADY ESSEX
So what is a Spanish, French and English-speaking criminal
doing here in my house? Antony, I think you try to force us
into war again with Spain. Into active war. This Perez is
obviously some sort of messenger. But how can our Elizabeth
be forced back into war with Philip? By hinting, perhaps, that
the French may close with Spain to form a new alliance? Is that
it? Your silence tells me everything. I fear you, Bacon. I fear
your conspiracies. I feel such crepitations in my soul. The
Queen's all decoration. She has no heart. Her body is as cold as
Arctic ice. She'll make my husband carrion in the end. I know
it. I smell her on his clothing, constantly. We must be careful.
There are traitors everywhere.

[*Exit* LADY ESSEX *who sweeps past* UNTON *and* PEREZ,
who award her unrequited bows.]

UNTON
She knows what we are up to.

ANTONY
Of course she does. She won't say anything. There's nothing she can do about it, not without compromising her husband. Unton, how did the Queen receive the news from France?

UNTON
Suspiciously. She is secretly uneasy. I am ordered to return to France immediately, and to report on things.

ANTONY
You have Henry's ear?

UNTON
He thinks I am his spy.

ANTONY
Good. Well tell him to stand firm. He must receive you like the North Wind, with public coldness. Insist, though, that he writes immediately to the Queen demanding that she joins in league with him against the Spanish. And you Perez -

PEREZ
Señor.

ANTONY
You must write a letter to the Earl. He must tell the Queen that sending Unton's made the whole thing worse. That he expects a sudden quick attack by Philip. Emphasise the king's desire for peace between us. That he cannot understand our country's policy. Some mystery, perhaps, lies unrevealed. And so on.

PEREZ
Fines principum abyssi multi. The Earl will eat my Latin and the Queen will breakfast on its rich complexity.

ANTONY
The Queen will be suspicious, but with care this may just tilt the balance. Hurry now. Tomorrow's tide must see you on the way.

[CURTAIN]

SCENE IV

Greenwich. BESS *is sitting at a table, peeling an orange. The room is shaken by distant Spanish guns bombarding Calais.* UNTON, *returned from France, is at her side.*

BESS
Another salvo. Look at that! The plates
are leaping from the table. Spanish guns!
Bombarding Calais! So much for a
secret alliance with the French. It's the Spring!
The sun's got to the Spanish once again.
Another bang. It's damaging my silver.

UNTON
Your Majesty, something must be done.

BESS
Why must something be done, Mr. Unton?

UNTON
The citadel holds out. We must send aid.

BESS
Why must we send aid, Mr Unton?
For all I know it could be a French trick.
Surrender Calais, draw us English in,
then make us pay to drive the Spanish out.
That's how I would see it. From the French
perspective.

UNTON
                    Essex waits at Dover.
He's restless as the metre of the sea.
He'll swim across the Channel for your sake,
or walk across the water.

BESS

                    Will he now?
That's just what I'm afraid of. We must not risk
the fleet. The French could turn on us, join
forces with the Spanish, both invade
our land. The French have men and weapons. They
may well relieve themselves. No! The cost would be
enormous. Burghley! Where is Burghley? Fetch
him in. (*Shouting*) Burghley! Burghley! Burghley! Ah!
He comes! No. I do not trust the French. Nor
for that matter do I trust the Dutch.   [*Enter* BURGHLEY]
And I certainly mistrust the Spanish.
Ah Burghley. Here at last. You must have been
delayed.

BURGHLEY

              All delays me now, apart from death, Your
Majesty. I bring you news. The citadel
has fallen. And so shall I if I do not
immediately take this seat. Its guns fire
on the town.

BESS

              Poor Burghley. Come my friend.
What it is to be old! I understand
your suffering. I know it all too well.
But you at least still have your doctor.
And mine is dead. Licked up by the dogs.
Converted into fire. He freed me of disease.
He healed my anus, cleansed my abdomen.
Understood my thighs, my toes, my loins.
Entered my most secret, hidden womb,
my bladder and urethra. Everywhere.
All my person. Every part of it.
And now he's gone. Flown into the air.
Who will save my body now from sin?
Our God is much displeased. Sit down, Burghley.
Sit down by the fire, and rest your gout.
That foot is badly swollen. Come and
rescue me. I'm now all indecision.
I must try to rise at dawn. Drink a full

glass of warm water. Encourage
morning movement of the bowels. Brush my last
remaining teeth. And scrape this coloured tongue.
Put myself in tune with nature's moods.
Respect her cycles of existence, egh?
Tell me now. How does one read the mind of Spain?

BURGHLEY
What reply to that do you expect, Your
Majesty?

BESS
     Deviously.

BURGHLEY
              Exactly, Your
Majesty.

BESS
     What's all this din across the Channel?

BURGHLEY
It is their cannon-fire, Your Majesty.

BESS
You misunderstand. Why all this cannon-fire?

BURGHLEY
To draw our fleet to France. To lure our arms
abroad.

BESS
     Why?

BURGHLEY
           So they can send a force to
Ireland, Your Majesty. Rebellion
is simmering again. The Catholics
are threatening our troops. You understand?
That is why the Spanish build a fleet.
Their next armada.

BESS

Something must be done.

BURGHLEY
Undoubtedly.

BESS

Shall we attack Cadiz?

BURGHLEY
It would seem prudent to attack their fleet
before it's fit to sail. To sink it in its
harbour.

BESS

But that would leave our country
undefended. Our nation's one protection
is the fleet.

BURGHLEY

The Irish have no navy.
A few coracles perhaps. We should have
to square the French, of course. And maintain
sufficient ships back home.

BESS

Decision time.

BURGHLEY
Decision time, Your Majesty. Your father
was the same. He loathed decision making,
all ultimate responsibility. (*He sighs.*)
You cannot let the common people doubt
your right to rule. That would be a terrible
mistake. To doubt your divine sanction, that
would strike at God himself. At God himself.
Roma locuta. Causa finita.
Never change your mind once you have come
to a decision. That's how your father
dealt with things. Or make some other man
decide. Or simply keep postponing.

As you, of course, prefer.

BESS
                    It is the
only way to exercise control.
The world is filled with rampant activists,
enthusiasts, mad military men
all roaring out for glory. Their logic
is immaculate. Their motives are
impeccable. Their danger is immense.
Not one of them can giggle at himself.
You only have that art.

BURGHLEY
                    And my reward
is flattery, and general deference.
So now you're forcing me to make the choice.
I'd rather not, of course, but what's the use.
Astraea has decided. So the point
at issue is which hot-blood takes control.
Raleigh's just returned.

BESS
                    I mistrust him.

BURGHLEY
Yes. Essex has a claim to lead the troops.
Lord Howard would be Admiral of the Fleet.
He would keep our Essex well in check.
The Earl is too impetuous. All he does
is act upon the moment. As you know,
action is the means and end of all
as far as he's concerned. The man is brave.
The handsome dashing hero, full of fire.
He'll lead men from the front. But into what?
I fear a Spanish ambush is prepared.

BESS
With Howard in command. I wonder. No.
I don't think that would work out very well.
They'd quarrel over tactics. Undermine

each other, then advance their rival claims.
Who would sign the letters? The Admiral
or the Earl? Which name would be on top?
Out first? The point is most important.
And Raleigh there as well to stir things up...
How would they attack? By land, or sea?
Raleigh is a first-rate officer
but will they let his counsels sway the day?
It's not an easy thing to fit a fleet
with victuals and munitions. Not at all.
As usual, my life's in children's hands.

BURGHLEY
One thing at least is working to our good.
Their adversary's the Governor of Cadiz.
He led the last armada to its doom.
Medina-Sidonia is a fool
who's even more imprudent than the Earl.

BESS
An omen, then, that God is on our side.
You'll take a chance on Essex. Fair enough.
Astraea is contented, and with luck
he'll fill his ships with plunder. We shall see.
Fortune, after all, will govern all.

[CURTAIN]

SCENE V

Essex House. FRANCIS and ANTONY BACON.

FRANCIS
Our patient sails. I hear he's found good forewinds.

ANTONY
All accelerates. The Earl has full control.

FRANCIS
He's blown into great dangers. The court is in a ferment. If Essex fails... *Ruse contre ruse.* (*Pause*) Meanwhile I have written to the Earl for his good offices. Concerning my future. As everybody knows, Pickering is dead and Egerton, the Master of the Rolls, has been appointed his successor.

ANTONY
You hope to take up Egerton's old post.

FRANCIS
Not unreasonably, I trust. In spite of the confusion that attends this mighty expedition, the Earl has written to the chief men of the bar to press my claim.

ANTONY
Watch out for the Old Fox. Have you heard the news of Bodley? Cecil is made secretary. Now Cecil holds her pen. They say he is already practising her signature... The Queen is crafty. She waits till Essex has embarked, and then appoints his enemy. Poor England. You need a man upon the throne, and not a vacillating woman. She knows no honour. She blunders, stutters, slips and hesitates and leads all to their ruin. She is nothing but inconstancy, indecency, a parody of virtue. Her life is one long passionate postponement, the problem of a body that's grown old and past producing children, whose only satisfaction lies in anger. She is a most preposterous old hag. The Earl should lead, and she should follow, or be put to bed forever, then thrown away with all the other offals. Fate is a relentless ironist. The master plays the slave and so accommodates the mistress.

FRANCIS
It's strange he has an influence at all.

ANTONY
The reason is obvious. Quite ludicrous. He satisfies the cravings of some ancient twisted virgin who has never lent her body to a man. The vanity of the woman! Three thousand dresses in her wardrobe. Ten for each day of the year. Miles of golden braiding. Pounds of jewels to mask her dying carcase.

Gloriana. The wandering Shekináh. The splendour of the Holy of Holies. The bride of God. Just look at her. The land is sick. Needs red blood for the throne. Yet underneath I think she loves the Earl. *Stet fortuna domus.*

FRANCIS
Of course she does. The two are two alike. Far too alike. He is the reflection of the Queen. Her counterpart. The image of her mind. Her endless fluctuations, to and fro. The servant and the rebel, both in one. As full of contradictions, dark conceits, as a verse by Donne. All fantasy. All paradox. Like her, he has his weakness. It may well prevent him from the highest seat of power. You see he lacks a fixed malignancy. There is no abiding viciousness in what he thinks and does. His evil is his anger, and that's gone thus (*clicking his fingers*), as quickly as a flash, a tinder-spark. I fear for him, he's far too close to her. And she's a dying woman. I fear, at times, they're far too close, the two of them, for either to outlive the other's death. I'm sure they love each other, mother, son. Yet neither understands the height, the depth. I fear he plots the gravest crime of all. As yet it has not formed inside his soul and so he still sees it in another. Such as Lopez. And she, she lures him in towards it, step by step, still understanding nothing.

ANTONY
If we should gain Cadiz...

FRANCIS
Well, then our danger will increase one hundredfold. We need to write. Advise. Essex is an unusual General. His grasp of tactics is extremely poor. He prefers to work from fantasy, an impulse. A poet? Yes. But reader of the soul? I greatly doubt it. If he should win, the Queen would not endure it long. Two suns can't shine at once inside the court. One must seem the dullness of the moon. Our lady would go green with jealousy. Emerald with envy. Well, we shall see. As usual in these things, success and failure work quite equally to put the Earl in danger. We shall need to brief our lord extremely carefully. *Post equitem sedet atra cura.*

ANTONY
Panta rhei. All is in a flux.

[CURTAIN]

SCENE VI

Whitehall. CECIL, *recently promoted.* SECRETARY.

SECRETARY
Have you seen this, sir?

CECIL (*glancing at the proffered document*)
The true relation of the action at Cadiz on the summer solstice by the Earl of Essex, sent to a gentleman at court by one who served. Common propaganda. Printed and distributed to prepare us for the Earl's arrival. To spike the opposition's guns. Rather an unusual version of the truth, from all accounts. Extremely orderly. And simple. (*He throws it into the fireplace.*)

SECRETARY
Where is the Queen?

CECIL
Killing deer at Richmond. Sticking them with arrows till they bristle like a hedgepig. Artemis is angry. We are in for a great storm. A truly magnificent frenzy. She's been planning it for weeks. The expedition's bankrupt. No *spolia opima.* Not one single piece of eight. The Queen is owed some fifty thousand pounds. Essex has no cash to pay the troops. Imagine what will happen when he asks for subsidies to help him pay them off. Meanwhile his sailors take away his booty, sell it for a penny, and drink themselves unconscious in the Strand.

SECRETARY
Does she still refuse to see him?

CECIL
Yes. Of course. She's stoking up her angers. The whole furnace
is about to explode. Essex has behaved in character. He has
committed three unforgiveable sins. One. Proclaimed himself
the Governor of Cadiz without her royal warrant. Two. Dubbed
six dozen knights without her nod. Three. He missed the
Spanish fleet, with treasures set at twenty million pounds, just
off Cadiz. No wonder she's been slaughtering the deer. Careful.
She is coming. On your feet. And watch your words. Silence is
the key.

[*Enter* BESS, *flushed with anger, in male leather buskins. She
is splashed with blood. Two huge bucks are dropped mid-stage
by bearers, who then scurry off immediately.* BURGHLEY
totters after her, followed by GENTLEMEN 1, 2 *and
courtiers.*]

BESS
I killed the bucks! They fell down dead as stone.
Full speed before my crossbow. Just like that!
My bolts burst through their hearts. They dropped like meat.
Their blood gushed up my buskins. Look at me.
A blood-stained butcher! Smoking Artemis.
Am I not the equal of a man?
A dozen in one hunt. In two hours' work.
Three horses dropped exhausted. They were shot.
All creatures have to keep up with their Queen.
These hands were born to slaughter, were they not?
No mercy when these fingers twang the string.
No mercy when they arch the silver bow.
One day, they say, I'll slay the unicorn!
Lure him to my garden. Shoot him down! Then
one quick, ceremonial incision! Ah!
I fired at them. They fell. My will was strong!
Poor creatures. Silent. Absolutely dead.
Take them to the kitchens. Let them hang.
Tomorrow we hawk herons! What a day!
This hunting seems to renovate my blood.
It makes me so much younger, luminous!
Am I not possessed of endless youth?
I've made a pact with Fortune, Age and Death,

and so my charm continues, constantly.
In thirty years I'll be a girl again.
Yes. Six or seven galliards a day
are better than all physic. Look at me.

CECIL
Your Majesty grows younger, hour by hour.
A virgin, and eternal. All can see.

BESS
I keep quite free from major suffering.
I have my minor ailments, nonetheless.
My generation passes to its grave.
I see them all, my former ministers.
Leicester. Brother Warwick. Walsingham.
Thomas Randolph, Croft, and Shrewsbury.
Hatton too, so beautifully he danced!
They all have closed their eyes upon the world
and I alone grow younger, see them there
all sleeping in the earth, all turned to bones.
Well, what's the news? How's London? Full of drunks?
The Thames awash with brandy? And the Strand?
They tell me whores are roaring everywhere
to celebrate the failures of our lord.
You there, with your face embossed with boils.
What's my golden gunman done today?

GENTLEMAN 1
Awaited your pleasure, Your Majesty.

BESS
Then he will wait all day. All week. All of the
month. All of the year. I hope his clothes
are warm. His feet well shod. By winter he'll
be hungry.

GENTLEMAN 1
        I fear the Earl grows angry at
his wait.

BESS
                That's excellent. Well, let him write
sonnets on his body. Embroider clocks
upon his stockings. I'll make him stand and stand,
immobile as a horse that's stilled with piss
and daren't disturb its bladder. I have heard
that at their coronation, Irish kings
must copulate with mares, with huge white mares.
My own was less uncomfortable, but long.
Poor Burghley! Are you ill?

BURGHLEY
                        Your Majesty,
today my hand can scarcely lift a pen.

BESS
How much you must desire to get away
from all these plots, these sly petitioners
and slink back to your lovely summerhouse,
to Theobalds. Well, I shall visit you
with quinces and with curling cucumbers.
And there we'll sit and while the day away
with talk of Essex, all his victories. (*to courtiers*)
We'll bring him in then? Hear what he can say?
What epic can revive my fallen sun?
I trust by now he's overcome with rage.
He's boring when he's sober and correct.
I feel it's now the time to let him in.
I hear the Spanish like to sport with bulls,
provoke them to a frenzy so that they
can demonstrate their courage and control
by killing them. Well, fetch our ox in here.
[*Enter* LORD HOWARD *and* BOB, *silently enraged.*
BESS *sits on a dominating chair.*]
Our Bobby! Prince of chivalry! At last!
I can't say how I've missed you all these weeks,
anticipating all you'll say and do.
We long to hear the wonders you have done.
The booty you have brought back to the court.
Our paragon of honour. Red Cross Knight.
What? Silent, my lord? This is a most

unusual collapse in adoration.
No words? No sentences at all? All thought
quite stifled at its birth. Quite limp? Still-born?
Then let your Queen revive your memory.
A hundred vessels, some ten thousand men
must cover the horizon east to west.
Their sails are round, a huge display of cloud.
There's Raleigh in his flag-ship *The Ark Royal*.
Essex in his craft *The Due Repulse*.
Howard in *Mere Honour*, on they come.
They cut into the blue face of the sea
that shears before their timbers. In their ports
the cannon glare like madmen, iron eyes
that glower at the mainland, at Cadiz.
It glitters on the skyline. On they scud!
It's Sunday, and the Sabbath. They arrive.
Great Essex claims the right to land the first.
For he, of course, is leader, in command.
The sea is rough. The wind blows half a gale.
The first two boats are loaded. Thirty men.
Their skiffs are caught amidships by the waves
and empty in the isthmus. Down they go!
Their armour fills with water, and they drown.
Raleigh now advises, "Go by sea!"
The galleons and the loaded merchantmen
are riding in the harbour. Howard fires.
He pounds the craft for hours, round on round.
The air grows black with powder, swirling fumes.
The Spaniards cut their anchors to escape.

BOB
Her Majesty is accurately informed.

BESS
Some, caught by the tide, are swept ashore.
Other boats capsize, but not before
the Spanish fire their boats. Their sails ignite.
The pigments and the gildings of the ships
are split by flame. I see it! How it runs!
It rips up through the red embroidery,
the bearings on the decorated wings,

and swallows whales and tritons, crosses, lions,
white saints with crimson symbols, mermaids' forms,
and rages through each panel. Up they gust!
The flames rush out like streamers, rags of fire
devouring every banner on the boats,
the name of each commander. Agonised
the sailors try to flee the burning pyres.
Many leap stark-naked in the sea.
Others hang on rope-ends from the sides,
their heads above the water, howling prayers
or swim into the waves with grievous wounds
and crying like the souls that boil in Hell.
A drumbeat on the deck of *The Repulse*
begins its sombre ritual. Thud by thud,
it pulses through the timbers of the fleet.
The boats fill, and their oars strike through the sea.
They thrust out through the bodies of the dead,
drive on through the dark diluted blood
that clogs the outer harbour. Then, they land.
They drop into formation, band on band,
and fall on the defenders. Robert leads.
His victory is certain. For, you see,
the Spanish are outnumbered, four to one.
Four times the fire to pour upon their power.
Four times the swords to flesh within their sides.
Essex is protected. Effingham
makes sure he does not venture through the worst.
Victory's a mere formality.
An army, made of children, could have done.
A pity, though, about the merchantmen.
Those forty merchantmen. What happened, Bob?

BOB
Sidonia saw them flee into the harbour.

BESS
And sent an offer for their safety?

BOB
                              Yes.

BESS
Two million ducats?

BOB
               Yes.

BESS
                    Two million ducats.
For forty merchantmen.

BOB
               It was enough
for the cargoes.

BESS
          Those boats were worth ten millions.

BOB
Perhaps.

BESS
       Perhaps? *Perhaps*? There's no *perhaps*
about it.

BOB
        Howard did not secure their
safety. Medina-Sidonia delayed
for several hours.

BESS
           For several hours.
And what did he do then? Egh? He fired the fleet.
Our ransom sank into the harbour. Howard,
what was the ransom for the city?

HOWARD
One hundred and twenty thousand pounds.
Essex showed them great humanity.
Churches, priests, were spared. Three thousand nuns
were taken to the mainland with the
greatest courtesy. The Spanish had not seen

such chivalry. Many were ecstatic.
He was, they said, the noblest heretic
that they had ever seen. The Spanish fleet
was totally destroyed.

BESS
                                    But where's the booty?
Great negligence, my lords, great negligence!
While you're engaged in games of chivalry
and kneeling to the skirts of papist nuns
the merchant fleet is fired. All burns in flames.
Twelve million ducats all go up in fire.
Don't scowl like that, behind those bloodshot eyes!
What do you expect that I should do?
Welcome you with rapturous delight?
Fill the air with glittering metaphors
when this has cost me fifty thousand pounds?
Fifty thousand, for this escapade!
What then have you brought me in reward?
Just more demands for money. And for what?
To pay your seamen's wages. It is all
exactly as expected. Everyone
has lined his open pocket from all this
apart from me. And I, I have to pay!
The Spanish have confessed that they have lost
some six or seven millions. What then is
the sum of what returns? Thirteen thousand!
Thirteen thousand! There's a lucky sum!
Where then are the strings of flying pearls?
The golden chains, the buttons made of jewels?
The chests of sugar, casks of quicksilver?
The silks and damasks, barrels of red wine
supposed to be predestined for the Queen?
The waste! The waste! The great disgusting waste!
I keep faith with my creditors. I eat
into my capital to pay for wars
before I ask the Commons for a grant.
What happens to the plunder you've obtained?
It's hidden in the chests of thieves and whores,
squandered on gross pleasures, drunken lusts
from London down to Plymouth. What a band!

Your seamen are a rabble, just a mob!
Marauders and deserters all of them.
They leak disease. Their officers are worse!
What happens to the man I send with you
with orders that he supervise my plans?
He rapes and burns and plunders with the rest
and you, of course, go knight him. Just like that.
You call it all a glorious victory
to celebrate with bonfires through the land,
but how am I to pay your drunken men
when my exchequer's empty, all my cash
is pissed into the sewage of the Thames?
You come back with that beard upon your face
and hide your true complexion, mask your wish
to mock me, make my throne a laughing-stock
for every reeking lecher in the land. (*Wincing suddenly*)
The pain! The pain! Such overwhelming pain!
The blood cakes on my buskins! They constrict!
I have this running ulcer on my leg.
The veins swell up like snakes. I need to rest.
(*to a servant*) You! Bring in my physicians! Loose my boots!
At times I think this world will poison me.

BOB (*rather insolently*)
You are angry at my absence, that is all.
A touch of melancholia, now made worse
by exercise, this hunting. Be advised.
A woman of your age who's growing old
cannot expect to live like lissom girls.
I've often seen old women in your state.
The dawn is thick with listless heaviness
and blacker than the teeth left in their mouths.
Time has scattered meal upon their scalp.
Their skin is cracked with anguish and despair.
No face to go a-Maying with the young.
Each ray of light assaults their sleepless eyes,
but later, when the sun has climbed the sky,
they find their sadness fading, gradually,
quietly, imperceptibly at first,
and then, at dusk, when summer's flames have gone
their horror and their sickness seem quite dead.

Then they can sit and reason, smile again.
This business of the ships is very bad.
What matters is that Philip has been crushed.
I was not the sole man in command.
Others were responsible as well.
If you had stood beside me at that time,
if you had sniffed the powder in the air,
had heard the wailing cries of dying men
and tasted Spanish blood upon your lips,
licked it in the sweat upon your skin,
had battled, hand to hand, in narrow streets,
experienced war, the violence of its art,
if you had heard me argue in Cadiz
of whether we should march deep into Spain
or sail out with the ships to the Azores
to intercept the plate-fleet from the west,
or fortify the city, wait until
the ships themselves arrived, then fall on them,
if you had seen me fight my brother men
to try in every way to change their minds
and bring you back the booty you had lost
you would not turn on me as you now do
accusing me of all the negligence
belonging to the others. Oh, if you
had battled through such storm-walls, lived in ships
that shivered like the ague, seen their sails
ripped open by the fingers of the wind
and scattered on the dropsy of the sea,
had torn your men from timbers, staunched their wounds,
bound limbs that bled from bullets, pikes and swords,
you would not sit like this and scatter me
like refuse to my enemies at court
with such black acts of slander.

BESS

What have you
brought back to me? Egh? Debts! Books! The library
of Jerome Osorius! And starving, unpaid men!
You'd argue with me, sir? Then you must feel
the dame's cane. You, Sir Insolence.
I'll make you hew my wood and muck my dung.

Life settles soon the fate of the unfit.
I'll have you gathering faggots in the woods
and gleaning fields of stubble. I'll make your face
as grave as rainfall, pale as woodman's ash.
Your eyes are red as pox-fires, wilder than
a cock fed bread and water. You bristle, like
some Irish Grey, at me?

BOB

                    Your soul is blacker than
a crow's. A winter rook's. A chattering daw's.
God! What is this that's happening? Who speaks this?
Is this great Essex? These my fiery eyes
that weep now with this anguish? Whose is this?
This hand that starts to stiffen on this sword,
these fingers that caress its silver hilt?
Am I some boil, some ulcer she must rub
to derogate my triumph? Who is this?
Must I endure these insults from this chit?
Must I, the ancient aristocracy,
prostrate myself before these female feet
of some Welsh bishop's butler? Who is this,
that all must grovel, crawl upon their knees,
and I, who am so loved, and judged to be
the best, the noblest earl in all the land
by all the thinking men in Christendom,
am scourged thus, by this other? Look at you.
Everything you do is devious.
You wait until the day I sail away
and then you make this Cecil Secretary,
this twisted twig, this bent serenity
whose head's as wrenched and crippled as his limbs.
What happens to my suit, my candidate?
You cast him off, you set the man aside
while I create your glory in Cadiz.
I sail back, bright with honour, full with bliss,
a sun fixed in the zenith of its joy,
and all you give is sickness, jealousy,
then order me a penance for my soul
because I've been too faithful in success.
The hostages I bring back from Cadiz -

you steal them from me, sweep their ransoms off.
And what of my thanksgivings through the land?
Oh yes, you let a few of them be held,
but not in York or Bristol, Winchester,
no, only here in London, where your spies
can eye me, note the popular response.
These sycophants that swarm about your court
like flies around the shambles, look at them!
Cripples as decayed as their estates,
men destined to be sexless anchorites,
without the strength to hold a human sword.
Foxes, crows and ravens, pigs in corn.
Through them you lost the whole West Indian fleet.
If they had kept the plan that I had urged
to stay just off the coast of Portugal
one hundred hulls of plunder would be yours.
But no. They must oppose, prevaricate,
play politics, achieve some compromise
that leaves my scheme in ruins. Cowards all,
men terrified of action, never born
to dignify the language of true war.

BESS (*rising to her feet in anger, approaching him*)
I tire of hearing this young madman's rant.
This General of feathers, puffs and plumes.
All bluster, wind and gases, all of him.
Stand still, my lord, and face me front to front!
I do not speak to shoulders! On your knees!
You're *opiniastre*. Unreliable.
You've been extremely lucky, until now.
I tell you plainly, straight into your face,
you are not made to be my General.
You know not who you are or where you go.
All lifts up from the mystery of your moods,
odd, sudden dominations of the heart,
intense, absorbing, contradictory,
things utterly at variance, each with each.
Politics one moment, verse the next.
You dally with the women of the court
then off you fly to pray in cold St. Paul's
and stare upon some death's-head hour on hour.

In cities you will dream of solitude,
in solitude you hanker for the court.
You mock, admire, delight, exacerbate,
you vacillate when needs you must stand firm
then stand erect and obstinate at times
when you should bend the knee and compromise.
You alter like the weather, spin as wind,
half man and half a woman, lunatic.
You find the state of love in everything,
let every contradiction have its place
then end in pure confusion! Look at me!

BOB (*turning slowly*)
The court! The court! What Hell on earth is this?
A place to climb a ladder made of knives!
A place to live like beasts, huge ocean fish
that swallow one another, head to tail.
Where conscience comes tomorrow, not today.
Better far to go back to the wars
and slice the Spanish scarlet. There one knows
the nature and the shape of enemies.

BESS
You see how I am loved? The way that I,
the Lord-appointed ruler of this land,
am bludgeoned thus, by idiots? So, my lords,
must I then shape my acts to other minds?
Am I allowed to rule, provided that
I seek this man's permission, and his gang's?
Have I then been set here, to lead for them?
Am I the Queen of England, or its Fool?
Was I, or some impostor born to reign?
Have I an orb, a sceptre, a true crown?
Did Ascham train this fine Italian hand?
And was it this, or some white duplicate
that lifted every morning, wrote out Greek,
started with the Testament and then
continued with the works of Sophocles,
with Aeschylus, and sly Euripides,
Isocrates, Demosthenes as well?
Each afternoon it studied Cicero,

Livy, then Lucretius, Virgil too,
Melanchthon, then the wise St. Cyprian
who wrote on statecraft, royal theology.
I was, all said, a regal paragon.
The type of girl that Aristotle loved.
Beauty, stature, human industry.
My mind possessed no female weaknesses.
Men schooled me with their cruel diligence.
All found I was notoriously quick.
I had real love for learning. Unlike you,
you court buffoon. Who do you think I am
to put into the corner of your eye
then wipe away? Must I die at your glance?
Smile when you abuse me, thank your brain
for ridiculing every word I say?
Some faint light in your mind still calls me Queen?
Egh! Answer me!

BOB (*turning his back*)
You are insufferable!

BESS
                You turn your back!
Take this, then this, and this, then this again! (*She cuffs him
round the head and kicks him repeatedly until he half-doubles
up with pain. With a cry he draws his sword, to general
consternation, and is bundled away by his supporters.*)

BOB
The man has not been born to bear such things
without retaliation!   [*Exit* BOB]

BESS
                Damn the man!
Damn his cheek! And damn his insolence!
Still he runs his wheels across my feet
and sets his iron tyres upon my toes.
He bites away the buttons from my coat,
plunges for the hanging bag of oats,
then kicks away the ladle from my hands.
I'll govern him. I'll make him haul my cart.

I'll train him to the traces, make him tame.
I'll place him with his proper stablemates
then feed the hay on which he should be fed.
(*She brushes aside the thronging courtiers.*)
No, leave me. I desire to be myself.
(*She pauses, breathes deeply, then turns to* BURGHLEY.)
A strange man! Such an overhasty Earl.
To draw his sword before me. What an act! (*She laughs.*)
I goaded him to treason. All could see!
Well Burghley, did I win?

BURGHLEY

                     Win, Your Majesty?

BESS
You're right. I need rebuking. Thoroughly.
One gains no virtue, harassing a child.

BURGHLEY
Oh, he'll be back. All charm. Eventually.

BESS
These quarrels age me. I feel as old
as an apothecary's rose. And Spenser's gone.
No longer reads to me. His throat was like
a well-soaked wooden trumpet. Very strong.
Not like my recent British courtiers
that scratch my ears like insects. Lopez. Dead.
And all his benedictions. I must dance.
Need music, leaping music, for my soul
is growing sick with Saturn.   [*Exit* BESS *slowly, followed by*
BURGHLEY, CECIL *and courtiers.*]

GENTLEMAN 1
The Queen went strangely silent.

GENTLEMAN 2
                       It's her way.
She's always placid, once she's picked a fight.
It smoothes her ancient body, like a kiss.
The Earl is overhasty. His estate

is chained by many luxuries and debts.
The Queen maintains the purse strings. One quick nod,
and Essex is a bankrupt, nothingness.

GENTLEMAN 1
To draw his sword in public was unwise.
To others it would bring immediate death.
With Essex, though, the rules are different.
He prospers where another man would fall.
He'll clamour for another trip to Spain.
His luck will hardly smile a second time.

GENTLEMAN 2
Ireland's far more likely. Time will tell.
No one sails the Irish Sea unscathed
or comes back with his character enhanced.
A trip to Ireland well might dig his grave.

[CURTAIN]

SCENE VII

Essex House. FRANCIS and ANTONY BACON *discuss their worsening predicament.*

ANTONY
Is the Queen sane? Did you hear how she received the French Ambassador, de Maisse? Dressed up like some common Wapping tart! Three dresses she wore yesterday. The topmost in black taffeta, cut in the Italian fashion, with gold bands, huge sleeves both lined within with crimson. Then underneath, another in white damask, and then a third, a pale chemise. All three of them cut right down to the waist, yes, even lower! The poor man blushed vermillion, red with shame. Didn't know where to look! Each time she spoke she tossed her red wig back and pulled apart the soft folds of her dress. The poor man stared point blank at everything - the stomach and the navel

and the hair. And there they sat in discourse, hour by hour, as she tied long strings of pearls about her arms and twisted jewelled bracelets round her wrists. [*Enter* BOB, *preoccupied*]

BOB (*nodding his head curtly*)
Francis. Antony. [*Exit* BOB]

FRANCIS
Her womb's dead as a leather purse. It's shrunk up like a walnut. She feels angry, unfulfilled. And so she plots, manipulates. Plays one off against another, the way a child manipulates the love of its parents. Her mind grows ill, I fear. She seeks an illusory security by living in a state of compromise, a tension of opposed malignancies that she alone believes that she can rule. All of us are caught up in the act. Statesman fights with statesman, king with king. Musician with musician, priest with priest, while poet vies with poet. Her skill is strange. Uncanny. All of us are trammelled in her nets. [*Re-enter* BOB]

BOB (*nodding*)
Antony. Francis. [*Exit* BOB]

FRANCIS
We are all exploited to the point where each of us is vulnerable, radically exposed. The Queen has not emerged from virgin adolescence. No more has he, our everlasting boy. (*He nods in the direction of* BOB*'s departure.*)

ANTONY
He's hardly a virgin. He longs for power, prestige, but underneath he's weak. And he conceals his weakness from himself. Such natures like to drive. To force their fellow beings into situations that may prove their personal misgivings to be false. Or try to. But such soon overreach. Like tragic fools they find they are committed to an end that ruins them by bringing into light that truth they most require to smother. At last they turn the glass towards themselves. By then, of course, self-knowledge is too late, both for themselves, and for their followers. England is not fragrant to the nose. It does not leave a sweetness on the lips. Spenser's left. He found the flute

Athene threw away and challenged Artemis. So now he's flayed
alive. Figuratively speaking, of course. Metaphorically. The
Earl, too, plays in the Phrygian mode, Cybele's sound. We
know our lady's ways. If we continue here we shall certainly be
compromised. We may even lose our heads. On this we need to
think, and think again. Must graft upon what's real, what is, in
these uneasy days. Meanwhile our Earl diverts himself with
girls. Too many girls. The Queen is growing jealous. Soon
must blaze.

[CURTAIN]

SCENE VIII

Whitehall. BESS, *angry*. LADY MARY, MAIDS OF HONOUR,
stitching nervously.

BESS (*her lips quivering slightly*)
All minds, in every nation, all agree
that there is something shameful in the way
that men and women couple. Something that's
at odds with perfect purity, the ideal
of total holiness. We find among
the Nazarenes, the Essenes of Judea,
the holy men of India, far Cathay,
the monasteries of distant Tartary
the same unaltered legend. Each records
that, right at the beginning, when there was
just one man and one woman on the earth,
that woman would not sacrifice her state,
surrender her most perfect virgin flesh,
not even to re-populate the world.
The gods then honoured her and granted that
her womb should then conceive by sight alone,
the mere gaze of her spouse. Virginity
became the parent of humanity.
The parent of humanity. Virginity.

You are my vestals, your continence
safeguarded by unusual penalties.
Your presence has great power. By thought alone
you foster the well-being of the state
and purify all England, just as I,
your Virgin Queen, by being celibate,
I cleanse its whorehouse lords' impurities.
Many men at court will say to you
the loss of your virginity is less
than leaf-death. Their mottled consciences
inform you more is gained than can be lost.
Such men are liars, enemies of God.
My daughters must be chaste, not alehouse jests.
Read Thessalonians 4. Verse number three:
"This is the will of God, that ye should be
holy, and abstain from fornication.
For God will shut such out." One must not grieve
the Holy Ghost. Such actions fan God's wrath.
Mary!

LADY MARY
        Your Majesty.

BESS
                        Your glances stalk
our Essex.

LADY MARY
        Yes, Your Majesty.

BESS
                            Remove
your dress.

LADY MARY
        Your Majesty?

BESS (*moving towards her*)
                        I told you to
remove your dress. Immediately. Or I
shall rip it from your back. (*Touching the dress as it is removed*)

                        Such handsome velvet.
The border's fine and silver. Powdered pearl.
You think that it would suit me? Answer me!

LADY MARY
Your Majesty. The dress is far too small.

BESS (*prodding the dress with her forefinger*)
And unbecoming? Ah! What's that? And that? And that?

LADY MARY
Nothing, Your Majesty. I see nothing.

BESS (*holding the dress*)
Look Essex's arms were here. And here again.
His hands have smoothed these haunches. Touched the breasts.
And there! You see? The navel, then the thigh.
The scars are irremovable, I fear. (*Setting it against herself*)
You're right about its size. It fits me ill.
It pinches at the shoulders and the waist.
I cannot dance in this. It stinks of sin.
Uncomely for a vestal. What's to do?
I think we'll have its bodice sewn with texts.
Pin its pleats with verses culled from Job.
Ecclesiastes. Not the Song of Songs.
I'll set it in my chapel, on the wall
to hang like an escutcheon. It will be
a hatchment of your passion. What shall we do?
Embroider it with pictures of his tricks?
Show the way he sailed away to Spain
to greet the gleaming plate-ships from the west?
Poor Essex. He's so full of fantasies.
Don't worry. We shan't burn you in the streets.
God is always nearer than the skin,
as the priests say. I envy you. Go. Dress.
Don't weep so much. It's time to dry your eyes.
What's love, my dear? A transient caprice.
A momentary beauty, here then gone.
I've heard it said when love's full joy is there
one vanishes, experiences a death,
a temporary extinction, like a swoon.

I also find that place of timelessness,
that state where pain and suffering are gone
a little while, in anger, while I rage,
then afterwards I'm calm, and clear again.
I was born a virgin and a queen.
A woman, and a danger to the throne.
Women like to marry, fill their womb.
But if the queen should marry, what of that?
All the world is jealous of the power
that's wielded by her husband. So, what then?
Great internecine strife, long civil war.
She takes a foreign suitor. What of that?
Is England made a province, say, of Spain?
Of Germany? Or France? May God forbid.
Nobody who's sane, intelligent,
would choose a female ruler. But, I'm here.
My father did so long to have a son.
There Mary, put your dress back on again.
The Court's so dull without our fiery lord.
I think it's time his love returned again.
But no doubt he'll be sulking for a while.
He needs some expedition to restore
his confidence. If that is what he needs
then I must find the means to give him one.

[CURTAIN]

SCENE IX

Essex House. FRANCIS *and* ANTONY BACON, *clad,*
unhappily, in black.

FRANCIS
Things deteriorate.

ANTONY
The Earl sulks. He eats his sheets at Wanstead. Speaks to no
one but himself, then dresses up his retinue in black. This
dangerous black! (*Brushing his sleeves*) I do dislike this cult of
melancholia. Look at his servants. All wandering around
unbuttoned, their brains hidden under huge, broad-rimmed
hats. Their eyes are always travelling down the floor or staring
at the walls. All mimic alienated malcontents.

FRANCIS
I believe the Earl intends it as a sign of love-sickness. But the
Queen can only read it as a show of political disaffection - that
the people are unhappy with the state of things, both at home
and abroad. These actions feed her paranoia. I have tried to
reason with the Earl. But he takes no notice of my words. None
at all. He prefers this phantasmagoria, this graphic self-
indulgence. I start to feel that our alumnus is beyond
correction. He's too restless, far too headstrong for the bit. It's
strange, though, that the man's still popular. The people will
forgive him anything. Any blunder, any murder or seduction,
any act of lust.

ANTONY
The people are idiots. And the Queen, too, will finally relent,
allow him his desires. To draw that sword before her was
absurd. Others would be punctured on the spot. But not our
Essex. We must anticipate events more fully. Prepare our
moves. Examine our allegiances. This Irish question darkens
daily. The Council's now a battlefield. One half would aid the
Dutch, our noble fellow Protestants. The other would conclude
a peace with Spain. As you know, I've always held that peace
with Spain remains our only chance of victory in Ireland. The

rebels there are draining our resources. A peace with Spain deprives them of the money that they need and prevents their reinforcement. Dublin's in confusion. Tyrone in arms again. The whole of Northern Ireland is at war.

FRANCIS
The situation needs a complex politician. Someone with a grasp of subtleties, a man of compromise, of endless patience. Someone who can play the waiting game more deviously than any of the Gaels. Yet Essex thinks he's to the manner born. To appoint the Earl would be to sentence him to death. He, of course, would be quite blind to what was happening. Others would be drawn into his fate. You and I be nothings, like the rest. We need to put out feelers to the Queen. Our talents and experience are great. Perhaps the time has come to leave the Earl to his own devices. We must watch how things develop, carefully.

[CURTAIN]

SCENE X

Whitehall. BESS and BURGHLEY.

BURGHLEY
I believe the Earl awaits you.

BESS
                              Ah!

BURGHLEY
He is dresssed in black. As are others of
his faction. All sighing darkness.

BESS
                                   Let him wait.
Have you ever loved, old man?

BURGHLEY

                             Ever loved?
Well there's a term that's hard to analyse.
I once was young and tired away desire
with sighing. But all vanished in the wind.

BESS
I lack desire.

BURGHLEY

                   It's not part of your nature.
You were made celestial from your birth.
Predestined our Astraea by the stars.
A woman born to rule and to control.

BESS
My loins are ice. I often wish they sinned,
that I could know the pleasures of real vice.
Instead I have my angers.

BURGHLEY

                        That is true.

BESS
I do not trust these modern patriots.
Their breath is black as cannon-smoke. All day
their throats are open, gape for human blood.
Our Essex is the worst. Always we
are quarrelling.

BURGHLEY

                  That's true, Your Majesty.

BESS
Some animals achieve perfection
without effort. A movement and a rhythm
without check. Some gun-dogs are the same.
But others must be curbed incessantly,
punished till they're conquered, schooled until
they're docile and obedient as the rest.
I'll ride my boy as tamely as a mare.

Yes. Soon I'll have him perfectly turned out,
in burnished brasses, gleaming leather straps.
He'll jump for me, or canter at a touch.

BURGHLEY
I grow old, Your Majesty. Be wary
of the Irish. Trust none of them. Not one.

BESS
Burghley, you and I should go to bed.
And there I'll lift rich food into your mouth.
I'll feed you pheasants, fresh-hung partridges.
Pour wine into you, till you feel refreshed.
All of us are hastening to our deaths.
You, and I, and Essex, every one.
But I'll die upright, standing on my feet.
Death won't take this woman in a bed.
Fetch Essex in to me.

BURGHLEY
                    Your Majesty.

(BESS *takes a look at herself in a hand-mirror, alters her
features somewhat, then picks up a mask which she sets upon
her face, then discards, sitting in a conciliatory posture as*
BOB *enters, arrayed like a malcontent.*)

BESS
Bobby! Little Bobby! Come to me.
Forget that wretched business of the fleet.
Come near to me. Walk over! Kiss my ring!
(BOB *stands coldly, ignoring her overture*)
It's time to work as friends, not enemies.
Why persist in this rebelliousness?
Your course is full of peril, can't you see?
You see how you're encouraging your foes.
Have you forgotten those who were your friends?
Have you forgotten this great land of ours?
Have you not given us good cause to blame?
Are grounds for scandal really offered you?
Duty and religion, policy,

all enforce, encourage you to yield.
Submit to your true sovereign. Look at her!
Perform the highest action you can do.
Lie, and set your hands beneath her feet.
Do this, and please your sovereign, and you'll find
your country will receive great benefit,
your friends shall comfort from it, be advanced,
your enemies weep wormwood, tears of gall.
God himself in heaven will smile with joy.

BOB
My actions do not wrong myself at all.
Your conduct, and not mine, has made this so.
How could a man of honour act but thus?
How could he serve his country once his Queen
had forced him to an exiled style of life
where he must speak to books and stare at trees?
For she, she has dismissed him and discharged.
Not he. The only duty that he owes,
the one great indissoluble bond
is this, his duty of allegiance. That he gives,
gives without a question, without check.
In that he's never failed, nor ever shall.
What has this servant failed in? Only this.
The duty of attendance. Only that.
And that's not wholly binding. His duty
is an Earl's. An Earl Lord Marshal's.
But though he's served Her Highness with a sword,
he'll never haul her coals, nor be her slave.
What thought of hers could make her action just?
What guilt is there that now should make him yield?
Who justifies her imputation's truth?
No cause was given, no real cause at all.
All's born. All's suffered, all indignities.
All lips now taste the scandal, smirk and grin.
Does God require that I should kneel and sue?
Are queens like she unable to do wrong,
their will, their power quite infallible?
Must all men cower, flinch and bow the knee
when a queen coughs, her bowels begin to move?
Is earthly power wholly infinite?

Are subjects quite unable to be wronged?
No, I am not the fool of Solomon.
Won't laugh when I am struck, or grin when kicked.
Smile with vile subservience when a queen
spits publicly upon me. Hypocrites,
dissimulators, men of policy,
those who make their profit from the throne,
let those men have no sense of injury,
let them acknowledge total earthly power,
its absolute existence here on earth
since they cannot believe in heaven it is so.
But as for me, I'm no such heretic.
I'm wronged. I know it. And my cause is good.
I feel it. So do you. Whatever now
may happen, be inflicted and oppress,
no man can show more strength and constancy
than I do in opposing to the end.

BESS
You were rude to an old woman. And for that
she boxed you on the ears. You're piqued. That's all.
Offended. As for me, perhaps I was
ill-tempered. Angered. As for all the rest,
there really are no principles involved.
And as for this oppression, what is that?
When have I oppressed you? Look at me.
Would persecution have the least result?
What would you do? Leave court? Leave public life -
devote yourself to boring scholarship -
you, who are so passionate, confused?
Just look at all your violent entourage.
Cuffe. So cynical and rash. Your sisters,
so ambitious. Your mother - still my
life-long enemy. Or Mountjoy, whose
liaison with your sister is well-known.
There's no one there to check you, hold you back.
I know you well. I prize your qualities.
Your pride, devotion, military zeal.
Be guided by my intellect, my love.
Together we'll accomplish miracles.
Throughout the country every town appears

to hold you as their hero. The city too -
the city that's so hostile to my court -
believes you are a pillar of the faith,
a perfect, God-affirming Protestant.
You've also been elected Chancellor
of Cambridge University. We need
each other, don't we, my dear sun?

BOB (*relenting, impetuously prostrating himself before her and placing his head beside her shoe*)
                                        Forgive me.

BESS (*rising, then starting to saw at his neck with the edge of her shoe*)
That shows real affection. I decapitated
my sister, you know.

BOB
                              Of course.

BESS
                                        My father
decapitated my mother.

BOB
                              I know.

BESS
I might even decapitate you, if
you disobeyed me.

BOB
                              Perhaps you will, Your
Majesty.

BESS
                    A slender and most pleasant neck.
As graceful as a swan's. As Dr. Lopez
would have said, you are suffering from
Saturn. Saturn square to Saturn. It is
foolish to believe a man your age

is totally mature. You wear a mask
of valour, but that only covers up
your radical uncertainty. Oh yes,
you are entering the true world, taking on
real duties. Oh yes, I grant you that.
You've responded to the summons, I agree.
But in your personal affairs you lack
rich subtlety of judgement. They still
require developments. Alterations
must be made. You embody, as dear
Lopez would have said, four other principle
planetary turning-points. Also the Moon's
nodal reversal. My poor gay boy,
you are at the most aggressive, the most
susceptible time of your life. One that lays
the real foundation for all future change -
should there be much to come. So you
experiment with power, with love. With war.
With poetry, religion, politics
and women. In fact, with anything.
Your aspirations for development
keep knocking up against the outside world
with all its set assumptions. The fear
that you experience, that can lead
in different directions. Glorious
success, or blank, disastrous failure.
Traditional values, such as I your
dear established Queen so represent,
the girl who holds your head upon her foot,
can clash against your personality
and all that seething vigour that it feels.
You see real chinks in her authority.
She also, like those things you'd once defend,
reveals herself uncertain, fallible,
shot through with contradiction. This can cause
real crises of identity. Do you
experience such discord?

BOB
             I do.

BESS (*kicking him gently with her toe*)
Do you begin to fear untimely death?
You'll die before you're thirty?

BOB

                                      Yes. I do.

BESS
You feel the need to put the past behind you?

BOB
I do.

BESS
    I do. I do. I do. It's like
a marriage service. *I do. I do.* Are you
increasingly aware of time? The restrictions
that it imposes upon you?

BOB

                                          I am.

BESS
Poor, poor young man. Such a difficult age!
Saturn sextile Saturn. Uranus trine
Uranus. Then the progressed lunar
return. Neptune sextile Neptune, then the
lunar nodal reversal. Then, just before
thirty, oh dear me, Saturn return!
So what happens when so many cycles
congregate together?

BOB

                               Crises.

BESS

                                  And what
does the Greek noun mean?

BOB

                                  Fractures.

BESS
                              Go on.

BOB
Breaking up.

BESS
                    Then?

BOB
                         War.

BESS
                         And?

BOB
You're hurting me!

BESS
                         And?

BOB
                              Arriving at a
conclusion.

BESS
                    Exactly. Reaching a
conclusion. Such is a crisis. A
time where nothing goes unchallenged.
No value's seen as absolute, hence
nothing's seen as totally correct.
You suffer such a crisis at this time.
Such tempests of emotion. So, what's to do?

BOB
I must get my life together.

BESS
                              Correct.
The unity you seek must rise in you.
Develop spirit. Genuine purposes.

Be, when such is called for, radical.
At others, most reactionary. Saturn
sextile helps you there. To leave the past behind
need not mean death. In no way. Not at all.
It ought to mean renewal. Lopez knew.
That man was wise. He knew the rules of things.
The patterns and the order of events.
Don't strive to be this mother's favourite.
Let's both become real adults, both of us
developing together to real goals.
Let's walk no more in mourning. No more black!
It's time to cede from Eden, move away
from mothers, and all crafty female ways.
Come on, now. Strip that jacket. And those shoes.
And what about that hose? Remove it too. (*Undressing him*)
Let's sever now with everything. Strip off!
Be naked, male, the General that you are!
Create yourself, or else destroy your self!
Which of these are you now going to do?

BOB (*half-naked, on his knees*)
Ireland has no General in command.
Bingham's dead. He died on his arrival.
He lies, inert, in Dublin. I must go.

BESS
I think not.

BOB
        I know I am your man.
The court is not the centre of my world.
You know that my vocation is to fight,
to fight for you no matter what your tongue
advises. I know that for your sake
all danger is a joy, and death a feast.
My breath is only wind. My reputation
tinder for your use, to light with fire.

BESS
Ireland is our country's Netherlands.
It ruins all who enter. No one leaves
unwounded. You know what Burghley says.
Our army has been beaten by O'Neil.
O'Neil is subtle. Also has the craft
to play the politician as he trains
his hordes of Irish tribesmen, who, I hear,
walk naked all the winter, live on skins
and hold their wives in common. No. I think
that Mountjoy is our man. He must go.
He's almost like your brother nowadays. (*Walking round the room*)
In Ireland we have sewn the dragon's teeth.
I fear this strange O'Neil. He hisses like
the spirits of the dead. He brags like giants.
His words cause havoc everywhere he goes.
He agitates the cities of your Queen.
He bellows like a warlock through the towns.
The man's possessed. His words, self-worshipping,
keep boasting that his sword's invincible,
as magical and flawless as his lance.

BOB
I'll use him as my sacrificial bull.
I'll drag his huge head downwards, cut his throat
and let my shield fill slowly with his blood.
I'll drink him in with ewe's milk, drop by drop,
then twist my steaming weapons in his flesh,
revitalise their spirits with the dead.
This arm has carved the bravest. Trust its strength
then you shall need no other pharmacon.

BESS
You all desire your sacrificial meat!
Machaireus the carver. What a sight!
No. Ireland is no place for men like you.
Ireland is a place of barbarous rites.
The Gaels rejoice in human sacrifice.
All is like a dream-world, full of ghosts.
It teems with exultations, weird ordeals,
with drummings and imagined animals.

There dead souls can be rescued and returned.
Magicians throng the darkest underworlds
and meet with bearded monsters, speaking snakes,
or climb through every level of the heavens
to talk with gods and heroes, prophesy
the meaning of the present, of what comes.
(*Suddenly stopping, as if struck by a new idea.*)
Who would be your General of Horse?

BOB
Southampton.

BESS
           I expressly forbid it.
He raped my Maid of Honour. Several times.
The man is a disgrace, as you well know.
I know the type of character he has.
He'll wait till his commission has been signed
and then, when he's alone and far away,
he'll dole out what appointments that he wills.

BOB
How beautiful you are, how fine you seem
once you are flushed with anger. I must change.
(*Removing his hose*) Cast away this darkness, dress in steel!
On this we must speak further, heart to heart.
I'm now your mind, your will, your counterpart.
Ireland will be Eden. You shall see!
Your eyes will smile forever, never frown,
illuminate the world like sapphire stones.
I'll cleanse all Ireland. Call down thunderbolts!
I am no mild Melanippus. I'll rail
like all the seven. Capaneus. Yes.
Adrastus, with all his famous names.
Hippomedon, who screamed like a Bacchante.
Maddened Tydeus. Parthenopaeus
with Sphinx-stamped shield. Amphiaraus
and filial Polyneices, battle-scarred.
I am the greatest warrior of them all
and you, my inspiration and my queen! [*Exit* BOB, *manic,
running naked, brandishing his sword.* CURTAIN]

SCENE XI

Essex House. LADY ESSEX, BLOUNT.

LADY ESSEX
Poor Blount. To Ireland you must go. The Queen's
decree is irreversible.

BLOUNT (*sadly, struggling to fill a long pipe*)
                    It is.
Damn this black tobacco! Just look at it!
It crumbles in the palm like Irish peat.
Or snuff, or dust. An omen. (*He lights his pipe, and coughs.*)

LADY ESSEX
                    Your hands are
shaking. I fear you are unwell.

BLOUNT
                    Unwell?
Oh, I'm as well as all the rest of our
menagerie.

LADY ESSEX
          Be sure to take warm clothing.
You're looking very ill.

BLOUNT (*coughing*)
                    My lungs are bad.
My throat is bad. My stomach's bad. My legs
are bad. Everything about my health is bad.
And I'm about the best knight of the bunch.
Nonetheless to Ireland we must go,
agues or no agues, aches or none. How's
the Earl? Still having second thoughts, or third?

LADY ESSEX
Every night he grips me like a child.
He lies inside the darkness of my arms,
confessing his adulteries, his sins.

Everything he's criticised and done
has robbed him of the chance of an excuse.
His enemies are moving heaven and earth
to help him. Keep paying him more rope
to hang himself. Whatever comes of it
he'll be the one responsible. The Queen
has seen to that. Success alone will do.

BLOUNT
Defiers of the high gods tend to sink
as quickly as the sun. The Queen so fears
his spirit. It was a masterstroke
to offer him the heart of his desire.
The Queen has such a quick instinctive wit.
She uses it like magic to avert
the menace in the men that threaten her -
like Oenomaus used, against Tydeus.
They tell me I have sixteen hundred foot
and thirteen hundred horse. Enough, perhaps,
for nothing. Well, something must be done,
some gesture must be made to please the Queen
or Essex will be taking all the blame
as one who held the water in his hand
but would not move to throw it on the fire.
The army leaves in March. The populace
will cheer us, as they stand, drenched to the skin.
The mighty expedition! There's a thought!
I see it in my mind. The rain will fall.
Rusts will brown our armour, blunt our swords.
Our horse sink through the bogs and Irish mud.
Pray for us, but don't expect success.

[CURTAIN]

SCENE XII

Essex House. FRANCIS *and* ANTONY BACON, *who is scanning a letter.*

FRANCIS
Well?

ANTONY
It is all much as we anticipated. The Earl has fallen straight into the trap. The Queen ordered him to attack, but Essex allowed the Irish Council to change his mind, so the battle was postponed till early June. By then, they said, the grass would be much greener, and the army's cattle fat.

FRANCIS
Where did he go? Ulster?

ANTONY
No. To Leinster. Without one word to any of the Council, or the Queen.

FRANCIS
The Queen is apoplectic at the cost. The progress costs one thousand pounds a day. He keeps on dubbing knights, but none has fought a battle. Everywhere the Irish welcome him with loyal peals of laughter. But when he's gone the town-gates shut, the rebels pour the whiskey out again. The Earl attacks an army, then finds he's charged a brake of gorse. So on it goes. Each mirage dazzles him. The waters of the ocean part before, then close behind him calmly once he's gone. Ireland has seduced him - like a whore that lets him rub his fingers down her back while she empties out his pockets of their gold.

ANTONY
And the Earl?

FRANCIS
Well, the Earl returned to Dublin in July. The army's spirit's
broken. All it's done is capture one small castle. He's slunk
back like a dog that's caked with dung. His tail is stiff with peat
and rotted bogs. It seems he has a mania. He gambled. Either
peerless glory, or total loss. And ruin won. Three quarters of
the army are in garrison. He makes all of the mistakes that he
complains about in others.

ANTONY
What choices are before him? He must march against Tyrone.
He cannot win.

FRANCIS
Or go over to the enemy. Apparently, according to my spies,
Tyrone has been approached. To ask for talks. Not to negotiate
a battle. Tyrone is sure to tempt him. What can he offer?

ANTONY
A chance to join the rebels. To become the greatest man in
England. To be king.

FRANCIS
Exactly. Treason! At Michaelmas the farm upon the customs of
sweet wines falls in. It is the mainstay of the Earl's estate.
Without it he'll be bankrupt. Unruly horses lose their
provender. The Queen is certain to withdraw it. No money, no
more power. And what of us? Our state will be most desperate.
Perhaps the time has come for us to switch allegiance. Our
legal skills must soon find ready takers. We must act
immediately, before his last defeat. We need to put out feelers,
rapidly.

[CURTAIN]

SCENE XIII

St. James's Palace. CECIL, BURGHLEY, CAPTAIN,
FRANCIS *and* ANTONY BACON. BESS *is hysterical with
laughter.*

BESS
What a coup! Our English Duc de Guise! What
a passionate fiasco! Imagine it!
Three hundred of them, clashing up the Strand.

CECIL
With Blount in front.

BESS
$\qquad$ *"Saw! Saw! Saw!"* he yells.
"Tray! Tray! Tray! Saw! Saw! Saw! Tray! Tray! Tray!"

CECIL
"Saw! Saw! Saw!"

FRANCIS
$\qquad$ *"Tray! Tray! Tray!"*

CECIL
$\qquad\qquad$ *"Tray! Tray! Tray!"*

BESS
Braying like a donkey. Yelling like a
bellman. *"Tray! Tray! Tray!"* (*Suddenly serious*) And how did
the citizens respond? Did they man the
barricades? Not one of them. And so
he changes tune. *"A plot's laid on her life!*
The crown is sold to the Infanta.
Take arms now for the Queen! Arms for the Queen!"

FRANCIS
There was great pathos in the scene. The streets
remained impassive. Motionless.
As silent as the shutters. Here and there

a face stared like a painting, quite unmoved.
Behind him came the herald's counterpoint
denouncing him for treason. Not one
insurgent joined him. All he saw
was windholes and the whites of frightened eyes.

ANTONY
His face went pallid, then contorted. As he walked
his followers all quietly slipped away
and left him there, a nothing, just a noise
that died into a void. We blocked him off.
He charged, and was repelled. A page was killed.
The Earl fled to the river, straight back home.
He entered by the water-gate and then
began to throw up barricades. He burned
his letters. But when artillery
was turned upon his doors, he rapidly
surrendered.

BESS
    And now his flesh is in the pen.
He's as useless as a musket in the rain.
How does treason seem? No longer in the
sheen of its condition, I suppose?

CAPTAIN
He's no April eclogue. He stares into
the earth like dirt's interpreter. The sky's
a lake of poison green.

BESS
    The tower is a
sombre type of house. Its floors are damp and chill.
As luminous as pewter, cold and grey.
Poor Essex. His enthymeme is argued.
The victim of a premiss unexpressed.

CECIL
He now awaits the exodus of death.

BESS
To be all corpse, all corpse. My mother, she
was carrying my brother when she died.
Arrested for adultery with five.
For incest with her brother, then, with
two weeks' time to organise her soul
the woman was beheaded. Cranmer
nullified her marriage. Thus the act
reduced me to a bastard. Nothing more.
Yet why should I feel shame? I bore no guilt.
My father then was parentage enough.
He wiped away adultery. His word was Jove's.

BURGHLEY
Your Majesty!

BESS
            I was a problem as
a child. No one knew my rank, or how
I should be treated. I was very short
of clothes. No gown. No kirtle. Petticoats.
No linen to run up some decent smocks.
And now I have three thousand gowns to wear!
My big teeth came through slowly. In great pain.
One is structured by one's sufferings, I think.
Precociously intelligent, at six
I seemed as grave as forty. Memories
befoul. My father longed to have a son.
I was born. Late afternoon. A Virgo.
The river turned. The Thames began to flood
through London, over banks and snags of mud.
My mother was the mistress of the king.
No Salic law in England. Thus a girl
could squat upon the throne. But nonetheless
there's always room for legal argument.
My mother was his folly. What a king!
While I was in her belly I had caused
the English revolution. When I kicked,
Rome fell. All were sure I'd be a boy.
No one dared to contemplate a girl.
One thousand years of Catholic belief

were cut at my conception, rubbed away
in one hot torrid night. All prophesied
that I would wear a penis. They were wrong.
My name had been decided in advance.
Henry. Henry the Ninth. Or Edward.
But Henry would be better. But alas,
poor Henry had a vulva! That was all!
A nothing with no sceptre, and no orb.
Virtually the richest bed we had
was carted down to Greenwich for the son
and there I lay. My mother failed the king.
Her metal tongue made many enemies.
A week or so, just after I was born,
most knew she was already in eclipse.
My father's lust in others. There we were.
She had to be the mother of a prince
or nothing. My birth debased her. I
cut away her head, her lovely head.
So I have much to answer. Very much.
Bonfires filled the city, bells were rung
rejoicing that the king had lost his wish.
God was praised, then praised and praised again.
Have I not been much stronger than a man?
Who leads the prosecution of the Earl?

CECIL
Edward Coke.

BESS
           He's too full of abuse. He would create
great sympathy for treason.

CECIL
                    I agree.
But Bacon will be helping. Guiding him.

FRANCIS
Your Majesty. My services are yours.
I know the argument. I'll keep the
prosecution to the point.

BESS

We'll pay you well.

A thousand pounds, at least. Or more perhaps,
depending on the quality of trial.
The Earl can call on massive sympathy,
not least among my courtiers.

FRANCIS

I understand.

Your Majesty's most generous. I think
a quick trial, just a week or so, no more.
And then the execution. Hanged and drawn
then quartered, don't you think? As Lopez was?
The traitor's death, deterring other souls.
Or something less demotic? Like the block?

BESS

That's up to you. You take the money, so
you also bear the burden. Did you know
he burst into my bedroom - you have heard -
and found me wig-less, naked, head to toe.
Nobody had gazed on such a sight
but Lopez. Though just once the King of Spain
observed me through a keyhole. Noisily.
Men that see the nude skin of a queen
and desecrate her pure virginity
deserve to die. I'm sure that you agree.
Taboos must be defended, to the end. (*Silence*)
History's a strange conspiracy.
I am not a tyrant. I can see
the world from his perspective, all too well.
Tyrants cannot take their victim's part.
I admit to being in the wrong.
My fate has been that I must speak for God.
A God, though, who is difficult and strange
and hard to understand, like all of us.
I'll send a holy chaplain to his cell
to question him and point the path to light.
He'll frighten him with virtue. Purge his soul.

[CURTAIN]

SCENE XIV

BOB's *cell in the Tower of London.*

BOB
I have always been most interested in
myself. I sensed from the beginning just
how different I was. I was a long
mysterious tale. Much of me was scarcely
credible. All that I said and did
enshrined some hidden meaning, dark conceit,
a type of secret message that I knew
I never would decipher. Yes, a code
that Walsingham himself could never solve,
a language that some skilled interpreter
might just begin to turn towards some sense
that normally is far beyond us all.
I feel I am some universal truth.
If I could but uncover what that is
I might then just discover who I am.
Then nature, man, and even God himself
might open to my vision. Yes. We need
to learn from one another what we are.
I feel that I am loved. That I am thought.
Encouraged, hated, balked and then destroyed.
Plotters have been watching, pulling strings,
scanning with the grey rays of their eyes
my most unusual nature. Who they are,
their names and nature, permanent address
is difficult to fathom, but they're here.
I, a holy ruler of this land,
am ruled, still, by the Other. What is this -
the actions that I've fashioned and performed,
this sequence of brief stories I have lived -
who authorised their contents, gave them life,
each episode a message, with a deep
emphatic repetition? But of what?
I find that if I look back on my life
then I can draw two different columns up:
on this side, things that I have overstressed:

on that side, things that have understressed.
I *over*rate. I *under*rate. What does this mean?
It is a most elaborate lesson that the Queen
is teaching me. That she should go to such
expense is touching. Such a cast
of monitors! But she will never kill me.
Kill Essex, and she'll surely kill herself,
will vitiate her own eternal soul.   [*Enter* GAOLER]

GAOLER
Your food, my lord.

BOB
                    I do not wish to eat.
I'll see that chaplain now. So many men!
And all assembled here to frighten me.
They'll play at passing sentence. Afterwards
the Queen will then forgive me and we'll be
as once we were, still are, will always be -
pure lovers, blent forever in the Ghost.
Yet Bacon's turned his coat.   [*Enter* CHAPLAINS 1, 2]
                    Yes, do come in!

CHAPLAIN 1
                                        My lord!

BOB
That Bacon should so turn against his friend
and patron. Should guide the prosecution.
His words will move all hearts to gain his wish.
Who are you? I have seen your face before.
Are you Bacon, dressed up in disguise
to lecture me on virtue?

CHAPLAIN 1
                    I am, sir,
your chaplain. I am sent here by the Queen.

BOB
The trial is arduous.

CHAPLAIN 1
                    The trial, my lord,
is over.

BOB
        Over?

CHAPLAIN 1
                Over.

BOB
                    The verdict?
I heard no verdict.

CHAPLAIN 1
                    Guilty of high treason.
With Blount and Danvers. Merrick. Cuffe. You
were sentenced, my lord.

BOB
                        Sentenced?

CHAPLAIN 1
                            To death.

BOB
I heard no sentence.

CHAPLAIN 1
                    You stood there in the
dock. So proud. So self-possessed. You smiled
towards the judges, quietly.

BOB
                    I smiled?
Yes. People find my smile is beautiful.
My smile has charmed the world since I was born.
You say that you are sent here by the Queen.
No doubt you bring me news of my release.
The Queen has taught me lessons. But, you know,
not one of them has been so strange as this.

CHAPLAIN 1
You will not be hanged and drawn and quartered.

BOB
Get on with the joke, then. See it through.

CHAPLAIN 1
You will be beheaded.

BOB (*unreally*)
                  Indeed? What with?

CHAPLAIN 1
With an axe. But with one, I trust, that's sharpened.
I'm sent here to acquaint you with the form
the execution takes. You will stand thus,
(*showing him the correct formal way*)
accompanied by three clergymen. You will wear
a black cloak and a hat. You'll take it off
and bow to the assembled dignitaries,
then make your last oration which will be
your ultimate confession and a prayer.

BOB (*smiling and amused, imitating his bow*)
I confess my sins.

CHAPLAIN 1
                Exactly so.
You confess your sins. Your youthful lusts
and your uncleannesses. Your vanity,
your pride, those individual faults that you
remember. You will beseech your Saviour
Christ to be your mediator with the Father
for this bloody, crying, most infectious sin
you have committed. You will pray then for
the Queen, and then confess yourself prepared
to die. You will forgive your enemies, remove
your cloak and ruff, then kneel down by the block
in a black doublet. There you will pray for
the estates of the realm and repeat the great
Our Father. The executioner will kneel

before you, asking your forgiveness, which
you'll grant. You'll then rehearse the Creed, repeating
it quite clearly, phrase by phrase. And then,
bare-headed, you will look upon the world
for the last time - your hair lifts with the wind -
to separate from us, part utterly,
be warm no more, and feel no human care.
The Queen will then be severed from your mind.
Your everlasting courtship will be gone,
its promise of delight, of earthly bliss
be cut away forever.

BOB (*with mock solemnity*)
                              You speak well.
Men fear death as children dread the dark.

CHAPLAIN 1
Turning, you will bow before the block.
(*Lying down on an imaginary block*)
You'll stretch out both your arms and lie down flat
upon the scaffold, your head placed sideways, thus,
for the axe. *"Lord be merciful to thy
prostrate servant!"* you will cry. *"Lord into
Thy hands I commit my spirit!"* There will be
a pause. The headsman whirls the axe
into the air. It flashes downward. Once! Twice! Thrice!
The head is severed. All the blood runs out.
The headsman bends and grips it by the hair
then lifts it up before the witnesses (*Rising*)
while shouting with full strength, *"God save the Queen!"*

BOB
You are a first-rate actor. Are you from
The Globe? She has sent you here to frighten me.
Life for her without me is unthinkable.

CHAPLAIN 2
We are sent to save you from the pains of Hell.

BOB
Hell?

CHAPLAIN 2
There are two kingdoms in this world. Two rules.
They war together, till the end of time.
There is no hope of truce. King Jesus is
the ruler of the one. And Satan the
usurper of the other. We are
clearly taught that all men are true subjects
of the one, or slaves unto the other.
Oh yes! There are the neutrals of this world
who dream that they can view indifferently
the battle-scars and wounds of other men,
who never wish to fight or get involved
but these, in truth, are finally deceived,
for Jesus has Himself proclaimed the truth
that those who are not for Him are against.

BOB
Is that the case? The scripture says that's so?

CHAPLAIN 1
It truly does.

BOB
It's not your false translation
of the text?

CHAPLAIN 2
Hell is terrible. Already
I smell suffering. The traitors base the hells.
I see you there, transfixed, a fly in ice.
Translucent, like an insect set in glass.
Around you I can see your fellow souls,
some scattered flat, some upright and some bent,
their faces on their feet, all waiting to
be torn, torn naked, torn and torn again,
lacerated through all future time.
Repent while you still can. Repent, my lord,
while grace and God's forgiveness still avail!

BOB (*turning on them*)
Get out! Get out! I'll rip away your heads!

GAOLER (*restraining him*)
My lord! My lord! Remember who you are!

BOB
Get them out! Get them out! The Queen's a crone.
I understand at last what she intends.
What she's intended always. Fetch her here!
I'll rip away her wig of crimson hair.
I'll use her as a lover should have done.
A brothel-girl from Wapping. Fetch her here!
I wish to see my lady. Let me plead.
I only have to speak, to look at her
and all her ice will shatter.

CHAPLAIN 2
                              Remember
this. No one can be neutral. Either we
subscribe to righteousness, and love it, or
we do not. If we do not we sin,
and sin exacts its natural punishment.

BOB
These officers of conscience drive me mad!
(*He hurls a jug at them.*)
Out! Out! Out! Take both these men away!
The Queen is cool as moonlight. Brightness
without warmth. I must create a moral
alteration of her mind. Gaoler!

GAOLER
My lord!

BOB
          Haul these torturers outside!
(to CHAPLAINS 1, 2) Go! Go! Before I break your necks myself!
                              [*Exeunt* CHAPLAINS 1, 2]
(to GAOLER) Bring me a pen and ink. I need to write.
My words must work, before I meet the night.

[CURTAIN]

SCENE XV

In a chamber with a far view of The Tower. BESS, *asleep.*
LADY MARY.

BESS (*awakening*) Hah! Ho! Ho! What's this? Am I asleep?
Is this a dream?

LADY MARY
                    A dream, Your Majesty?

BESS
I dreamed I was the goddess of the moon.
Shepherding the stars across the night.
Changing with my phases. Suffering.
Leading them towards an abattoir.
I heard a voice. A dark black voice. Saturn's.
He said that I was entering the time
of dissolution. Who is it that I am?

LADY MARY
Elizabeth, Your Majesty. The Queen
of England and of Ireland and of Wales.

BESS
I disengage. I disengage. What do
the others expect of me?

LADY MARY
                              Your attendance
at an execution.

BESS
                    I'll not go there.
I'll spend my time in deep self-contemplation.
But not my thick external image. Not of that.
I'll pass my time defining what I am.
Discovering and uncovering my soul.
I'll interact with archetypes, my girl.
For one is not the one one thinks one is.

I pass through every room inside my house.
It gives me the capacity to save.
You understand, my child?

LADY MARY

No, Your Majesty.

BESS

Nor should you yet. Nor should you, my dear girl.
Strange sensations creep into my soul.
A tender time precedes the last renewal.
One lets go of attachments. Lets them go.
Poor Essex must be one. He must be one. (*Picking up a mask*)
Demeter is about to lose a son.

[*Enter* CECIL, BISHOP, CHAPLAINS 1, 2]

Well chaplains, did you minister to our
braggart?

CHAPLAIN 1

We did, Your Majesty.

BESS

Good. Good.

I trust you left him altered, utterly.
The flames of Hell so agitate the soul.

CHAPLAIN 2

They do, Your Majesty.

BESS

Well, the outcome?

Did they singe his imagination?

CHAPLAIN 2

He has lost all self-reliance, self-respect.
He grovels. He confesses. Cries aloud.
He implicates his false associates
more readily than if he felt the rack.
Danvers, Cuffe and Mountjoy, all of them.
His sister is denounced, Penelope.
He sends you this, a letter.

BESS
>Tear it up.

CHAPLAIN 1
You wish me to destroy it?

BESS
>Utterly.
It irks me, the deciphering of his script.
The Marshal is a traitor, tried, condemned. (*The letter is torn up.*)
What say you bishop? Should he be reprieved?
I am the queen of everything that's dead.
What course of action should I now adopt?

BISHOP
Whatever is most loving in this case
is right and good. One's attitude and one's
intention determine what is moral.

BESS
Nobly said. I catechise you further.
What is love?

BISHOP
>Agape is spiritual love.
It shows itself by feeling true concern
without the thought of gaining some reward.
With agape one needs no rules or laws
since Love itself creates them. For, you see,
the end of Love must justify the means.

BESS
And what of killing? Chopping off a head?
Is that an act of agape?

BISHOP
>Depending
on the circumstances. Yes.

BESS (*growing angry*)

       And so I serve
the needs of agape by lopping off
his head! How simple! How straightforward!
How well you seem to grasp the finer points
of human limitation. How proud I am
to practise such an altruistic act.
How final, when my knowledge of the good
is at the best unsound, and quite unsure.
You theologians argue over hairs,
pay scrupulous attention to one dot
but show a monstrous ignorance of life.
I've never had great mastery of facts
nor faced my motives with great confidence
nor known for certain what my acts would bring.
Often it's the best thing one can do
to throw one's whole unknowing onto God
and hope some stray solution filters through,
though often it does not. To live, or die?
To leave like apples parting from a tree
in a mild night. The soft thud of a plum.
Politics makes terrible demands.
One's forced into these acts, and afterwards
who knows what pangs of guilt one must endure?
Who knows from whence they come and what they mean?
I only know I love him, love him still
with all his sins, with all his miseries.
His father was my lust, my lifetime's dream.
I felt more like his mother from the first.
Yet he rebels against me, me, his Queen,
and I am forced to kill him, kill my son.

BISHOP
God guides through all.

BESS

      Such rich simplicity.
I lack it. Am an atlas, full of sadness.
God guides through all? I wonder! I believe
he speaks behind a curtain when I'm there.
My soul is like a privy used by whores.

Between this world of matter and our God
hang seventy thousand veils. The inner ones
half light. The outer ones half darkness.
Through all these different veils the soul of man
must travel down from godhead to this dust.
Each veil of light retains some quality
of heaven. Each veil of darkness adds
the gravity of earth, its misery.
We weep when we are born upon his earth
for then the soul's disjunction is complete.
In sleep a little child will often cry
because it still remembers what it's lost,
the glory and the splendour. So it is.
But how to travel backwards through those veils,
reclaim the seat of glory, that's the task.
You'll answer me the task's already done.
I know. But I don't feel it. Not at all.
What then is the motive and the force
that drives us back but love, this worldly love,
this bridge by which we try to climb to God.

BISHOP
Your Majesty.

BESS
                Speaks heresy. Her heart.
Once I heard love's whisper everywhere.
I heard it in the dancing of the leaves,
the music of the brown birds in the trees.
The doves that set their heads against their necks
then loved and loved in mutual delight
as we do, too. For I have heard men say
that when we love, and couple, limb in limb,
the angels fly from paradise above
and join us in our ecstasy of joy.
They take us in their arms and sing their songs,
each mystery of heaven and its bliss.
For those that do not love are fictile clay.
So be love's slave and then you will be free.
Enjoy its pain, and happy you will be.

CECIL
The warrant, Madam. It needs your signature.
Just here. The quill is inked. How could you trust
the Earl again, when you are sixty-seven
and he's disgraced you so? His deceit
is moral, mental, and material.

BESS
You have the ceremonial sense of life.
You know when just to act, when to desist.

CECIL
The scaffold is an instrument of state
and many princes tread her eager steps
from many noble lines. For most, in turn,
must greet her. If not now, then later on.
All waits on your decision. For its ink.

BESS
The people will not thank me for this act.
Their Barak dead, Deborah's mighty man.
How often has he threatened, suddenly
to take a metal horseknife to the fire
and seize it with his hands, all bright with heat,
and plunge it with full force into his side
to let my healing lips, my woman's tongue
with crimson kisses seal his holy wound,
and heal it with my spittle? How he's bragged!
Offered me his hands and both his feet,
to tear away the eyeballs from his head
so he could write he loved me in his blood.
Such hideous conceits, hyperboles!
Now men will mourn his death, and poets grieve,
their jewel gone, the prince of chivalry.
The soul I once would live in will be dead.
I fired his flame, I did it. I alone.
Now I must scatter water on his pyre.
I am to blame. I gave him too much power,
more credit with the people than behoved
his over-eager nature. Men rebel.
Already he is yesterday. A sound

is rising through the earth, my mother's voice.
"Avenge my early murder. My sad death!"
And so I snuff the flame. (*She reads the warrant.*)
                        All's cold as earth.
Already I can feel it on my skin,
death's carelessness, the coming of decay.
Subjects rise to greet the coming sun
but when it falls, great troubles seize their sleep.
I think he'll be much happier in heaven.
He'll sing at ease, and wait a while for me,
then we'll be there together, endlessly.
A feather ends him. Light as perfect souls! (*She signs.*)
Perform the execution. Rapidly!   [*Exeunt* CECIL, BISHOP,
CHAPLAINS 1, 2, *each bowing as he leaves the stage singly.*]
I shall not attend this gory death.
Come, Mary, Mary. Come across to me!
No need to weep. No need to weep at all.
Come. Hold me up my mirror. No more masks!
Grip it so. More tightly. That's the way.
Let me see what picture will appear.
What wrinkles, heavy eyes and huge black teeth.
It seems they mourn for Essex, dark as coals.
Time has scattered meal upon my hair.
It fills this wig. It covers me like loam.
I look and see the image of a corpse.
She'll go no more a-Maying with the young.
But she will die, a virgin to the end,
her winding-sheet unspotted, pure and clean.
Just look at her. A walking skeleton!
She stiffens in the saddle, needs a stick
to travel up the staircase. Yet her heart
loved dancing, plays, and cards. Do hold it still.
She has her cupboard, stuffed with memories.
Leicester's final letter, full of love.
The window, now! You tell me when he's dead!
(LADY MARY *moves reluctantly to observe Bob's decapitation.*)
I feel I grow much younger as I fade.
I'm sharp enough. I see the end of things.
My eyes are keen as arrows, thick-tipped flints.
Always they are searching for the soul.
As Hatton said, I seek the inward man.

I deal with men quite well. My peering eye
is set on one, my ear upon the next,
my judgement's on the third, while to the fourth
I speak. You've watched me work. I move through all.
My spirit shifts through any company,
insinuates its essence, everywhere. *(She sinks into a slumber. A
loud cry carries through the window. She flinches, then her
head drops again as she falls into a deep sleep.)*

[CURTAIN]

DATE DUE

ILL (AVE)		
52352818		
4/24/09		